THE WORLD OF CYCLING ACCORDING TO G

GERAINT THOMAS

THE WORLD OF CYCLING ACCORDING TO G

Written with Tom Fordyce

Quercus

First published in Great Britain in 2015 by

Quercus Publishing Ltd
Carmelite House
50 Victoria Embankment
London EC4Y 0DZ

An Hachette UK company

A CIP catalogue record for this book is available
from the British Library

HB ISBN 978 1 78429 636 0
EBOOK ISBN 978 1 78429 639 1

10 9 8 7 6 5 4 3 2

Typeset by Hewer Text UK Ltd, Edinburgh
Printed and bound in Great Britain by Clays Ltd, St Ives Plc

For Sa. Not really used to saying things like this. Been a cracking six years so far, here's to the rest like . . .

Contents

LIVING IT

Bib Shorts and Bare Arms

In few sports is it as easy to get it wrong with your clothing as in cycling. Its most defining item, the bib short, is something that no fashion designer would ever consciously come up with. Perhaps if they were Austrian, you might argue, but even then the fabric is wrong. Pull on the bib short in front of a new ladyfriend unfamiliar with the garment and you can see the confusion and distress on her face: have I started going out with a deviant, or a Freddie Mercury impersonator?

The first time I wore bib shorts as a kid, down to a Maindy mini-league race in Cardiff, I wore pants under them. Why wouldn't you? I wore pants under my rugby shorts. I wore pants when playing football. It led to an awkward but important conversation in the changing rooms. 'What, you've got pants on?' 'Well, yeah . . . haven't you?'

You can try to fight these things, but in time you have to accept it. Cyclists do not wear pants, at least not when they're cycling. It's the same as shaving your legs. When you are a twelve-year-old boy in Cardiff you do not want to be rocking up at school with shaved legs. It's a matter of choosing which world you belong too, the 'normal' hairy-legged world of the playground, or the smooth, clean-shaven changing rooms of the velodrome. So I fought it until I was fourteen and away at a race in Germany where I thought no prying eyes could find me. Into a Portaloo with the cheapest disposable razor I could find, hacking away like a blindfolded lumberjack. I stumbled out of that toilet looking like Johnny Hoogerland's backside after he was knocked off by a car straight into that barbed-wire fence during the 2011 Tour: wild gashes, blood everywhere. Mixed in among random hairy patches over my calves and thighs.

It takes some longer than others. Aged fifteen you would still see girls wearing thongs beneath their bib shorts. You never thought of saying anything, because you were fifteen and you could see girls wearing thongs.

My first proper cycling jersey was in the luminous yellow of Maindy Flyers. While the design these days is more subtle, I look back on the dayglo years with pride. The top was of its era, and it comes with its own set of special memories. I've kept a jersey from every club or team I have ridden for precisely that purpose: a sartorial time-travel machine to bring the past back to life.

Even in the late 1990s, there was neither the beautifully designed cycling clothing of today nor the number and size of bike shops. What you could buy in the shops that were around cost you a year of prize money. I used to get my gear from the car-boot-style sales they held in the car parks outside the various velodromes, where you'd find random items hanging off coat racks and plastic tubs of gloves or caps. You'd pick up a horrendous multicoloured jersey for a fiver and wear it with immense pride. At one place, I bagged a pair of T-Mobile team shorts. Grey panel down the side, three stripes down the leg. If it had been possible to wear them to bed and school as well as in the saddle I would have done so.

There was seldom a thought for the practicalities. If you reckoned it looked the business then that would trump everything else. It's raining? If being dry means you can't see my multicoloured magic then soak me to the bone. Have you seen my T-Mobile shorts?

Technology was still in its scratchy infancy. The jerseys made you both hot and cold at the same time. The shorts very rarely maintained their shape. At one race on the Manchester Youth Tour, when I was thirteen, our rain jackets were black bin bags with holes cut in them for our heads and arms. You wouldn't see that in a Rapha store. Not at a bin-bag price-point.

You learned through osmosis. Either that or hypothermia. I remember going out for an evening winter ride, snow falling heavily on the streets of Cardiff. The lad I was supposed to be meeting was late, leaving me riding up and down a rapidly disappearing stretch of tarmac with my legs going the same colour as a Welsh rugby shirt.

Eventually he arrived just before snowdrifts cut the road off like a mountain pass. 'Whoah, what's happened to your legs? Why aren't you wearing tights?' 'What do you mean, tights? Is this like the pants thing?'

By the time I got home I was so cold I had to be helped directly into bed, kit stripped off, wearing a thick woollen jumper, jogging bottoms, three pairs of socks and curled up under two duvets, shower forgotten. I couldn't move. Every ten minutes my mum would come running upstairs to make sure I hadn't died.

Things came second-hand – a helmet also worn by the British team, imbuing its teenage wearer with the same sense of cool. A first pair of cycling-specific shades, loved so much I barely wore them. In fact I hardly took them out of my bedroom. Very little fitted. Skinsuits were not suited to your skin. It was like wearing a onesie that had gone wrong in the wash.

As in every sport there was always one kid who had all the gear: bike, replica kit, shades, team gloves. Helmet? We thought so.

It didn't so much make you jealous as desperate to beat them. There was a lad called Ben Crawforth who was very evenly matched with me. We'd trade victories: whoever didn't win that day would always be in second. 'There you go,' my dad would say; 'He's in ordinary kit, and he still wins.' The next race Ben rocked up on a pimped-up bike. I beat him. Motivation.

Don't think the pros have got everything right. You might not see the ultimate horror – a lad putting on his arm and leg warmers before anything else, and his girlfriend waking up to see what appears to be a floating limbless torso backlit against the bedroom wall – but mistakes abound. Bloodied backsides hanging out of shorts are a common sight after crashes in the peloton. At Barloworld, the young Chris Froome decided his team-issue skinsuit had the wrong dimensions, and took some nail scissors to the sleeves. Skinsuits are seldom flattering. They're even less flattering when they're entirely sleeveless. Barloworld, to make matters worse, was an Italian team. If you are going to get away with a skinsuit with no arms and ripped shoulders, it will not be with an Italian team.

'FRRROOME! You cannot go out like that!' There were no spares. Instead, he was made to borrow a suit from an Italian teammate who had just finished a twenty-kilometre flat-out effort in 25°C heat. Lesson learned.

These days there is no need to rummage in the car-boot sales. At Team Sky we begin each season under a mountain of bespoke kit: three sets for winter, four regular, three summer, two made from mesh, three skinsuits. Some last longer than others. Socks and arm warmers fall victim to light-fingered teammates who have misplaced their own. Mesh tops are quietly left to one side, a little too *Fifty Shades* for the more modest rider. I've never been on a bike and worried that my legs felt too hot. Mesh on bare chest must be an acquired taste.

Most is worn hard. Little lasts long. First to fall are the white socks, victims of mass genocide in the washing machines that are running twenty-four hours a day on the Team Sky bus during stage races. Crashes see off more kit. Inadvertent error takes care of other items. On the bus we have a compression device to help our legs recover after a race. It requires you to strip down to your underwear to be treated. After one punishing day I limped to the back of the bus to reunite with my trousers, only to become aware while walking into the hotel a few moments later that I was giving it the full Jay Z – waistband round my thighs, backside on display for the world to see. Just as I had begun to fear that I had somehow lost two stone through the day's brutal exertion, I spotted my giant teammate Christian Knees staggering about wearing black tights and a confused expression. Ah, Christian. It appears I may have picked up the wrong pair. What's that? You don't wear pants off the bike either?

The best item of day-to-day wear I have now is the merino undervest. Warm when you want to be warm, cool when you don't. Garmin are rightly proud of the skinsuit they have, which features a letterbox-style slot an inch above the groin (farewell, soggy chamois; hello, easy urination on the move), while every other team has copied the filled-in helmets we debuted to so much scorn at the Tour of Qatar in 2010.

The single finest piece of cycling clothing I've had the pleasure to wear is also Sky team issue: their Rapha rain jacket. The fit is perfect, with minimal pinch-points or flapping. It's warm. It's waterproof. On those days when the rain is no longer individual droplets but a three-dimensional wall of water, it keeps you riding.

Not all the kit is entirely practical. The label on one garment states that it must only be hand-washed. It would do well to receive this treatment at my mum's when she's bored, let alone on a three-week stage race populated by exhausted men who can barely be bothered to hand-wash their hands. The worst? White shorts are never good. In any sort of rain your private areas become instantly public, which reminds me too graphically of an old teammate at Barloworld for whom the distinction between private and public spheres just didn't exist.

I say spheres – if it were just those on display it wouldn't have been too bad. Instead, this was something that no teammate wants to see, even if it was medically intriguing: the act of climbing off the bike after hours in the saddle triggering a reaction in his bib shorts that, shall we say, quickly became a pressing concern. The rider himself couldn't have been more proud, strolling round the bus with a delighted expression on his face that seemed to say, 'Look at that! Just imagine what would be happening without five hours of pedalling behind me!'

Worse still was what I had inflicted upon me as a teenager while racing for a British representative team for the first time. We were in Germany, riding for the British Schools Cycling Association. Bear in mind that this was a time when merely crossing the Severn Bridge from Wales into England was enough to make our whole minibus start booing loudly. So imagine the reaction when I found out that the British kit – rather than the usual combination of red, white and blue, or even the strange green they had for a while – was plain white with a red St George's cross. There was genuine outrage. I thought my dad was going to head straight to the airport and fly back to Cardiff. In the end, I wore it for the minimal time possible. Literally seconds after slamming on the brakes over the finish line, I'd torn the jersey off and thrown it back at them.

Jump forward a decade and those wrongs were being righted in spectacular fashion. By the 2008 Olympics, being part of a British cycling team meant you looked like an astronaut and felt as if you could fly to the moon. Our track kit looked sensational. What it did for our performance was even better. Did you feel 2 per cent faster, or sense 0.05 seconds slipping over your streamlined back? Not really. But when you knew how long it had been tested for, the hours Chris Boardman and his fellow secret squirrels had spent studying wind tunnels and equations on coefficients of drag, you felt something far more powerful: you felt like a superhero going into battle. You had a special something no other team had.

It took a little getting used to. Putting on some of the skinsuits was like climbing into a drainpipe. So obsessed were the designers with getting an aero advantage that, after one fitting, my pursuit teammate Ed Clancy offered to have an inch taken out of each of his collarbones to reduce his front-on profile to acceptable levels.

You would do your warm-up, sweating from both exertion and nerves, and then try to slip into this unmalleable plastic second skin. So stressed was sprinter Jason Kenny that he once inadvertently put a huge tear in his. There was always a spare on hand, but the worst part of any race is the *longueur* between warm-up and gun. Trying to swap your race numbers over with shaking hands, knowing that one more rip is your Olympic Games gone – I feel a little sick just thinking about it.

By the next Olympic cycle, some of our rivals had caught up a little. That was when the double bluff came into play. At the 2012 Track World Championships in Melbourne, just a few months short of London, our Australian arch-rivals treated it as a full Olympic run-out – all their best kit, their latest innovations, their strongest team. Deliberately we did the opposite – ten-year-old jerseys, helmets with cracks, bikes a City boy might use at weekends.

Come the team pursuit final, we beat them by a full tenth of a second, breaking the world record in the process. In that moment we won Olympic gold. You could see it in their faces: if GB can do this to us now, in that ropey old gear, what are they going to do in their superhero cloaks?

Unexpected Consequences

I t's just about the speed, right? Just about being able to climb mountains or win sprints or ride flat out for five hours, through rain, sleet and parching sun?

Not all of it. Being a good cyclist has some magnificent fringe benefits.

Winning go-kart races on a stag do. Never bet against a cyclist on these highly competitive occasions. Why? Because they are experts at picking the racing line, at hiding in slipstreams and dive-bombing past, at focusing the mind into a fierce racing attitude, and they are likely to be significantly lighter than many of the normal chaps there. Only ignore this rule if there is a professional go-kart racer in the ranks, in which case lob all your spare cash on him.

Driving impeccably in dangerous motorway conditions. I appreciate that this may appear to contradict the previous entry. But, as a road racer, you develop almost a spider-sense regarding everything around you – what's happening a long way down the road, who might be behaving slightly strangely, what that road surface or bend will do to those close by. On the motorway you instinctively do the same, and thus insulate yourself against dangers others would never see. Plus, you don't panic when overtaking a lorry in heavy rain, because what can spray do to you on those rare occasions you are behind glass and metal?

Winning eat-offs. Simple. We're always hungry, and we're used to having to eat 6,000 calories a day. At my Sky team-mate Luke Rowe's engagement party, Pete Kennaugh and I ended up in a showdown: three large bananas and a massive slice of engagement cake each. Now, Pete K likes a banana, and at the halfway stage he had a substantial lead, not least because I badly underestimated how hard it is to eat three bananas at express pace. But he tied up badly on the thick marzipan layer in the cake, and with immense focus I was able to bring it back for a glorious victory at the death. There's another tale from the same party involving a lad called Tank and an entire Shaun the Sheep cake, but it ended messily, so I'll leave it there.

Ordering coffee in six different languages. And being able to say 'please' and 'thank you' to complete the order. I also know six different words for ham.

An instinctive sense of where you are. You're so used to going on long training rides from strange hotels that your mental mapping process is always in operation. Cyclists very seldom get lost. When they do, they tend to have a good idea of where they might be lost, if that makes sense. Having said that, before the 2007 Tour prologue in London, my Italian team based themselves in Surrey. As we pedalled out of the car park the rest of the riders looked at me expectantly. 'Right, Tom, where do we go?' Hang on, I'm from Cardiff, not Croydon.

Finding a light switch in a strange hotel room. You may mock, but you try going to the toilet in the dark when you have no idea if that door handle you can just about make out leads you into a bathroom, a cupboard or the corridor outside the room. As someone who spends countless nights in countless different rooms, let me tell you that there are only five permutations, and I know them all.

Excellent tanning. It's not just that your arms, legs and nose will be in the sun for most of the summer. When your tan has faded in autumn, the first hint of sunshine on a warm-weather training camp brings it straight back. As a result, I'm less susceptible to burning than most Welshmen, although that's not saying a great deal. Ed Clancy always insists that a tan is just damaged skin. But he would say that. He doesn't have the option.

Travelling with efficiency and calm. So many times a month do you find yourself travelling with outsize baggage through airports that very little can rattle you. Turn up two hours before the flight and you'll queue for forty-five minutes. Turn up an hour before the flight and you'll go straight through. Never stress about where the gate is, never queue up before it is absolutely necessary. And never stand by the luggage carousel when you can sit down until your luggage actually appears. None of this jostling for position at the carousel, getting so close you might as well sit on it for a ride. What do people think will happen if they don't take their bag off the moment they see it? What horrors do they think lie behind those rubber strips where the carousel briefly exits the room?

Cheap nights while out drinking. This is actually more complicated than I'm making out. Although endurance riders need very little alcohol to go bandy-legged (on account of our monastic existences for most of the year), our immense stamina means we can keep going for an awful long time. That's as long as it's not a one-off special like a stag do or wedding: on these occasions you hit it a bit too hard, believing you can keep up with the seasoned drinkers around you. It always ends badly, although it helps to have some other bike riders around that are even worse drinkers than you. It's a dangerous, although often highly amusing, combination.

Reliable with directions. Not only will we know exactly how far away something is ('6.6 kilometres, with a total climb of eighty-six metres') because of our road sense we can be remark-ably specific about the landmarks en route. 'One hundred and fifty metres after a garage, you'll feel a slight crosswind. At that point, bend right and hug the hedge until the third bollard.'

Patience under fire. No matter how stressful the scenario, you can always hear the voice of GB cycling's psychiatrist

Dr Steve Peters in your head. Can you change anything? Yes? Then change it. No? Then deal with it.

Sleeping anywhere. Plane, car, sofa, cinema, dinner table, thunderstorm, rock concert, rollercoaster.

The Perfect Ride

Is there such a thing? Let's believe there is. But since perfection is a personal thing, let's give ourselves a little wriggle room.

Short

We are in South Australia, freshly arrived from the dank greys and browns of the British winter into summertime in a land where the sky is such a deep blue it's as if someone was holding their finger on the contrast button of the remote control. It is early on an Adelaide morning, just before 6 a.m., before the fierce heat has begun to bake the streets and parks, but still warm enough to breathe gentle life into tired legs and keep long sleeves and leg warmers in the cupboard drawers.

Away we go into the Adelaide Hills – no frightening climbs, just a few gentle testers to get a pleasant sweat up, a few swooping descents and views, wheels whirring easily. No need for breakfast, legs moving on the remnants of last night's fresh fish. Easy company, soft descents back into the sleepy city and out the other side, down to Glenelg and the beach. Bikes leant against a cafe table, eggs Benedict, magnificent coffee. And then? The beach calls.

Medium

It's a crisp November morning in Cardiff. Omelette for breakfast to fuel the fun, rugging up with a good winter jacket and tights over the bib shorts, comfort and reassurance in pulling on the thick gloves. Leaving the house later than normal, allowing the South Wales roads time to thaw.

The afternoon before, Wales have recorded a resounding win in one of the autumn rugby internationals. I'd like to think a major southern hemisphere nation has been involved. I appreciate that's optimistic, but this is supposed to be the perfect ride. It may also be the only way I'll ever experience the feeling of victory over the All Blacks. If we have just beaten the All Blacks I'm sure it would have been a heavy night, so we'll leave at 10.30 a.m. Although seeing as it's November and therefore after the cycling off season, my drinking form is in peak condition, so a training ride is still possible.

We're going west, out towards Ogmore-by-Sea. The terrain is never more than rolling, and we'll stop for Welsh cakes and coffee at a little cafe in Llantwit Major. It's run by a guy who used to race bikes, so the welcome will be warm. He'll be showing highlights of the previous day's victory on the big screen. Bolstered by the caffeine and glorious slaying of New Zealand, we'll cruise back nice and steady, possibly breaking it up with a few spontaneous races to the next village or roundabout. Appetite awakened, we'll pedal straight past mine and up to my mum's for Sunday lunch. A retro ride, and all the better for it.

Long

Time: five hours. Starting point: Nice. Parcours: a good few climbs. Time of year: September, with the tourists gone and the roads quiet.

It's warm enough to tickle the tan but not so warm your jersey is heavy with sweat. The tempo is relaxed, and while good company is essential, I don't want anyone along who can climb quicker than me. Team Sky teammates Luke Rowe and Ben Swift would be ideal – they can climb, but they're not too keen – and because we need four of us, so that no-one is ever left on his own at the back, we shall have another Sky man Phil "Paddy" Deignan, too, as he's good for banter and can take more than his fair share of abuse.

The training effect will come naturally from the climbs. No extra efforts, no need to look at our power meters. Three decent hills, then a drop down into Italy for a Parma ham and mozzarella piadina and the best coffee in the world. Spinning back along the coast, autumn sun on our faces, light breeze at our backs. Who would want to be anywhere else in the world?

Off Season

There's nothing like getting away from it all once the long cycling season comes to an end – heading somewhere far away from the mountainous torture of the Alps or the cobbles of Flanders, far away from teammates and the road-cycling culture. Somewhere like New York, with your girlfriend, on a special surprise trip. Walking down those busy streets, yellow cabs honking, skyscrapers all around, nothing at all to remind you of the day job and – hang on a second, is that Wiggins?

The odds of bumping into someone you know in New York are slim even when you and your friend both live in New York. When one of you lives in Chorley and the other in Cardiff, you start to wonder if something strange is going on.

'Brad?'

'G?'

'All right?'

'Yeah, good. You all right?'

'Yeah, good.'

Then the freakiness of it all starts getting to us.

'So, you're in New York?'

'Yeah. Having a good time?'

'Yeah. You?'

'Yeah.'

'Right, see you later . . .'

'Yeah, see you later . . .'

There's a cliché that every Premier League footballer goes on holiday to Ayia Napa, where they spend their time with the same teammates they see all year. I now have some sympathy with that predicament. Us cyclists have such a small window – basically October – that you're immediately ruling out a load of options on the basis of inclement weather. Majorca we go to with Sky before Christmas. The Canaries hold painful memories of our training camps on Tenerife's Mount Teide. So that means either the southern hemisphere, which in effect means South Africa (warm enough, English-speaking, plenty of things to do, not as far as Australia), or the US. And if you go to the US you're likely to at least stop over in New York. But still, Brad. There are eight and a half million people in New York. Of all the streets in all the towns in all the world, you walk down mine . . .

America can feel like a true escape. Sometimes it can be an escape too far. The food is fast and liquor cheap. When I glance in a familiar mirror on my return to Cardiff I am always chastened to see that I appear to have left my cheek-bones on the plane. And who inflated my face? I glance down and feel a pang of solidarity with my shirt buttons, which are mustering all their mute strength to hold the material together. It means that I have to keep two ward-robes: my off-season one in Cardiff (loose, relaxed, belt notches in unfamiliar places) and my in-season one at my training base in France (considerably smaller).

There's a further problem now that we're all growing up: the off season is becoming by default the wedding season.

There are too many Sky riders getting married and not enough space each October to squeeze them all in. We are becoming bridezillas of the bike. If you want to get married, you'd better hurry up and pop the question – not because your future wife is dropping hints all over the shop, but because you need to nab that date before someone else books it up. Then there are the friends and family who have nothing to do with the rhythms of the professional cycling year but find their own special days shunted around by the desire to have random cycling pals present. I was asked to be the best man for two of my closest mates in Cardiff. A fine decision, but one that immediately meant no summer weddings for the brides-to-be. Sorry, Cath. Sorry, Hannah.

Years ago, before the cycling revolution turned previously obscure track and road cyclists into household names, you could holiday incognito wherever you went. For the big boys it has now all changed, as Chris Hoy found out in Thailand a few months after his three Olympic golds in 2008. What was intended as a beach retreat had become a daily autograph session. Because, if you are a pale ginger man with thighs that have a circumference of twenty-seven inches, there may be better places to hide than Phuket.

We're not quite at the levels yet of Indian cricket icon Sachin Tendulkar. To even leave a hotel in his home country he apparently has to wear a specially made disguise that makes him look like an old man. For our superstars, it's more a case of keeping low in your own back yard. Brad tends to get out of Europe. Chris Froome avoids South Africa.

Me? I try to keep my head down in Cardiff, but I can't pretend it doesn't sometimes work in my favour. A little while ago my girlfriend was trying to get into a local nightclub but had forgotten her ID. No chance, said the bouncer. Hang on, said her mate. You see that gold 2012 Olympics postbox over there? She's marrying the bloke whose postbox that is. Prove it, says the bouncer. Sara had a quick look on her phone and found a photo of the two of us together. The bouncer leant over. 'Oh, fair enough. In you come . . .'

Thoughts of the off season, of the good times you're going to have and the rules you're going to break, keep you going on those hard rides. It gives you something optimistic to talk about when you're lying on your bed in a lonely Campanile, legs in bits after a horror of a mountain stage.

So restricted are we for most of the year that even a flight that takes you on holiday, the part that most people simply endure, becomes part of the release. Normally we avoid eating airline food. Too salty, not enough nutrients. You certainly can't tuck in to a relaxing beer. In the off season you fill your boots. Simply turning up at an airport without a bike and in normal clothes feels like a revitalising break.

Not all nationalities break out in the same unbridled fashion. The Brits and the Aussies tend to do it properly, enjoying a few of the drinks considered illicit at other times; sampling items on the menu of a size and calorific content that would normally induce a week of guilt and masochistic punishment.

The Italians and Spanish tend to squeeze in a little more training, or at least they claim they do.

My Sky teammate Leopold Konig went to a health spa in his native Czech Republic and spent a fortnight getting massages and drinking green tea. You could understand it in the first week of November after a month of off-season blow-outs, but in place of the actual blow-outs themselves? The call of the burger, the lure of the rare steak, is too much.

The off-season holidays have changed over the years. Initially they were all about the drinking. I went away on trips to Dublin and Barcelona with a few of my close cycling mates. We had missed out on the whole student lifestyle, and those weekends were our release. They were the time to be normal twenty-year-olds, and they were messy to say the least. When I first met my wife, it was more about adventure than booze. Then we started going away with her parents, and it swung back rapidly the other way. Young cyclists cannot hope to match the alcohol intake of a pair of fifty-year-olds from the Cardiff suburbs.

Yet, without the good times, the hard times would be even harder to get through. The off season is the light at the end of the dark tunnel, even if that light turns out to be the flames grilling a half-pounder with fries.

Being cyclists, we're not comfortable doing absolutely nothing. A little adrenaline is required. In South Africa you might abseil down Table Mountain, go shark diving or, if you're feeling really gung-ho, ride your bike round Johannesburg without a local for company.

Back home, it is a time to fulfil commitments to your generous sponsors. There are also the less well-remunerated but more enjoyable commitments to old friends and kind relations. Before you know it, you're not so much resting as on a two-week tour of the country's motorway services, which has all the risks of shark diving but none of the buzz.

How to play Christmas? You can't go flat out with everyone else, because the Tour Down Under starts less than a month later. My tactics are to stockpile heavy training in the weeks before, not least during Team Sky's two-week camp in Majorca. That means the return to Cardiff around 20 December can see me plan training sessions around drinking rather than vice versa. Time on the bike will be shortened but become a lot more intense, which fits in well with the bad weather anyway. Christmas being Christmas, spontaneity will sometimes win out over good intentions. There was a New Year's Eve a little while ago that began conservatively in the Y Mochyn Du pub off Cathedral Road, accelerated into a random meeting with legendary Welsh classical singers Bryn Terfel and Shân Cothi, took in a detailed conversation about Eminem, picked up pace again as I tried to keep up with six-foot-four-inches Bryn on the local ales, peaked with me performing a version of 'Sex Bomb' to Shân and ended with me dancing with six sixty-something ladies. I remember this because Sara has it all on video. I know.

Occasionally you can try to buck the calendar. There is a little pocket of time after the spring Classics, but you have to be careful not to put any weight on. The Classics will already have done that – two kilogrammes gained in competition, another 1.5 kilogrammes in the five days off afterwards. We are in the land of the chip. It is dark and cold. It is inevitable.

You must also be lucky. A few years back I was desperate for some warmth and blue skies. I looked at a few shortish-haul options. Hmm. Egypt looks nice and warm. Perfectly safe, Egypt. Probably no chips, either.

It was two days into our outlaw break that the Eyjafjallajökull volcano in Iceland first started belching clouds of ash into the skies of Europe. You'd think three days' extra holiday for free would be a good thing, but there were two problems: phoning the bosses at Sky to explain that I might be back a little late, and Sa being struck down by a case of severe food poisoning.

After a couple of slightly awkward tables for one (do you ever eat so fast as when you're dining on your own?), I decided to use it more as a Konig-style holiday and drop some weight, albeit without the assistance of a ruthless virus. To help Sa in her own battle, I dutifully went to the local pharmacy (with the assistance of the Team Sky doctor on the mobile) to see what they had that might help. The chap behind the counter could not have been more sympathetic, recommending a series of medication and making sure I knew exactly what the dosage was. I thanked him profusely, which was the point when he winked, reached under the counter and offered me a special deal on some knock-off Viagra. Because when your girlfriend is collapsed in bed, feeling as attractive as an open sewer, the first thing you reach for is the Viagra, right?

Cafes

A long ride without a cafe stop is like a bike without wheels. So let me set out the conditions for the fantasy cycle stopover.

Indoor and outdoor seating. No great drama with this one: if it's warm, let the sweat dry in the sunshine and the cyclist's tan grow dark. If it's winter: let me in, please, I'm freezing, and each additional minute I spend outside in these damp clothes takes me a step closer to hypothermia. Ideally there'll be a place to leave bikes, because it's very hard to relax over your beverage when you've left several thousand pounds' worth of carbon fibre unlocked in the street outside. If there isn't, try the old trick of leaning your bike against the nearest wall and letting your fellow riders place theirs on top. Yes, there is a chance of a cosmetic scratch to the frame. But if some light-fingered individual decides to grab a bike when your back is turned, it's not going to be the one at the bottom of the pile. Undoing the quick-release skewers on the wheels also helps; unless it's a fellow rider nicking your bike, the thief won't have a clue what's happening when the wheels fall out, and will be even more confused when it comes to putting them back in.

Staff should be welcoming. It's not the easiest thing having a pack of sweaty cyclists piling in to your carefully arranged interior, clicking and clacking in their cleats and waddling like Lycra-clad ducks. If you're okay with that, we will reward you with a significantly larger order than most other mid-morning visitors. And not just on this occasion – cyclists are extremely loyal when it comes to their cafe stops, and will stick to a good one once found. Consider it an investment in your own future.

A proper coffee machine used by properly trained staff. The doomsday scenario is to go to the counter, ask what coffees they do and watch them reach behind for a jug of percolated horror. Probably with a tidemark halfway up the glass jug where the already gravy-like drink has evaporated over the three hours it's been sitting there. In that case it's not worth it – instantly switch your order to a pot of tea. It's almost as galling when they appear to have a long list of possible coffees yet, when the moment comes, appear unable to differentiate between a cappuccino and a latte. You can't expect every little place to know what a macchiato is. But a bucket of brown milk with some foam on top is not a cappuccino. On that subject, be warned: a cappuccino in Belgium is not as we would understand it. It's black coffee with cream. Cheeky.

A wide range of attractively presented cakes. On an early morning recovery ride it's a delight to stop for a proper egg-based breakfast. On a longer run, at the right time of year, it's all about the cakes. Usually I'm under harsh dietary restrictions so, if I'm going to have something, I might as well go the whole hog and have something really bad. I don't want to just see a couple of stale flapjacks crumbling on a doily. I'd like to see carrot cake, fruitcake, possibly something from the Bakewell range and ideally some bara brith with butter. Or Welsh cakes. Although for the latter two you'd have to be in Wales to get anything like the authentic quality a lad raised in Cardiff would hope for.

At least two toilets. Otherwise you'll spend the whole of your half-hour break standing in a queue while your fellow riders fumble with their bib shorts and slip over on the tiled floors in their cleats. I'd probably use a quiet lane on the way in just to be on the safe side.

Companions with change. When the bill comes, make sure it gets paid. With a generous tip. There's always a tightwad who works out that his coffee was £2.40 and his lemon drizzle cake £2.30, so can he have thirty-pence change from his fiver, please? Look: what goes around comes around. Chuck your money in and be gone. Having said that, I often forget my money completely. That's far worse. And I only realise after I've eaten the weight of one of my arms in scrambled egg.

Respect on both sides. In return for all the above, treat your hosts as you would like to be treated. Do not strip down to your bib shorts and merino mesh vest, in the style of *Little Britain*'s Daffyd. Do not hang your clothes over the back of every chair to dry. Your gloves may not smell to you but they do smell to everyone else: do not toss them onto a neighbouring table, and do not put your feet up on the soft furnishings. It's not your front room.

You'll sense that cafes have played an important role in my cycling education. An early favourite as a kid was in Cowbridge, about a forty-five-minute ride west from Cardiff. It was very much a cups-of-tea-and-bacon-sarnies sort of vibe, as popular with bikers as it was with cyclists. The two cultures would coexist rather well, the bikers outside in their leathers and us lot shivering inside in thin sportswear.

There was a lad we rode with in our teens called Stephen Roche. Not the former Tour de France winner and World road race champion, but a local a few years older than us. He was famous for nailing eight cups of tea on every ride. Another couple of chaps his age had a quiet word. 'Oh, Roche, it's about time for something called coffee.'

That started us all off. Initially it was like your first few pints of beer. You couldn't stand the taste but you threw it down because you knew you it was the right thing to do. The next thing you know, you're hooked. Give it a few more years and you're an out and out coffee snob.

That brought a new cafe into play, a charming establishment up in Usk. The standard of coffee was far superior to Cowbridge. Don't get me wrong, it wasn't Rome, but you could order a cappuccino in confidence, and the owners were very friendly people. They passed the critical test of refilling your water bottles for free, as long as you didn't lean your bike against their plate-glass window or block the little door to the flat upstairs.

There was something we called the Usk Cafe Rules. It was actually more of a Rule: whatever you've ordered, you have to finish everything on your plate. It might not sound that bad – we were hungry lads – but when you ordered a scone, you were given enough cream for six of them. That's a lot of dairy when you've got big hills to climb.

As my horizons have expanded, so has my appreciation for such places. I hope I'm not the kind of coffee snob, like my former British teammate Andy Tennant, who will refuse to join you unless you're going to exactly the right place another two kilometres up the road. There are times when Starbucks does the job, even if it's not in the same class as the great little cafes. At least you know what you're getting. You can stop for a coffee in Menton in the south of France – a beautiful setting where you sit overlooking the beach – and be served a coffee so terrible you need to throw in three sugars just to down it. You then pedal a mere five kilometres down the road into Italy and can get a great coffee anywhere. How does that work? It's as if any knowledge of making good coffee is wiped from a barista's memory at the border, like that crazy pen thing in *Men in Black*.

Nothing is as heartbreaking as ordering coffee in the US and receiving a large vase of tasteless murk. Nothing is as alluring as a stop in Bordighera, just across the Italian border from my training base in the south of France, where the piadina can bring tears to a Welsh lad's eyes. And, when I'm home in Cardiff, there's a little Italian place opposite the castle where the tiramisu is as good as in the homeland and the owner even indulges my appalling efforts to communicate with him in his native tongue.

Then there's Australia, where the coffee is not only uniformly outstanding but the weather is always warm enough to sit outside. They love their sport, they love their cycling. And then when they find out you're actually Welsh, when they'd assumed before you were English – well, I've seldom seen hospitality like it.

Rain

'**D**on't worry about the rain, butt,' my old Wales coach Darren Tudor liked to tell us. 'Skin's waterproof. Crack on.'

GB coach Shane Sutton used to make a similar claim: there is no such thing as bad weather, only bad clothing. Thus speaks a bloke from Australia, not one born in South Wales and matured in Manchester.

Offered a choice between skin-peeling heat, farewell-fingers cold, capricious winds or relentless rain, you would choose rain last. Particularly if it's cold rain.

There are some races and some riders where heavy rain becomes an excuse. People won't refuse to start, and they won't step off their bikes halfway round, but you can see in their eyes that they have given themselves a reason for failure.

It doesn't happen in the Classics, because there's always the chance of rain in the Classics, and you have to love it when it does – the harder the better. But if it comes down hard and chilly on the Tour, or on the Giro, you will see riders getting depressed about it. On the week-long races, or during a race on a circuit, passing your team bus lap after lap, knowing how nice it is inside, is a cruel form of toasty torture. Oh man – as if what we're doing isn't tough enough already . . .

There will be someone on every team who starts the moaning. And one misery guts is all you need to drag everyone down – so you have to stay clear, stay strong and ignore the prophesies of doom. No-one is going to cancel the stage. No-one is going to cancel the weather. We will be racing unless it turns cloudy with a chance of meatballs, so you might as well do it properly: attack with teeth bared rather than sitting in the spray at the back feeling sorry for yourself; ride hard rather than quitting at ten kilometres and spending the next four hours shivering in the team car, feeling more disgusted with yourself with every mile.

But it changes everything. An already jumpy peloton becomes a shifting mob of stress. Elbows dig and tempers unravel. Fights break out over the kingpin slots at the front, because with every metre further back in the pack, the more likely you are to be devoured in a crash. Your ability to brake fast and where you want begins to drift. The road turns into a skid pan. There is more shouting, more swearing, more fingers tight on bars and more dirty looks. On a climb, there is an indecent sprint for the top, because everybody wants to be as far forward for the descent as possible, rather than being out the back and having to chase flat out on those treacherous descents. There might not be a crash, but the peloton is likely to split. Even a five-second gap is too much. By the time you hit the flat road at the bottom you'll be going balls-out to close it up. And that will hurt.

In pro cycling you seize upon every advantage fate throws at you. Of all those battling in the peloton, there are only a very few who can match my involuntarily perfect preparation for such conditions: Cardiff for the first eighteen years of my life, Manchester for the next eight. Silver linings to the most permanent of clouds.

It's a very simple equation; you can't be a bike rider in the UK if you don't like riding in the rain. As a kid I used to actively enjoy it. It was more of a challenge. On one ride we were heading back into Cardiff on a road known as the Newport flats. It had been hammering down all day and night, and there were huge puddles everywhere. Being kids, we ended up riding through them, faster and faster, making as big a wave as possible. What we failed to realise, at least until I hit a huge crater and catapulted over my bars, was that where there were puddles, there were also probably holes in the road. On the up side, the water was so deep it was like landing on a wet mattress. On the down, while I was unharmed, both front and back tyres had blown. I had to get a soggy lift home from one of the other kids' dads. Lesson learned.

As I've grown older, I've grown grumpier, but those early years have still toughened me in profitable fashion. Whenever there is bad weather at a race there will be a Briton in the showdown – Cav, Swift, Sky teammate Ian Stannard. What is a convenient excuse for others becomes a soggy-bottomed opportunity for us. We can handle it where others cannot.

We have had our moments. After the Track World Championships in 2005, Ed, Cav and I returned to Manchester. We had an easy couple of hours planned to get over the travel. It was a typical Manchester day, rain and 6°C. So we left later than usual, fighting the urge to stay in. *Bargain*

Hunt was on the telly, something we'd never ordinarily watch, but even that was more appealing than the ride. When we eventually made it out, we were all thinking the same thing: 'What the hell are we doing?' Five minutes down the road we stopped at a set of traffic lights and almost as one came out with it: 'Sod it, I'm off home.' Ten minutes is better than nothing, right?

Everyone remembers the 2013 edition of Milan–San Remo, where the snow was so bad that the race was stopped. It was certainly deeply miserable, being frozen to the internal organs, climbing onto the bus and desperately trying to warm up and dry off before the inevitable resumption. But it was actually far worse the year after, when it hammered down, chilling us like fish fingers, before stopping – allowing us to get hot enough to strip down to basic kit. Then, as we came round a corner, the weather gave us the meteorological middle finger: a sky as black as bib shorts and rain like an igloo wall. Our domestiques tried to get back to the team car to pick up fresh kit, but every team in the race had the same idea. Logjam at the back of the peloton, human icicles at the front and middle.

When it does that you will see every rider in the race wearing their own version of the 'Rain Face'. This is the expression one adopts when being scoured by raindrops like cold stilettos: face off to the side, one eye shut, the other only half open. It's far from the ideal perspective when you're going at 26 mph surrounded by eighty other cycling Cyclops, but since your glasses steam up and do not come with wipers, you are left with a dilemma: leave the foggy shades on, gambling that you'll miraculously see that kerb sticking out or that hole in the road, or take them off and deal with the spray. By the finish, should you be lucky enough to make it there unscathed, your eyes will be bloodshot and ruined. After a Belgian Classic you will be on the team bus and unable to see. You stick in eye drops but, until the morning comes, the world sits behind a grainy blur. With every hour that passes, more grit and dirt ooze from the corners of your eyes. When you wake in the morning, it has sealed them shut as effectively as Acme quick-drying cement. You feel your way into the bathroom, shove the end of a towel under the tap and start to dab.

As a result, we become obsessed with the weather forecast. Temperature, percentage chance of rain, where it will fall, where the wind will blow, how strong it might be. If you see Bernie Eisel looking at his phone, he's most likely to be studying an app called Windfinder. I'll look at three or four different forecasts to get the most accurate prediction, and then immediately ditch it in favour of the one that is most optimistic. Three say 90 per cent chance of rain, one says 40 per cent? Forty per cent it is.

Just as rain rewrites the racing rules, so it changes training. If you're a club rider and you pull back the curtains to see it coming down stair-rods, you can sack it off in favour of some time on the turbo or a little R&R. We can't. And we end up going out on our own, because if you go out in a group there will always be someone soaking in the spray of a rear wheel.

You become obsessed with having the right gear. At home, wet-weather clothing used to mean a transparent plastic cape that was like wearing a sweat jacket. It's remarkable how much difference a merino base layer, soft jersey and good rain jacket can make, with overshoes to keep the worst of it out of the socks for a while and a cap to keep the head warm. Digging out that sort of clothing can feel like you're readying for battle, pulling on your armour and preparing for the nastiness ahead.

The best way to keep warm? Ride hard. Still cold? Ride harder.

Trouble is, it's more difficult to ride fast on wet roads around Nice than back in Cardiff. In that part of South Wales there are plenty of flat, straight roads. In Nice it's either up or down, left or right. And going downhill isn't good when you are trying to keep warm.

Warm rain barely counts as rain at all. Richie Porte thinks he grew up in the rain, but that was the 20°C stuff of Tasmania. That's not rain, it's a spa treatment. Only when it comes down in torrents, as in a summer thunderstorm in the south of France, do you have to take notice. Because then the roads become first streams and then sewers, all sorts of horrors washed out under your wheels. If you're lucky, there might be a team car following behind where you can stash dry gloves and an extra top for the shivering descents, but that doesn't happen often.

More often, you're on your own, heavy legs made twice as heavy again by your sodden clothing. You try to hide under a tree or in an old farm building, until the realisation comes that it's settled in for a long innings. Then the calculation changes. From worrying about mere water, you scan the sky for lightning strikes. There is a lot of metal on a bike. Okay, our tyres are made of rubber, and that will insulate us. But will the lightning know that there is rubber right down there before it has scorched all the way through rider and frame? We all know the theory. The practice feels something more of a gamble.

PEOPLE

Brad

There are two different Bradley Wigginses.

There is the confident, jovial, successful Brad; all impressions, all gags; the man who called Sue Barker 'Susan' at the 2012 BBC Sports Personality of the Year; the extrovert who, at the wedding of our teammate Steve Cummings, nicked the band's mic to entertain the expectant crowd with some impromptu Usain Bolt/reggae rapping and his tie around his head.

Then there's the man who maybe hasn't had a great day, who is low in confidence, who is seriously tired. That one just comes down to the team dining room, silently eats his food and leaves. The foreign riders who don't know him are totally baffled. 'Where Brad go? Where the jokes?'

When he's up, he's a remarkable character to be around. I first met him in 2003, when the velodrome in Newport opened for the first time and held the European Derny Championships. Brad, having won, was holding court in the bar afterwards with Dave Brailsford, us fresh-faced juniors hanging round him. At one point after midnight he and Dave were chasing Ed Clancy and me round the car park. Shortly after that, someone ended up in the pond out front, and was last seen trying to backstroke through the muddy water. It's fair to say times have changed.

Brad is someone I've always looked up to, because he's always done what I wanted to do. And because he's not that much older than me, I've seen him do it: winning the Junior Worlds, winning Olympic gold; even at the velodrome in Manchester, winning national titles as a kid.

On the track he would always turn up with a purpose. He was always motivated for the efforts ahead, just the same as Chris Hoy. Others might be struggling, or fearing the pain, and Brad and Chris were probably feeling exactly the same, but it didn't show.

We would stare in admiration. They were always the first up for the next effort: 'They're up again, they're going for it!' They knew what they were training for, and so they did the work: that rubbed off on the whole group.

Brad with the endurance squad, Chris with the sprinters. Each was like the godfather. Their attitude spread to us.

At least, it did in the end. At the start of it all, when us young lads were among the first intake to the British Olympic Academy, I shared a house with Mark Cavendish and Ed Clancy. On my birthday in 2005 I went to the pub for a few beers with Irish rider Matt Brammeier – a few beers that, watching Liverpool come back from 3–0 down against Milan to win the Champions League final, turned into many, many beers.

It was buzzing – through extra time and then penalties, drinking away, so inebriated by the time it all ended that we piled into the branch of Subway down the road and bought every single cookie they had left. Back to ours, frisbeeing these cookies around, waking up Cav and Ed, turning over the sofas.

Cav was furious – so furious that he rang our coach Rod Ellingworth. The next morning, we had an interview at the house with Larry Hickmott, a journalist for British Cycling. I was frantically cleaning the house – at least until the Hoover broke. I had to borrow the neighbour's. Getting ready for training, I couldn't find my cycling shoe. I rang Brammeier to ask if he knew where it was. No idea. Five minutes later, he called back: 'Ah, I think I stuck it in the freezer . . .'

The following day, a big meeting was called. Head coach Shane Sutton was in terrifying form. 'G, mate, the buck stops with you. This is your fault. So you're not riding the Five Valleys [a big race in Wales I was really looking forward to] – you're going into the Peaks with the big boys.'

We were sent off with Brad and Steve Cummings on a monstrous punishment ride. They had been told to stick a wheel on me and, going up the long Cat and Fiddle climb out of Macclesfield into the Peaks, that was exactly what they did. Brad had just returned from riding the Giro and was in shape, while Steve was in fine form. We had to do effort after effort in the hills, and then lead-out after lead-out in the Cheshire lanes. Brutal.

I learned my lesson: don't go back to your own house after a night out. Head over to Brammeier's instead. A little later, Brad decided to pop over to mine for another training ride. At the time I had just moved into the first house I ever bought, a modest property in Newton-le-Willows, one of the tougher parts of the north-west.

Brad being Brad, he turned up in a brand-new pearl-white BMW M3. My first thought was, 'That won't be here when we get back.' We went out for a five-hour ride. When we returned to see that car still gleaming outside my house, I could hardly contain my relief.

If Brad is high in confidence, he is unbeatable. He'll just go out there and smash it and be great. But if he's a bit doubtful, he'll barely turn up at the race.

He's always been like this, even training for the pursuit in Beijing, four years before he became the first Briton to win the Tour de France. When he was training for the Tour he took his preparations to a level that most of us had never seen before. What you ate mattered far less on the track. But in 2012 it was as if the coaches and nutritionists wrote his programme on their laptops, pressed enter and it went straight into Brad's brain. It was almost like he was a robot, carrying out instructions by remote.

I had never seen anyone so focused. The two and a half years from his disappointing first Tour for Team Sky in 2010, all the way through until the end of 2012, he lived like a monk. It was no surprise that he crashed off that afterwards, because no man could sustain that intensity. It was the most impressive thing I've ever seen.

Yet, even in his days as a knight of the realm, the scrapes have continued.

We were training in Majorca, just Brad and I, doing a long ride, going through the mountains, a good six hours. We had raced the infamous twists and climbs of Sa Calobra and blown our doors off doing efforts – hanging off the bike, starving hungry, ready to turn back for home. And then we came across a landslide blocking the road. So we had no option but to go back up the long climb of the Puig Major and down into the distant town of Soller, way across the mountains from our training base on the coast at Pollensa, neither of us with a phone, food or money.

To others this would be a disaster. With Brad it was just the start of the fun. We stopped in a little cafe, ordered food and copious drinks. Brad borrowed their phone, called his wife, Cath, at home in Lancashire, and instructed her to call the velodrome in Manchester to get Team Sky directeur sportif Dan Hunt's number, then call Dan to tell him where we were.

Two hours later, Dan arrived, already pissed off, to watch Brad just climb into the car without a word and shove a massive bill in his hand. All in the name of Wiggins fun. Good times.

I've learned a lot from Brad, on and off the bike. I'll miss him when he leaves the continental scene.

Unsung Heroes

What gets a rider to the top? Determination, for sure, and some raw talent, and great coaching, and a little luck. But we are only one cog in a smooth machine. We succeed, not on our own, but because of all those human components around us. You might never see them. But, without their constant action, neither would you ever see us.

The mechanics. The best fringe benefit of being a pro bike rider? Climbing out of the saddle at the end of a long day, handing over a dirty, knackered bike and being given it back the next morning with everything working to spotless perfection.

Imagine never having to clean your car, or fill it with petrol, or check the oil, or tune the engine. Imagine making the mother of all messes in the kitchen, filthy pans and plates all over the place, food up the walls and sink over-flowing, and coming down the next morning to find it all so clean it looks like you've moved into a show home.

That's what it's like having a team mechanic.

When you're training at home, you never fix your bike, unless it's absolutely necessary. You barely pump up the tyres. A quick squeeze as you head out – ach, that'll do, even when you know it probably won't. You forget to recharge the batteries on your electronic gears. Gradually everything gets clanky and squeaky and full of rattles.

Not at a race. Brakes run smooth and actually stop you. Tyres are sweet-rolling perfection. Gears change with hardly a whisper. Everything is where it should be, where only you and your body's idiosyncratic dimensions want it to be.

It's wonderful for us. For the mechanics it's a working day that never ends. They are up before anyone else, fettling and fiddling. When the race starts, one will be in a team car, ready to make adjustments – not only by the side of the road but leaning out of a car window at 35 mph if need be. Another will be driving the truck to the next hotel, getting what is in effect a small workshop put up and taken down every single day. They are the last men down for dinner and the first to have their schedules ripped up.

There is never an easy day. If it's a time trial the following afternoon they will spend all that day dialling in everyone's unique position. If it's cobbles, they may have to build entirely new bikes, like those that featured little suspension units in the rear stays that we used at Paris–Roubaix in 2015. There may be fresh livery, as with the special green bikes Team Sky used in 2011 to show their support for the Rainforest Foundation. There may just be a rider who seeks solace in constant micro-adjustments, like Nicolas Roche (a tweak of the saddle every time he stops) or Ben Swift (so sensitive to tiny changes he's the cycling equivalent of the princess and the pea).

And they are always away from home. You can't fly trucks full of bikes from one race to another, which means their race begins three or four days before anyone else's: chugging all the way down from Belgium on Europe's motorways to the start of the Vuelta in Marbella, or having to take the cargo ferry to Majorca for our winter training camps. Head mechanic Gary Blem will be away from his family in South Africa for three months at time. That's some sacrifice.

But the mechanics love their job. They love all the new kit. They could talk gear ratios and tyre pressures all day, even if you're not too bothered about it. Before the Classics, they love all the extra problems they have to deal with. The new suspension bike. Double-tape on the handlebars or gel inserts? What tyres? What pressure? Now then, G, fancy these wheels for the morning? Mechanics are the kings of bike porn, the dedicated followers of bike fashion.

The greatest irony of all? They never get to ride the bikes themselves. Dave Brailsford and head of performance Tim Kerrison have their own Pinarellos to ride. Not the mechanics. They don't have time. They are the chefs who work in a Michelin-starred restaurant but must exist on takeaways. Dedication doesn't even come close.

The nutritionists. It used to be that nutrition was about standards: get this much carbohydrate down you; consume this many grammes of protein after finishing a ride. Now it's about specifics: how many grammess of carbs you'll need for today's mountain stage rather than the flat one yesterday; exactly when in the day you need that protein so that your body can absorb it most effectively.

Our long-term expert at British Cycling is Nigel Mitchell, not only a leader in his field but also the most pleasant man in the team hotel. A meal eaten next to Nigel will fuel not just your body but also your depleted reserves of humour and goodwill to others. Within Team Sky we now work with James Morton, known informally as Danny Murphy – not only because he too spent much of his career at Liverpool FC but because, off the pitch at least, you could be talking to one of them for half an hour before you realised you had the wrong man.

With each year the focus tightens. It began with the success Brad had in 2012 after becoming obsessional about his diet. It continued in 2013 when Chris Froome followed in Brad's nutritional and Tour tyre-tracks. There could be no wriggle room after that: this approach works, we should all be doing it.

The innovations don't always come in the areas you might imagine. We now eat Greek yoghurt rather than the fat-free stuff, happy to take on the extra fats because they are natural rather than processed. Plus we are doing our bit to help our Greek friends through their financial crisis. We pay more attention to what we eat on rest days after a tough stage than what was consumed on the previous evening, because we are eating for the tests to come rather than the day just gone.

In the weeks before a stage race I will cut back on my coffee intake so that my body gets a bigger kick off it when it needs it during the race. On the bike it is now more a question of constant grazing than two hours of hard riding followed by a chunky panini. Every twenty-five minutes we will eat something – a rice cake, an energy bar. If you wait until your body tells you it is hungry, it's too late. You will already be in energy deficit.

These aren't the sort of rice cakes you might see babies sucking on. They are custom-made beauties, a soft pudding rice baked with apricots and jam, hazelnuts and almonds, Speculoos or dried fruit, compressed into slabs and chilled in the fridge until the next morning, when they will be chopped into pocket-sized squares and wrapped in foil for us. Not only do they fuel you beautifully, but you genuinely look forward to eating them. And the same cannot be said for all riding food.

The old cycling traditions, the classic post-race meals of big steaks and big bowls of pasta, are as outdated now as steel frames and leather saddles. They are too difficult to digest, they stay too long in the gut. Rice has taken pasta's dominant role. It has less gluten, it clears your stomach more easily. The Italian teams will never abandon pasta. But for us, unshackled by cultural considerations, the argument is over. Eat a little too much spaghetti or fusilli over three days and you can feel the weight coming back on.

They look back to the pasta. We look to the future.

Directeur sportifs. Every team has one, but not all are created equal.

The role should be a straightforward one: on the road, the DS organises the team. Quite how they do it can be the difference between a team and leader that achieves their goals and those that are left with nothing but what-ifs and why-nots.

The perfect DS is assertive. They are clear both in their communication before a stage starts and when you are knee-deep in the day's racing. Confusion should not be given the chance to spread. They can stress all they like in the car, but as long as they are unambiguous and forthright on the radio, that's all that matters.

Sometimes they will be harsh. Come on, you know you can do this. But the iron fist always comes gloved with empathy – I know what you're going through, I know how hard this is. They are constantly calculating tactics and time differences but they are not just a computer. They have a rational brain but also a heart. Our old DS at Sky, Sean Yates, was a master at this, demanding and harsh. Straight-talking, but also sympathetic and understanding. He knew how hard it is.

They too will feel anxiety. This cannot be communicated to the riders. On a big set-piece climb, when it is all kicking off, attacks going everywhere and the pre-arranged plan going up in smoke, they must understand that they cannot vent their anger down the race radio. For a start, few can actually hear them, because everyone is flat out. There's nothing worse than chatter down the radio when you're head-deep in lactic acid. Short instructions. Necessary instructions.

There must be a deep understanding of the race and each of its myriad nuances. There must be the ability to decide the correct tactics but also to abandon them should the situation on the road change. The team needs someone to make a call. Whether it turns out to be right or wrong matters less.

It's more that the decision needs to be made. A great DS is one who gets his riders doing exactly what he wants, when he wants. He has the respect of the man on the road. What he says goes. No questions.

DSs are getting younger, their careers in the saddle more recent. There are a few guys I have ridden alongside at Sky who have then popped up as a DS the following year. It feels a bit like a lad from your class at school rocking up as a supply teacher. Nicolas Portal was the first to make the transition, becoming one of the youngest-ever lead DSs to win the Tour de France; and there is our pair of tamed Norwegians, Gabriel Rasch and Kurt Asle Arvesen. The promoted man will usually start as the second DS, learning the ropes from the weathered, more experienced lead. But even the second DS on the team cannot afford any sloppiness. When they plan the day – what time to get up, when breakfast should be served, what time to arrive at the start – they must get it right to the minute, for the tired rider needs every second of sleep he can get, and the weary, grumpy rider is no use at all on the road.

The big don'ts: overtalking, overcomplicating. Changing your mind, changing your style. Babbling when you should be brisk. It is a hard job. That does not mean it cannot be done right.

The partners. It is hard to be the girlfriend, wife or boyfriend of a professional cyclist, and not always in the ways you might expect.

I will go out for dinner with Sara. As soon as we order she will be feeling self-conscious, because while she quite rightly goes for a nice pizza or a steak, I'm restricted to ordering a tiny piece of steamed fish and some spinach. Then, when the waiter returns with the food, he will instinctively put the steak down in front of the gentleman and the flake of fish in front of the lady. You may as well put a flashing neon sign above the table: 'I EAT THREE TIMES AS MUCH AS A HUNGRY MAN.'

It can be lonely for them. As a rider you are away so much that it's like dating half a person. Cycling comes first. I missed Sa's graduation because I was at the team's pre-Olympic holding camp in Newport. She has had to get used to going to big events on her own, when everyone else is coupled-up – family celebrations, birthdays, the weddings of good friends. She almost lives two lives: one at home in Cardiff, another with me in the south of France. Now, there are worse places to move to, although Nice sadly has no equivalent of Cardiff's infamous Chippy Lane – not even a Rue de Pommes Frites. You need to be comfortable on the road, on your own, cooking two separate meals each evening (one for the normal person, one for the weirdo sportsman) or forcing yourself not only to enjoy the taste of quinoa, but to be able to pronounce it well enough that you can ask for it in the local supermarket.

In the brief periods you are together, your energy levels are often wildly out of sync. The partner has been looking forward to catching up, to getting out and about, to doing exciting things. The rider just wants to sleep. When they are awake, they will still be so drained from their racing exertions that the conversation will be limited to grunts and shrugs. If the partner doesn't understand or recognise this, they can fear they've done something terribly wrong. Why aren't they replying to me?

Sometimes, as a rider, you just want to be on your own. You have been away for so long that you don't want to go out. It becomes a treat to eat in your own house, to lie in your own bed. You just want to slump on the sofa and watch something on the BBC. Because it's the BBC, a channel you don't get when you're away, you don't care what's on. If you are training hard you will be gripped by hunger and unable to satiate it properly. If the training session has gone badly you will be grumpier still. Your partner needs to be both a psychologist and entirely selfless, because you will be locked in your own world rather than reaching out into theirs.

Cycling can provide a comfortable financial cushion. It can also be a social manacle. You wriggle out of pleasant engagements because it's not far enough to drive yet you're too tired to walk there, or get somewhere and leave almost immediately because you are not drinking and have to be in bed by a reasonable hour so you can train in the morning. You can't stay overnight at a certain hotel because there's nowhere to ride your bike the next morning. You can't go to a certain restaurant because the menu is all burgers, gourmet or otherwise, and burgers are eaten by cyclists as often as bikes fly.

And so your partner begins to feel like a cleaner, a chef and a taxi driver rolled into one. Cycling always takes priority. Cycling has first claim on every day.

When they come to a race it can take days to get there. Twenty-four hours in taxis, planes, trains and on foot, all to watch it on a TV screen until they see you flash by at the finish. There are no family seats and no family time. When the racing is done, there's no time to chat at the bus, because you will be swarmed by autograph hunters, and then you return to the team hotel for massage and dinner. The space for the two of you shrinks to an awkward twenty minutes in the hotel lobby, fighting the hangers-on.

The team will try to help. Before one stage in the south of France, just before the Sky bus drove off and left Sa standing by the side of the road with her suitcase, one of the swannies dashed out to make sure she had enough water. Hot on his heels came Dave Brailsford, giving Sa his mobile number and telling her to call him if she needed anything. I could picture the scene: four hours into the day's racing, everything kicking off, Contador has attacked, the team is chasing full gas behind, Froome's punctured. Sa calls Dave. 'Hi, Dave, do you have any numbers for taxis in the Toulouse area? I think I'm lost . . .'

That's classic Dave. Not just running an entire team but concerned that your wife might get on the wrong bus to the airport.

The unsung unsung. Who never get mentioned, even when discussing those who never get mentioned. The physios, who not only fix your body but also ease your mind, and are rewarded by having to work late into each evening, while the riders and coaches are halfway through their dessert. When I fractured my pelvis at the start of the 2013 Tour, I would see physio Dan every morning and every evening, and his chat was as important in getting me to Paris as his treatment. Few things worked in alleviating the excruciating pain like a detailed conversation about the British and Irish Lions tour of Australia (good job, Wales, plus a few extras from the other nations). Neither do these physios just physio. They have to help with luggage, work on feed stations, operate on-bike gadgets. All so we can go out and break ourselves afresh in the morning.

The media team, the press officers and web guys, act as a buffer between you and the outside world so that you can focus purely on the riding. The Tour is like a soap opera. These guys stop you getting tangled up in the subplots.

Our two Scandinavian chefs, Heinrich and Søren, take over strange kitchens and produce sensational food, day after day. In doing so they hold the key, not only to our health and nutrition, but to our happiness. During a Grand Tour, riders can get very tired and very cranky. A dinner to make every other team jealous is often the highlight of a bad day.

Then there are the least appreciated of all, our bus drivers Slarky and Claudio. Perfection in navigation is one thing, particularly when one wrong turn in three weeks will see an unjustifiable amount of abuse thrown their way. But it's everything else on the bus – making sure that a coffee machine that is grinding and steaming every minute of the day never packs in, that the showers always drain, that the projector at the front works and both interior and exterior are cleaned every night, that there is always fresh rice to eat and recovery drinks to hand, that the toilet-roll holder never spins in your hand to show itself as nothing but brown cardboard. Otherwise the shout will go up. 'Oi, Slarky! What's up with this?'

Dave B

I've heard Dave Brailsford described as a cross between the Dalai Lama and Colonel Kurtz. I've heard him compared to a free climber, all risk and reward. I've heard him described as the best sports coach Britain has ever produced.

Here's how I prefer to encapsulate him: your best mate's dad.

I appreciate that's not quite as evocative, so let me explain. Your best mate's dad has seen you grow and mature. He's seen you at your worst, much more drunk than your own father has. And that creates a lovely bond between the two of you: close but not too close, stern without being a brute, years of knowing each other, years of him keeping a partially paternal eye on you.

It's the 2003 Junior Track World Championships in Moscow. Matt Brammeier and I are bored. We start messing about in our spartan hotel room, throwing a rotten old banana at each other. It's hardly Jagger and Richards, but it gets a little messy: banana up the walls, black marks across the carpet and on the ceiling. We pop down to breakfast, intending to clean it up when we get back, only for the Russian maids to find it first. And they flip – shouting, wagging fingers, scaring the life out of these two skinny kids on their first big trip away. Before you know it, they've told management that we've smeared poo all over the wall.

Hold on, we protest. All right, we might be silly. But we're not animals, yeah?

Back at the velodrome in Manchester, the poo narrative seemed to have travelled better than the banana bit. Dave called us in to see him and delivered the most terrifying telling-off. Terrifying, not because he was ranting, but precisely the opposite. Not once did he raise his voice. All the usuals were in there – colourful language, the 'You've disgraced yourselves . . .' line, the 'You're supposed to be representing your country . . .' stuff. And all the time he was bending a pencil between his hands, the flex in it increasing with each quietly furious statement; Matt and I staring at it in dread fascination, wondering if it would snap and what the snap would signify if it did.

You'll hear different theories about Dave Brailsford. His predecessor at British Cycling, Peter Keen, came up with the Dalai Kurtz idea. Chris Boardman, godfather of the cycling revolution in this country, chose the climber analogy ('A free climber will always be the first to the top of the mountain, but there will also be a big pile of them at the bottom who didn't make it'). From someone else I learned that Dave, remarkably, was an undercover investigator in the perfume industry before cycling came calling. He's still coming up smelling of roses.

Everyone wants to know his secret. Having gone through the system at the same time as his rise to the top, I can tell you that it comes down to one key ability: getting the right team around him.

You can break that down further. Recruit the right people – not necessarily the ones with the biggest reputations, or with the best track records, but the ones who will both bring something different and grow at an advanced speed. Push them. Improve them. Get the best out of them.

Dave trusts those around him. He works with the top three or four – a coach like Shane Sutton or Rod Ellingworth, a sports scientist like Tim Kerrison, the psychiatrist Steve Peters – and lets them do the same beneath them. No-one is allowed to stagnate. If you're not up to it, you're moved on.

The two of us met when he was assistant to Keen and I was a hopeful nobody. All these years later – after Olympic gold medals, the idea of Team Sky, the Tour de France-winning reality – he is the same: definitely your boss; still a friend you can speak to with total honesty.

Dave hasn't changed. His bank balance and the cars he drives have. And he wants more: more success for Sky, a better way of doing things. Rivalries spark, die off and are reborn – with the Aussie track team, with Tinkoff-Saxo, with individuals like Jonathan Vaughters or Alberto Contador.

All he cares about is cycling. You never see him relaxing, only hammering at his laptop. On the team bus, when his nine riders are lying there with their feet up, Dave will be figuring out what went right or wrong and why. If anything, he loves it more than us riders. Sky is his team. His baby.

He struggles to switch off from it all. He can never stand still, never settle down. Because he has always been on the move – trying to make it as a pro rider in his late teens, becoming a soigneur in his mid-twenties, getting involved with British Cycling as the magic started to fire, dominating the Olympic velodrome in Beijing, somehow repeating the trick under immense pressure in London.

Boardman made that free-climber comment in relation to there being a British winner of the Tour de France. Most people couldn't conceive of a British-based team, let alone a Briton winning. Dave could. When he had one winner, he wanted another. He got it. He then wanted three in a row. Now he wants to win all three Grand Tours in the same season.

He will let his hair down; he used to do it in style. Like all of us he learned that there is a time and a place, and that place is no longer in public.

Dave was a good drunk: one of the lads, twice as funny, a little lairy. In short, a classic Welshman.

In 2005 the Track World Championships were staged in Los Angeles. On the final night a glorious mood of collective mischief settled over everyone – Dave, head coach Simon Jones, Chris Hoy, us kids. In an eerie replay of the banana incident two years before, another foodstuff was thrown around and accidentally smeared all over the walls of a restaurant. In this case it was tomato sauce – which wouldn't have been a problem if a passer-by hadn't mistaken it for blood. And decided to call the cops.

The point in an evening out when the police are called is never a good moment. The point when you remember that you're in LA and that the cops are quite a serious bunch is even less good.

Dave realised that more quickly than the rest of us. Now when he has a few beers he keeps half his brain on the lime and sodas. After Paris–Roubaix one year, enjoying the end-of-Classics hospitality at our hotel in Kortrijk, we stumbled out into the street and started renegotiating my contract under the stars. My bargaining technique wasn't particularly sophisticated – I'd just add a zero to the end of every sum he mentioned – but I awoke confident that my financial future looked bright. Unfortunately, I had no recollection of the final amount we agreed on that night, only that what Dave eventually paid me was much less. He'll still bring it up today: no negotiating after drinking Belgian ales, G.

As a rider, you know he looks out for you. Though his profile has exploded, his demeanour makes you forget that he is now one of the top dogs in British sport. Even when he casually mentions that he's off for dinner at Arsène Wenger's house.

In different ways he is like all the great coaches: as innovative as Sir Clive Woodward but with more sustained success; as good as José Mourinho at distracting attention from his sportsmen so that they can focus just on the sport; as clever as Sir Alex Ferguson in never criticising his team in public but keeping them going flat out, year after year, incarnation after incarnation.

If he trusts you, if he knows you, he will look out for you. If you are one of his British riders he will protect you inside his bubble. If you are from overseas – and at one stage Team Sky's staff featured eighteen different nationalities speaking eleven different languages – he will give just as much or even more time to make you feel at home and part of the team. He'll even hire staff to help with the communication.

From Steve Peters he has learned the art of communication and reassurance. There is a significant difference between encouraging a rider and making him feel under pressure, Dave understands that. He will even work that magic on those around him. My partner, Sa, works for Welsh-language TV channel S4C during the Tour. When she had to interview Dave she was a little nervous. He spotted that and coached her through his own interview. By the end she felt like Jeremy Paxman. Then there was the time that Sergio Henao turned up in Majorca for his first training camp with the team. Dave got chatting to him in broken English in the hotel reception. After a couple of minutes of small talk – journeys, weather, that sort of thing – Sergio decided to take it further. 'So, what you do here? What your job?' Sir David took it well.

On the bus before each day's stage our directeur sportif Nico Portal will tell us what is to come and how we should handle it. He then will turn to his right. 'Dave, would you like to say anything?' The reply is always the same. 'No, no. But I will add . . .' And so follows the motivational speech. And it's never blood and thunder. Dave is too smart for that. Instead, he will leave you feeling both relaxed ('What's the worst that can happen?') and ready to ride yourself into the dirt.

And he cares.

He cares about the pure thrill of riding. On training camps or before a day's racing he will go out with the coaches for a blast and come back buzzing about how he whipped Tim on the climbs, or left operations manager Carsten Jeppesen for dead in a sprint.

He cares about the sport's history, and the part it has played in his own life. When the Tour of Britain passed close to his home village in North Wales a few years ago, you could tell that the sense of having come full circle made him very emotional.

And he cares most of all about the success of those he looks after. At the European Track Championships in October 2011 the team pursuit squad performed dreadfully. After a brutal year I was a broken man: the Tour Down Under, the Classics, the Tour de France, working my legs off for Cav as he won the Worlds. So were my teammates. With less than a year to go until the London Olympics we were in real danger of falling apart.

Dave saw that and acted. For six weeks he nursed us through a cycling boot camp, personally present at every single training session, rising at 6 a.m. each day and getting home much later than any of us.

The message was clear: your success means as much to me as it does to you. I don't know if that was because he genuinely cared about us as individuals or because he wanted to win for himself or his sport. But his commitment was extraordinary. In 2012, tilting both at the London Olympics and Tour de France, he never once spent consecutive nights in his own home. That's devotion. That's loyalty. That's Dave B in a sentence.

Soigneurs

Aka swannies, aka 'carers' at Team Sky, aka cycling's equivalent of roadies.

Soigneur comes from the French word for dogsbody. That isn't true, but it should be. A swannie has to do everything: massage, wash kit, dry it in time for the next day's racing, make rice cakes, make up hundreds of bottles of isotonic and carbohydrate drinks, carry bags, know every country like the back of a carbohydrate drink bottle, speak every language of every rider on the team, get up early, stay up late, lug bags, pack cars, soothe troubled minds, never get caught frowning, be willing to change habits of a lifetime at the slightest notice and not expect to be thanked for any of it.

A good swannie is thus a precious commodity. My first at Barloworld was Mario Pafundi, an Italian who transferred across to Sky at the same time as me. Mario personifies the art of swanning. He would see me in a hotel corridor and open his arms wide. 'G, you're my rider!' His massage is very Italian, all flicks and flourishes and signature moves, his attitude humble yet idiosyncratic. In his wake has come a posse of Slovenians, who enjoy being called Slovakians in the same way a Welshman likes being confused with an Englishman. They are masters, both of the deep but not damaging rub and the uncomplicated humour of the road. Different approaches, but unified by their adherence to the Secret Code of Swannies, which looks a bit like this:

Work bloody hard. You will do brutally long hours. You will get tired, and angry bike riders will take out their frustrations on you, not because it is your fault but simply because you are the nearest person.

Soak it up. You will be expected to be part agony aunt, part mother and part brother. The riders will sometimes want to just sit there and have a drink with you – beer for the swannie, lemonade for them. They will want to feel relaxed with you in a way they can't with a coach – have a moan, be reassured, feel that you at least are completely on their side.

Don't dish out tactical advice. This is one line that should never be crossed. It doesn't matter if you have raced as a kid, or been around pro bike racing for years; being in the middle of that madness is totally different to watching from the side. Don't advise on training, don't offer unsolicited feedback on how that day's racing went.

Gauge a mood in a moment. Your rider will get back on the bus or limp back to the hotel and see you first. In that instant, and often only from body language, you must sense what sort of day they have had. Do they need you to pick them up? Do they want to be left in silence?

Wash clothes as if the label inside were your gospel. The window for turning kit from grimy, sweat-soaked horror to freshly laundered and functional joy is small. It is also during normal hours of sleep, and will have to be achieved in a washing machine installed on a bus parked in the street. Despite this, you must get it absolutely right. The fabrics are likely to be sensitive to temperature and spin cycle: never put them on so high they either become attire for midgets or melt entirely. It has been done. If a rider gets their kit back in the morning and it's still wet, expect to hear about it.

Expect to be thanked in alcohol. Riders will often receive a large amount of the local tipple for winning a big race. They will be incapable of drinking it, even if they are allowed. You will be the lucky recipient. When I won E3 Harelbeke in 2015, I won my weight in beer. My prize is due to arrive at the same race a year later. I am expecting a lot of swannies to be putting their hands up for the Classics come March.

Double-check everything. You may think you have everything organised. It is worth being absolutely sure. On the first day of my first Tour de France with Barloworld, we arrived at the start to discover that the swannie in charge of the team's helmets had forgotten to bring them. Well, he took the blame anyway – the staff were mainly Italian, so fingers were pointing and accusations flying around everywhere. Apparently, he had put them in the wrong truck – one that was 100 miles away en route to the next hotel. We had to dash round London trying to borrow spare ones off the other teams. Complete panic. And to think you felt bad that time you lost your mobile.

Enjoy yourself socially, but put team harmony first. One lad with us was known for favouring the odd extra beer and a regular extracurricular relationship. After Paris–Roubaix one year, our always cheery nutritionist Nigel – a great guy to have around, always loud and friendly – noticed that this particular swannie had his girlfriend with him. He decided to make her feel welcome by introducing himself. 'Lovely to meet you, you must be the policewoman I've heard so much about.' A tense silence. 'No . . .'

A massage is a massage. Not an exfoliation, not a garden salad. Use enough massage oil that the rider does not walk away with friction burns: a tub of Nivea cream won't break the bank. But do not use so much that the cyclist will go up in flames if someone throws a cigarette our of a car window two streets away.

Be prompt but not pushy. Everyone likes to crack on with their more mundane tasks. But if a team programme says suitcases will be collected at 10 a.m., do not turn up at 9.30 a.m. and expect to see anything but a tired, naked rider getting out of the shower. Every second of rest is important.

Riders: be grateful. Swannies can feel like an overworked butler to a particularly insensitive young gentleman. Even if you expect them to be Jeeves, do not act like Wooster. Show them love whenever you can. David Rozman has a young family at home, but in the height of the season he will be away for eight weeks out of ten.

They will be up before you and to bed later. They have to drive to the races rather than fly, starting mostly from the service course in Belgium, where they have to help the mechanics pack all the luggage. Swannies will leave for a race at least two days before you, getting home two days after, travelling in far less comfort, eating worse food at less sociable hours and be paid a fraction of your own salary. And they have stressful days, so when you see them drinking beer and eating as much chocolate as they like, do not hate them for not having to obsess about their weight like you do. They are the lads of the team. Let them lad it out.

Cav

Whenever I see a colander, I think of Mark Cavendish. We've known each other since we were fifteen. We lived together as young lads on British Cycling's academy programme. We have raced against each other and for each other. And the colander story sums him up.

It's while we are sharing a house in Fallowfield, in south Manchester. It's the first time any of us have lived away from home. Also with us in the house is Ed Clancy, who will go on to win Olympic golds in Beijing and London alongside me in the team pursuit. Cav has already made his mark by turning up off the ferry from the Isle of Man like the original boy racer from the sticks: gold Corsa, stick-on skirts around the edge, big sticker across the windscreen saying 'GOLDFINGER'.

He has turned out to be obsessed with tidiness. And so, every time one of us has cooked pasta (and, as cyclists, that's an awful lot), the familiar refrain is bellowed round the house: 'ED! HOW MANY SIDES HAS A COLANDER GOT?'

Most people will just rinse out a colander after use. Some might give the inside a quick wipe. Only Cav – a Cav just out of his teens – expects it to be cleaned and polished inside and out until it shines like a guardsman's boots.

We had first met at the Junior Nationals. I was sitting on my own enjoying a tuna sandwich a couple of hours before a race when this loud, overweight kid came over with what sounded like a Scouse accent. 'What you eating that for? You don't want to be eating a tuna sandwich at this point. What were you thinking?'

More than a decade on, he's exactly the same.

He had been a champion ballroom dancer as a kid, which tells you less about his tastes than his attitude: if he does something, he has to be the best at it. Even back then he was always flash with his money. He liked his designer labels at an age when he couldn't afford them. You might have been able to get an identical shirt to his for a tenner in Topman. He'd look at you and shake his head. 'That's the Welsh in you, lad.'

He could be both maternal and paternal. Maternal because he was the mother of the house. Do this, do that, don't be out late, clean that up now. Paternal because he liked looking after Ed, who was probably the most naïve of our little group. Cav felt Ed needed to learn about life, or at least life as Cav understood it. If you were walking somewhere, Ed would often drift to the back of the group and drift out of the conversation. Cav would drag him back into both. 'Come on, Ed lad, get involved!' He also noticed that Ed, who didn't grow up racing on a bike (he was picked up by the talent team in his late teens), couldn't read a race like other guys. So Cav tried to help him – talking him through the last race, what happened, why it happened, what he did, what he could have done. He even tried to get Ed playing chess, to teach him to think a few moves ahead, stay on the front foot, anticipate what other people were going to do.

He meant well and wanted to help you out. It just didn't always come across that way. If he spotted you washing your bike in the back yard, he had to get involved. 'You don't want to wash it like that. What are you doing?' 'Thanks, mate, but don't worry, it's my bike, crack on with yours.'

Sometimes his interventions worked. Being a Cardiff lad, I used to add in an 'Oh' when referring to someone in conversation. 'Oh, Cav, where's the jam?' As ever, Cav had to have his say. 'Oh? It should be "Aye", lad, "Aye".' He'd then listen critically when I was on the phone to one of my best mates back in Cardiff – Dale, known to us all as 'D'. 'Oh, D, how you doing?' Cav would shake his head. 'If he's D, then you're G.' And so a nickname was born. Every time I see him now I can hear him coming a mile off. 'Oh! G!'

The one part of the game he wasn't quite on top of at that stage was his weight. It's true that fat sticks to him a lot more easily than most, but it's also true that he was fat because his diet wasn't as good as it could have been. None of ours was. We were eighteen years old, our mates back home were getting drunk every other night. By comparison, we thought, what were a few burgers or a pizza? But the coaches were on his back, along with those extra millimetres of subcutaneous fat. They'd tell him he was in danger of missing the cut. Cav would tell them they were wrong. Cav was more certain that he was right.

It made for a splendidly easy way to wind him up. One season our nutritionist Nigel Mitchell put him on a special diet, which slimmed him down but would also inevitably make him extremely hungry. So Ed would load the ingredients into his bread-maker and fill the house with the smell of fresh baking. I would roast some Welsh lamb chops, just to polish him off.

Everything was a song and dance. At one stage he decided he had a phobia of bananas, which again is somewhat awkward for a cyclist. Being Cav, he seemed to actively enjoy having the phobia. He would certainly make sure everyone knew about it, which made it interesting when one of his race wins years later meant he had to stand atop the podium brandishing a huge basket of ripe ones.

If you had sat next to him at my wedding, you would have found him surprisingly shy to begin with. And then, as he warmed to you, the Cav judgements would have begun, and the fun and fireworks would have started.

He has opinions on everything. He will read a story on a website about a bloke in China doing something Cav personally has no experience of, and that will be enough to fire up the engines. 'How could you even think like that? What the hell is he doing?'

He will never acknowledge that it's a situation that doesn't affect him, or that it's something he can do nothing about. It will nag away inside him until, two days later, the bloke in China gets it in the neck again. 'I mean, what is the guy thinking?'

It can cause him problems at times. He had a few at Sky. But our year together in 2012 had some wonderful moments.

At the Giro we were functioning beautifully as a team. There was a good group of us who were used to racing with each other, going back to those fresh-faced days of relative innocence, and we helped him to three stage wins. It was one of the great thrills: leading out my friend to take those iconic stages, a long way from messing about in the velodrome canteen.

We should have won more. Cav knew it and let us know. Not in the overly aggressive or negative way that he's sometimes portrayed as possessing: he only wanted men who were truly committed to the cause. And when he learned, minutes after the end of the final mountain stage up above Milan, that he had missed out on the precious points jersey by a single point, all that emotion came surging out. There, in a plain hotel room atop the Stelvio Pass, he sobbed into his hands. At those points there is no glamour in cycling, no glory. Just a borrowed room, a lukewarm shower and a grimy-faced kid, kit in a wet bundle on the floor, a long, lonely coach ride ahead.

He's not for quitting. Watching how he dealt with the pressures of going for the World road race title in Copenhagen in 2011 made me admire my friend afresh. We built for that day from two years out. Riding for a mate allows you to drag a few more miles or watts out of your legs. If you're Cav, you understand those sacrifices and make sure those weary compadres understand the depth of your gratitude.

That's just who he is: emotional, a little manic, struggling to keep it all under control. But this emotion comes from the desire and passion to be the best, whether that's sprinting on the Champs Élysées or performing a particular bouncy jive in a Blackpool ballroom.

The more attention he gets, the harder he finds it to rein it back. But when you get to know him you learn to deal with it. You understand that he will sometimes need to go off on one. You understand that sometimes you have to tell him to pipe down. And you know that his instinctive, emotional responses are great for the sport. Cav does not hide who he is. There is no generic with Cav, no clichéd answer or hiding behind platitudes.

And he is an exceptional rider. His cycling intelligence is remarkable. He understands things inside racing that many very experienced men do not. And in the pell-mell madness of a sprint, there is no-one like him.

Some of it comes from being small for his age as a kid. He had to learn how to ride to his optimum, learn all those little tricks that naturally bigger and faster lads never had to bother with. Some of it comes from his memory. He can tell you everything about the last ten kilometres of a flat, sprinter's stage – where there is a bollard, how long the slight rise with seven kilometres to go is, the fact that a shop with a red awning comes fifty metres before a right-hand bend that could see you get squeezed against the barriers. Much of it comes from his unparalleled racing mind: knowing where he wants to be, knowing how to get there, understanding instinctively where the best place is to throw the last fuel on the fire.

As he did with Ed in those academy days, Cav's happy to share with his mates what he's learned over the years. Before Flanders he will text me – a few words of good luck, a few words of wisdom, a self-deprecating disclaimer like 'but what do I know about winning Flanders'. Not everyone does that. On the bike, too, that understanding between us remains. Coming into the last three kilometres of a Tour sprint I instinctively leave space for him. Three kilometres before hitting a long, brutal climb he'll leave a gap for me. Still looking out for each other, still going hard in the same direction.

Fans

People say you can't beat the sound of supporters shouting your name. These people are not called Geraint.

Can it be so hard to get someone's name right when asking for an autograph? I've had so many pronunciations. Jer-ain't. Grrr-ant. Grey-nant. A chap I used to bump into regularly in Manchester just called me Gareth. I've had Grant.

At least they were having a go. Some people won't even attempt it. It appears to be one of those words that they look at and don't even know where to start, a little like the British with *pneu*. Or *mille-feuille* (memo to Francophiles: just ask for 'custard slice' instead). They'll simply move on past my Christian name and call me Thomas. Or Tomma. During the Dauphiné or Tour I'm constantly assailed with it – '*Allez, Tomma!*' There are those in the peloton adamant that these supporters are in fact referring to local hero Thomas Voeckler, but they can be ignored. As could my old directeur sportifs at Barloworld, who cut my name back to a simple, if inaccurate, 'Tom'. Throughout a time trial I'd hear it over the radio: 'Go, Tom! Good boy! You fast, Tom!' They may genuinely have thought I was called Thomas Geraint. At a race in Germany, one official tried telling me I was in fact wrong, and Thomas was my first name rather than my surname. At least I'm not the Seychelles 800-metre runner Gaylord Silly. Or German alpine skier Fanny Chmelar.

You think that at least your name is your own. Then you join social media, and find out that @geraintthomas is getting a little tired of 140-character missives about Gent–Wevelgem and rear cassettes. Unfortunately for him, @GeraintThomas86 isn't quite as obvious for those looking to get in touch with me, and every time I do anything, his account bears the brunt, just as Chris Hoy suffers every time Premier League referee Chris Foy makes a controversial decision.

'I see you've won a race,' the other Geraint will tweet me, slightly tetchily. At other times, it seems to get a bit too much for him. It appears that my win at E3 Harelbeke in March 2015 caught him at a bad time. 'AAAGGGHHH!' he tweeted. 'I AM NOT A CYCLIST!!'

The protocol of the autograph requires careful consideration. You might start by signing your full name, but doing 100 jerseys in a row soon disabuses you of that notion. At the same time, it must still unmistakeably be your autograph. It's no good simply scrawling your first initial and following it with a wavy horizontal line. My compromise is to go with a straightforward 'Gez Thomas', as that's what I was called in my early days at Maindy Flyers. It's simple, it's efficient, it's still me.

Profile dictates tactics. Each man has his own technique, if not a style, that renders his name visible. Pete Kennaugh goes for something relatively flamboyant. Brad is like lightning. Ian Stannard writes his full name like it's his first day at school. You half expect him to put his age in brackets afterwards.

Consider the material: jerseys are surprisingly hard to sign. Unless pulled very tight, the pen gets stuck in the thread. People ask for autographs on their bikes. Does this mean they will no longer ride them, or that they are happy to smudge the signature so it looks like a botched respray?

You might mock, but try being handed a black pen and asked to sign a black saddle. You're glad they have a pen, but it gets to you. Helmets? Advances in material technology are great news for those who prefer large air vents, but they're disastrous for the hurried autograph signee. As are the curved slipstreamed sides. Ge – gap. Tho – gap. 'Hey, check this – Gethos signed my helmet.' 'What, the musketeer?'

You do get strange requests. When the Tour was in Yorkshire, a random woman marched onto the Team Sky bus and asked for all the riders to sign her chest with a pink marker. You wouldn't mind, but by the time she got to me at the back she'd run out of room – or at least the sort of room an innocent boy from Cardiff could sign without going the colour of the Welsh dragon.

I was a childhood autograph hunter myself. When they held a track Grand Prix in Cardiff I thrust my programme at Rob Hayles and asked him to do the honours. I still remember how nervous I felt. My collection also featured Hoy and his fellow Scottish Olympian Craig MacLean, which makes it a little weird when you become friends with them as adults. But it serves too as a reminder: always make the effort, as if it's a teenage Geraint – or Garth, to quote another one – asking you now.

It may occasionally feel like a grind when you have just been peeled off your bike after a brutal day. But the time will come when the queues will wither to nothing. Enjoy it while it lasts – and apologise when you can't sign everything, like when you're dashing to register at the start of a stage and have to battle through a crowd. Don't be fooled by the dark Oakleys. Underneath, I'm feeling a very British guilt.

Some supporters will send you gifts, which are always appreciated. Beer, flowers, cuddly toys – I could open my own tombola stall at a fete. Unfortunately, if it's food, none of us riders can eat it. Although 99.9 per cent of it would be fine, we cannot risk any of it when we don't know who's made it and how, The last thing we want while racing is having to stop for an unexpected nature break every thirty minutes, and for the more suspicious, you never know if it's been laced with something illegal. Even our own CNP sports nutrition products are batch-tested. Which is logical, but when the package in question is a lovely stack of fresh Welsh cakes, it can also be an absolute heart-breaker. Happily our mechanics and soigneurs have no such compunctions, so if you're looking to empty someone's bowels for twenty-four hours via a lemon drizzle cake, they're the ones who are going to bear the brunt. It would be nice to think that Sky's budget would stretch to some sort of official taster, much like medieval kings or North Korean dictators would employ, but who would want to tell a rider at the end of a 140-mile mountain stage that he's not allowed to tuck into his rice until some other bloke has not only ingested it but waited for it to pass safely through his system?

With the way cycling's profile has gone through the roof in recent years, you'd think there might be packs of groupies roaming the sign-on zone. There are certainly some strange ladies who float around in the shadows, but it's not quite football yet. Not that we're less attractive, us sunburned men with the upper bodies of teenage girls and the legs of shire horses.

There are certainly distinctive tribes of fans. The stat obsessive: the one who knows my results better than I do. The bike obsessive: taking photos from every angle, firing a question about the geometry of the head tube that leaves me staring blankly back. The corporate newcomer: much more straightforward questions, as if asked by a twelve-year-old who has just ridden a bike for the first time – 'How many gears have you got?' 'Doesn't that saddle make your bottom hurt?' And the slightly disturbing ones: the ones who have a photograph of you aged twelve that neither you nor anyone in your family has ever seen before.

Belgians are the most knowledgeable. Italians are the most openly passionate. Others are as nervous as I was with Rob Hayles. They ask for a selfie, and then they can't get the camera app to open. You have to help them through it, which is something you're always happy to do, unless they're sprinting up the side of a road you're attempting to climb at a punishing tempo. No-one would jog onto the pitch at Wembley when someone is taking a corner and stand in the six-yard box trying to put an arm round the goalkeeper, but in cycling it's considered acceptable. In many ways that's a fine thing: in what other sport can you stand around chatting to one of the world's best, ten minutes before they start to compete?

Some give you the wrong pic to sign. 'Would you like me to write Ben Swift's name on that photo of Ben Swift, or mine?'

Some just walk onto the team bus as if they're walking through their own front door. 'Hey, what are you doing? Get off our bus!' 'But why? I only want you to sign this. It is a photo of you in your school uniform, taken with a telephoto lens. Thanks, Grant!'

Success can turn some against you in ways you wouldn't expect. On the Tour in 2013, as Team Sky dominated and Chris Froome owned the yellow jersey, a minority of French fans appeared to hate us. At the top of one mountain summit a seventy-year-old granny booed me like I was Will Carling running out at the Stade de France. Move on a year to 2014, when we were struggling, and everyone seemed to love us. By 2015, and another win for Froomey and Sky, it had switched back once again.

The finest fans I've ever experienced? The Britons who lined the route for the Tour's Grand Départ in Yorkshire in 2014. It was so rammed along the roadside that the only way you could stop for a natural break involved ruining some poor chap's shoes. Going up Holme Moss at the front of the bunch was like standing next to the biggest speaker in a nightclub. Even on the descents your ears were ringing.

Only the Tour of Flanders has ever come close to that before: up the Kwaremont climb, the stench of beer getting stronger, the noise louder, the pleasure even greater when a Belgian voice tells you to keep it going, Gerrard.

Froome

The word first began to spread about a talented white kid from South Africa* when I was riding with British Cycling's academy in Tuscany. He was racing as part of the UCI's team set-up at the World Cycling Centre in Switzerland, an academy for riders from lesser-known cycling countries. Coming up against him, two things were immediately obvious: this lad's got a huge engine, but he handles a bike like he sat on one for the first time a week ago.

A couple of years later I met Chris Froome for the first time. He was Barloword's young signing in 2008. It was unforgettable, and not only because no other cyclist turned up for their first pro team wearing hippy traveller jewellery and a backpack. The Italians further understood that he came from a different culture when he bowled round the hotel wearing a *kikoy*, also known as a sarong, also known as a towel worn as a skirt. A few moments later we learned that some South Africans have more in common with kilt-wearing Scots than you might imagine. He would come into your room for a chat and perch on the end of the bed. 'Mate, would you mind closing your legs while I'm eating, or at least pointing your knees the other way?'

---

* Yes, I know he's from Kenya. But he referred to me as English in his autobiography, so this is my little dig back.

He was a lovely chap – friendly, fiercely determined and as innocent as a schoolgirl. He knew nothing of cycling's history. He knew nothing of cycling's present. At dinner during the Tour Méditerranéen we were chewing over the day's stage. 'Who's that Cofidis guy? He looks pretty good.' 'Yup, that's David Moncoutié. Lots of big results. And he won it.' 'Oh.' The Tour of Oman, 2013, first stage. 'Who was that Astana guy? He's quick!' 'Mate, it's Nibali.'

It was rather endearing. Even now you can confuse the hell out of him by talking about Jérôme Pineau and Thibaut Pinot. One spring I found him looking somewhat put out. 'I can't believe I'm having to do this Roubaix thing. There's a race in Portugal I really fancy.' 'You want to miss the biggest one-day race in the world?' 'Why? Where's that?'

You could always see that he had something special: the way he could climb, the way he could time-trial. On his first Tour in 2008 I remember seeing him accelerating up the final climb alongside Denis Menchov and thinking, this guy is some talent. But he was so inconsistent, not least because of illness. When his big breakthrough came with that podium finish at the Vuelta in 2011, it was both a shock and entirely expected.

So Froome was different, in his background, his development, his outlook. Over dinner he would casually tell me stories about being chased by hippos and being locked by his brother in a pen full of angry ostriches. That doesn't happen in Cardiff.

He was self-sufficient in a way that cyclists who have always been part of an established system seldom are. When he wanted to ride the time trial at the 2006 World Championships he borrowed the head of the Kenyan Cycling Federation's email and entered himself without telling anyone. He then rode his one and only bike to the managers' meeting the night before the race to find out where the course was and what time it started. Because he couldn't afford to stay in any of the official hotels, he tried cycling to a budget place miles out of town and got lost en route. The race? He rode slap-bam into an official on the first corner, sending them both to the deck.

Chris is an intelligent guy. He picked up more Italian in his first month at Barloworld than most of us had in two years. At other times he would do things that left you scratching your head. Racing one day in Italy, he stopped well before the finish, stuck his clothes in a backpack and rode fifty kilometres home. His reasoning was that the finish was too far from where he lived, and that he had no other way of getting home.

I was both amazed by him and seriously concerned. He would always totally commit to the team, try to do what was asked and more. In the manic sprints of the Tour Down Under he'd do a long, strong pull at the front and swing over. Then, two kilometres later he'd suddenly be back, dive-bombing most of his teammates to get on the front and help again. 'Froomey, good job, but leave it to us now.' At times it was like watching a Clio with the engine of a Ferrari. There was the sense when you rode with him that anything could happen, that all that raw talent could be blown through some daft accident.

Even now the way he rides a bike amazes us. We talk about being at one with the bike. He looks like he is surprised to find one between his legs. It's so ungainly, but miraculously it works. At times you'll be following him through a tight corner and he'll hit it at ridiculous speed on a crazy line, and somehow gets away with. The rest of us are left shaking our heads: how the hell did he do that?

Because his cycling education was on mountain bikes along the red dust roads of Kenya's Rift Valley, Chris didn't learn to handle his bike in the way that those raised on road and track have. He also appears to have no fear, in part because he hasn't had enough big crashes to know how badly it can go wrong and also because his attitude to danger as a child was so different. In Europe you are cushioned from risk. When you grow up in the African outdoors you are not. Kids in Cardiff have gerbils for pets. He had a rock python. The only reason he kept rabbits in a hutch was to throw them live to his snakes.

Does he see the danger and laugh in its face, or does he just not consider it danger at all? Hammering down a descent, you often come up to a car travelling more slowly than you are. He'll pass it on the inside on a blind bend. 'Chris! What are you doing? The Tour starts next week! Just chill!'

He'll laugh about training. 'Isn't it funny how close you come to crashing on every ride?'

'What do you mean?'

'There's always a few close calls, no?'

'No . . .'

Like most cyclists, he gets a little giddy on the sauce. Before the National Championships one year he came to stay with me at my in-laws house in Cardiff. We went for a pub lunch and, after a few drinks, he decided to rustle up an old Kenyan cocktail favourite called a *dawa*. This was no ordinary beverage, and it was certainly better than the mojitos I tried to make, which ended up looking like gazpacho. The first of Froomey's concoctions tasted surprisingly good, as did the second and third ones. He stopped after three but happily made more for the rest of us. I told Chris that if he beat me in the time trial it was down to these cheap tactics. Two days later he did, by eleven seconds. Moral: when a Kenyan stops drinking *dawas*, you should stop too.

He has grown into his role as team leader at Sky. Where once he was quiet round the dinner table he is now the alpha. He knows he has to take the other riders with him, and he does so, not only because of his talent, but because his attitude is faultless. You know that he always gives it everything in racing and training, so you want to match him.

The success hasn't gone to his head. He can handle the mickey-taking – about how he stays upright on his bike, that he knows nothing about anything but cycling today. Tell him you're watching the Six Nations and he'll ask which six and why, what are they doing?

But he is blessed in that he has a Welsh grandmother, and he is obsessive in the right areas: about training, about efforts, about what his rivals have been doing – or say they have been doing. Nothing is done without a reason. No advance in diet or equipment escapes him. He is the embodiment of Dave Brailsford's mentality.

And Chris never gives up. It's not in him. During the 2015 Tour it was incredible with how well he dealt with everything that was thrown at him, figuratively and literally: the unfair abuse, the baseless accusations, the occasional cup of urine. His mental strength and endurance were almost as impressive as his physical gifts. In public, no matter how tired or upset he might be, he remained relentlessly polite and calm. Behind closed doors he would get it off his chest, but only in a quick two minutes before dinner. He would never let it hang over a whole evening.

I saw what it took for Brad to win one Tour. To replicate that over two separate years – the dedication, the sacrifice, the focus, the ability – is remarkable.

That slow start and difficult journey to the top has made him appreciate what he has now. He knows what he wants to achieve, and he will give everything in pursuit of that.

Hoy

Does celebrity change you? Do six Olympic gold medals hang heavy around your neck? Put it this way: such is the attention Sir Chris Hoy gets from autograph hunters and selfie obsessives when popping into the supermarket for his weekly big shop that he now goes disguised in a strange hat, sends his wife in to do all the legwork and shuffles down in his seat until she's loaded the car, at which point he drives home.

Fame costs, does it?

The first time I met Chris as a teammate rather than an autograph-hunting twelve-year-old was at the 2005 Track World Championships in Los Angeles. A ruptured spleen meant I was unable to compete, but with a plane ticket already paid for, Shane Sutton decided the nineteen-year-old Thomas would benefit from seeing how the big lads did things. Chris was a year on from winning his first Olympic gold. I assumed he would only speak to his fellow stars. Instead he had as much time for a gawky kid like me as he did for Brad Wiggins – talking cycling, sport and girls as if we were somehow equals. There were even trips to Krispy Kreme for doughnuts, which is the sort of thing you can get away with if you're a sprinter.

Don't think he ever took it easy. I'd sum up the man I grew to know in a single word: dedication. This is a bloke who packed his own espresso machine in his suitcase for the Beijing Olympics, because he couldn't stand the idea of getting all the way to the most important competition of his life and having to put up with substandard coffee.

Neither was that an isolated example. At a World Cup event in Manchester we had the unusual and, if I'm honest, rather pleasant situation of Chris using his room at the Holiday Inn as some sort of impromptu espresso bar. So good were his flat whites (he was particularly handy with the shapes and designs of the foam) that there was a queue of us in the corridor waiting to take advantage of his barista skills.

Maybe before anyone else, maybe before even Dave Brailsford, Chris realised that something big was happening with British cycling. He spotted that the old ways of behaving – the sort of thing that happened in Los Angeles with the tomato ketchup and visit from the LAPD – were no longer going to fly, and he adjusted faster than anyone else. He became aware that people were watching him, that camera phones could turn a casual remark into a national scandal.

Because fame hit him at a good age – he was thirty-two when he won those three golds at Beijing – he was able to handle an avalanche in the way that a less mature person would not. By the time Christmas that year came round, four months on from his return home from China, he had signed eight new sponsorship deals, been forced to change his mobile number three times, been feted by prime ministers and royalty, and shaken, on average, 200 strangers' hands a day.

Coping with that kind of intensity is impressive. But that was what he had always done. His first world title in the kilo (1,000 metres against the clock) was won by 1/1000th of a second. In Athens, when he upgraded that kilo world title into Olympic gold, he had to watch as the Olympic record was broken three times by the riders going out on track before him. It cracked some of his rivals. France's Arnaud Tournant switched to a bigger gear, went out like a maniac and died on the last lap like a feeble child. You can't blame him. That's what the ferocious strain of an Olympic final does to you.

Chris, aided by Dave and Steve Peters, knew better. In the build-up to the tournament the three of them had mapped out various scenarios and then tried to decide how they could cope with them. One of the situations that they gamed was exactly the one that came to pass: the bloke before you smashes the Olympic record. Chris's instinctive reaction was the same as Tournant's. Go out really hard, try to hang on. To which Dave replied: you've just thrown away two years' work right there. We have spent twenty-four months working on what you know to make you as fast as possible. Stick to the plan. It works. It's proven.

Most riders understood the theory. To trust it in that frantic moment, even on the deepest subconscious level, is something else. That is the ultimate.

And then Chris did something arguably even more impressive: once his preferred event of the kilo was removed from the programme, he mastered the completely contrasting demands of the Keirin and the sprint in the space of one Olympic cycle. Once again it was his dedication that did it. Constantly watching videos, relentlessly researching tactics, working flat out every day with coaches Jan van Eijden and Iain Dyer.

In the gym he was a heavy-metal obsessive; his thighs had a circumference of twenty-seven inches, each one a full four inches wider than Victoria Beckham's waist. Neither was he too posh to push. He could squat 237.5 kilogrammes, more than two and a half times his own bodyweight. Only try that at home if you can afford twelve months off work in traction.

He became a figurehead to those of us knee-deep in the daily slog at the velodrome. Some of the top dogs will keep themselves in their own bubble, especially when they are surrounded by eager young acolytes. Chris not only had an infectious attitude to training – 'Christ, this hurts, but you can handle it' – but he was always willing to talk, to chew things over, to offer calm advice.

When you train on the track, the precision measurement of every effort perversely makes your mood much harder to control. Dealing with such intense scrutiny can destroy riders. Elite sportsmen can drown in numbers, lie awake at night obsessing over minute percentages and fractions of metres. Chris was the same, which is why he could spot when morale was plummeting and say exactly the right thing.

His commitment was total. When you're an endurance athlete you can train on the road and get away from the velodrome and the Manchester weather – different countries, different climbs, different cultures. In summer we had the road race season to entertain us; we got to live in Italy for part of the year. Chris and his fellow sprinters? Nothing but the velodrome, and the gym at the velodrome, and the canteen at the velodrome, day after day, week after week. A lot of athletes could do that, I'm sure, in the lead-up to an Olympic Games. To do it from before Sydney 2000 and continue with the same intensity, every day of every week, until London 2012 is extraordinary.

And yet you could have fun with him. He was doing a big public appearance one evening and found himself badgered relentlessly by a very drunk Welsh fan with a very strong accent. 'Chris butt. You've said lots about you. What about our boy Geraint?' Chris, as ever, was all polite restraint. 'A good guy. He's world and Olympic champion. Fine rider.' This wasn't enough. 'He'll beat you, so he will!' 'Well, we do different disciplines. We could never actually race.' A cackle from the back. 'Hoy! He'll have you one day! Won't he? Right?'

Having heard this tale, I used it for my enjoyment at every opportunity. Whenever Chris came off the track as us team pursuiters were waiting I would hit him with the big shout. 'Oh! Hoy! I'll have you one day!'

He could soak it up. When the cameras aren't on him, Chris is a funny guy. Some of his jokes are far spicier than his public image as a knight of the realm might suggest. Before he settled down he also enjoyed a significant amount of attention from girls, and was not unsuccessful with them. He is also keenly aware of his appearance. There is always a large range of male grooming products in his hotel bathroom, and a small patch worn out on the tiles in front of the largest mirror. The chances of him blobbing out like many ex-cyclists do are minimal. When I saw him at the Tour Down Under he had been up with the sun doing thirty-second sprints up a nearby hill. Dedication.

He is a minutiae man. His suitcase looks like it was packed by a career soldier. His hotel rooms always look as if they have been organised with rulers. At the Olympics he knew the fine detail of every event in every sport. Lots of cyclists don't even understand football; Chris could give you the scoring system in dressage.

And he is a genuine hero. For kids watching him storming to gold after gold in Beijing – black helmet, visor down, white skinsuit curving over his muscles – he was like some mad robot, a Scottish Hulk. Even the way he rode spoke of total dominance: that's me at the front, you won't get round me. He won races in a style that made people love him. Coming through a non-existent gap on the final bend to win World Keirin gold in 2011. Somehow holding off Maximilian Levy after the German had come past him on the back straight of the Keirin final at London 2012.

Even though most people in Britain love Brad Wiggins, there is a small percentage who get wound up by his look and chat, unfairly or otherwise. Chris? Your mum likes

Chris. And your nan, your girlfriend and your niece. Everyone.

He could end up running the International Olympic Committee. Quite easily. In fact, I'd stick cash on it.

DOING IT

First Times

First bike ... was a mountain bike called The Wolf. Already you're beginning to appreciate why I liked it. On the handlebars was mounted a small box that could make big noises: police sirens, ambulances, fire engines. I'd race down the park on it, play rugby or football with my little brother and dad and then ride home. Great days.

First racing bike ... was a Giant, with shifters on the downtube and toe-straps on the pedals. As is the way with these things it was a present from my mum and dad, and I loved it. It was far too big for me – there was barely any seat post showing – but I would ride it round Maindy thinking I was hammering a stage in the Tour. As is also the way with these things, I didn't look after it very well either. I have to hold my hand up: I certainly made a lot of big promises, but I failed to back any of them up. It was left to my old man, not least because he was the one who'd had to fork out for it in the first place.

First time on a track bike ... was rather scary. 'What, no brakes? One gear? What is this?' Maindy Flyers put us through a five-day course, culminating in a flying one-lap sprint. The coach was a woman named Debbie Wharton. 'Can you go faster, lads? Can you go out the saddle?' 'I can, Debbie.' At least until, crossing the line, I attempted to freewheel, at which point I felt as if I was living the board game Buckaroo! The record for the flying-lap debut was fifty-four seconds. Debbie the motivator once again: 'Your dad will get you something nice if you get this, Geraint.' 'New football boots?' 'Possibly. Just try your best.' I did, and with that came another first: my debut record.

First long ride . . . was aged fourteen, up from Cardiff to the Storey Arms outdoor centre in Brecon, and then out further still to the Steps by Pen y Fan. It wasn't intentional. It was the club Sunday run, and I'd spent an hour wondering why I wasn't recognising much. 'We seem to be an awful long way out here. Bloody hell, is that the Storey Arms?'

That was when it began snowing. Riders started dropping off the group and heading for home. I'd have liked to have done the same, but I didn't have a clue which way home was. When we went over a bridge and the river underneath was frozen solid I began to worry a little more. 'If I get dropped now I may as well lie down under that bridge and wait for spring.'

What saved me was that Brecon to Cardiff is downhill. I hung on to the last wheel until Pontypridd. By that stage I was starting to bonk badly, but I couldn't let that wheel go. Not in Pontypridd.

I made it, and a new weekly adventure was born. From then on every weekend would be the same: Saturday night, Mum going to the Chinese takeaway to fuel me up on barbecue spare ribs and egg-fried rice. What I'd give to be able to eat like that now. A big old breakfast, jam sandwiches wrapped in tinfoil in my jersey pockets and off I'd go. It was almost as exciting as race day: new roads to explore, new hills, old boys – with their encyclopaedic knowledge of the lanes and loops – to pass on the knowledge. And with every ride you could feel yourself growing stronger and faster.

First race . . . was in the Maindy mini-league, racing round the bumpy old outdoor track. It was built on the site of an old rubbish tip, so subsidence has been something of an issue; the back straight actually has a big dip. I used to get so nervous. We wouldn't race far – you'd never go for more than three laps of the 450-metre circuit – but it was flat out. And awesome.

First win . . . came aged twelve. The primary sensation was shock. 'I've won!' My rival in those earliest days was Alex Burridge. I'll never forget his name. He beat me three times. I got closer in the fourth race, and then it came. And once I beat someone, they rarely beat me again. I'd focus on the next target. Dad would be quietly pleased on the way back home. 'Got a scalp today, Geraint. You've never beaten him before.' I'd be noisily pleased. 'Did you think I'd win today, Dad?' He would play along with it magnificently. 'No. I thought you'd get close, but . . . very good effort, that, very good.'

First race abroad . . . came in Berlin, as an under-14. At the time I thought that milestone had been reached in Palmer Park in Reading, but with age came the understanding that having to cross the Severn Bridge in a minibus to get there did not make England a foreign country. Germany proved a brutal baptism. I spent three days gasping at the back of the peloton, taking the kicking of my life. I'd never before raced in a bunch bigger than forty riders. And I'd never raced at a speed faster than my time-trial best.

First cyclo-cross race ... was at the 2001 Welsh Championships, on a borrowed bike. I loved every muddy second of it. I came in third and, having just changed clubs, decided to celebrate by zipping up my jersey as the line approached, just like the pros. Unfortunately, my momentum died in the thick mud, meaning I crossed the line with my arse in the air and my nose on the front wheel. I eventually slid to a halt at the feet of my old clubmates. Harsh words were exchanged.

First exposure to the big boys ... came at the World road race as a first-year junior. We flew out to Hamilton, Canada, which was exciting enough by itself. Then I realised we were in the same hotel as the pros. Sitting at the same dinner table. I didn't know what to say or do. The night before their race the British riders Dave Millar, Max Sciandri and Charly Wegelius ordered their breakfast ... of pasta. I felt like Alice in Wonderland.

First pro contract ... paid me a pro cyclist's minimum wage for two years. It was awesome. I was up in Manchester on the Olympic programme at the end of 2006, when I got a call from Shane Sutton. 'G, there's an Italian team called Barloworld, and they want a young British rider. I'm recommending you.'

I flew out to Italy to be fitted for kit. The team's wily old directeur sportif, Claudio Corti, examined me as I got changed. 'You have weight to lose. Not least from your legs.' By the time I got back to the house I shared with my fellow British mates the kit had arrived, along with a beautiful new Cannondale bike. The lads were staring at me as if I was suddenly someone shiny and new rather than the same old Geraint.

First pro race . . . came Down Under. I had to fly to Italy, then back to Amsterdam, then to Kuala Lumpur for eighteen hours of hanging round the airport for the connecting flight.

I was nervous. I'd been on the Internet before I left, looking up all the riders in the team so I would recognise them and know their characters and strengths as riders. I arrived at the hotel particularly intimidated by South African sprinter Robbie Hunter, who had a reputation as something of an angry man. I knocked on his door, and he answered in just his boxers. Gulp. 'Hi, my name's Geraint . . .'

He was as good as gold. I spoke no Italian, so he looked after me. And you don't want to be an enemy of Rob.

In our first training session together we were practising lead-outs for the sprint. With us were two big Italian lads: Enrico Degano; and Fabrizio Guidi, who is a now a directeur sportif at Garmin. I was told to go second. I thought: I'd better show these guys what I can do. I can show these guys, because I've got all this track speed in my legs.

I hit the front with 300 metres of work to do. And I ramped it, and ramped it, and the power came. One rider bailed off the back. Another tried to get past, just about got level and then blew up too. Only Degano, Guidi and Hunter were still with me. That single session won me the respect I needed to hold my own.

It was an education. I lived out in Italy in an old apartment above the town square in Quarrata. I rode with Hunter, Brian Cox and, in the second year, a kid with blond curtains from Kenya called Chris Froome. This, I thought sometimes, is remarkable. I'm being paid to race bikes!

First senior win . . . took a while! In my Barloworld years I was a track rider using the road as a tool to get fit, doing my job for the top guys while also living out my childhood dreams. My first win therefore didn't come until I was a fourth-year pro with Sky, in the team time trial at the Tour of Qatar. My first solo win was the British Nationals in 2010; riding the Tour that year in the GB champion's jersey was great for the ego.

First Tour . . . oh, what a month!

It was 2007, the year it began in London. Ahead of the first road stage, the five Brits in the race – Brad, Dave Millar, Cav, Charly Wegelius and me – were asked to pose for a picture, lined up together on Tower Bridge at the front of the pack, flanked by Beefeaters. Only two years had passed since

Cav and I were living together in Manchester as academy riders, dreaming of days like this. I nudged him with my elbow. 'Cav, man – we're in the Tour!'

I survived into France and the first up-and-down stage, five days in. The speed of it was frightening. With Hunter aiming for the green jersey I was sent back to the team car to collect four bidons. And I couldn't get back.

I started ditching the bottles, one by one. I'm going to get dropped, I'm going to get dropped . . . Desperately I clawed my way towards him, every man I passed hurting me horribly. I got within five riders. Four riders. Three riders. And then blew up.

I had one bottle left, and just lobbed it on the ground. Out the back I went, all the time thinking: this isn't even a hard stage. How can you come to a race like this and actually try to win it? Just to get round is nigh-on impossible.

The first proper mountain stage was the hardest of all. I was out the back on my own for 120 kilometres. Just chasing the *gruppetto* – the large posse of riders off the back of the peloton, the loose collection of the weary and the injured – taking crazy risks on descents in my desperation to get back. The team car was giving me bottles, other teams were giving me gels. Throw it all in the furnace. Get back. Get back. I went down the last descent like a maniac, came up the last climb and there it was: the tail of the *gruppetto*. I was safe. And saved, because the following day was a rest day. Lucky boy.

The biggest shock came on a flat stage. As a track rider I understood that I might struggle on the hills, but I assumed

I'd be fine on the flat. And then the crosswinds came, and the echelons worked their cruel spell. Spat out of the back of one group, into another, spat back out of that one. Holding a final wheel, I suddenly thought: I just can't do this any more.

For about half a second I freewheeled before another thought came barrelling in. Fuck no. You can't give up. Never give up. I sprinted to get back on the wheel. The thought cropped up again. You can't do it. Again I fought it, and again.

I made it through the hardest day I'd ever had. And, a week or so later, Millar cycled up to me, pointed into the distance and said, 'There you go, G – the Eiffel Tower.'

Climbing

Some fear it. I believe you have to relish it.

Why do we climb? To challenge ourselves. To prove something. To get somewhere that lots of people couldn't get to. To shut up the devil on your shoulder who whispers: why bother? This is stupid. Why not give up?

As a kid I loved to climb. I loved the hills the old boys would tell stories about, the loops that took you far from home and into a world you'd never seen before. I loved that I never gave up.

It began around Caerphilly Mountain, just across the M4 from the Cardiff suburbs, and in the lanes around Lisvane, the hills all short sharp things, as if you were in Belgium, the road rough and heavy under your tyres.

With each year that passed I would venture further out. The Rhigos (600 metres above sea level), starting by the grey industrial estate at Hirwaun, climbing past the old colliery, ascending from familiar South Wales to what felt like the Alps as you rode on through the pine trees and took on the hairpins with the steep slopes dropping away beside you. The Bwlch, a long, twenty-minute drag, picking your route from Cymer or Price Town or Treorchy. Up through the village, across the cattle grid, into the forest. Clouds all around. When legs were stronger, out to Abergavenny and the Tumble – hard pedalling out of the village of Govilon, up through the Blaenavon World Heritage Site, the temperature dropping and the trees giving way to wild bushes and then dank moss, over yet another cattle grid and past the pond towards the rocky summit.

These were big days out, a mighty challenge. Five hours of hard breathing and hanging on to wheels, dreaming you were racing the Five Valleys, a 112-mile local rite of passage that forced you up everything steep that South Wales had to offer. As a junior, fresh from winning the Welsh Nationals, I rode it for real, borrowing a Welsh jersey so I felt the part, using my years of practice on the Bwlch to drop more experienced riders and then spinning furiously in a 52x14 gear (juniors were allowed nothing bigger) on the descents to stay away. An education and a graduation on the same course.

These days I can whistle up those climbs in ten minutes. Back then, before I had experienced Mount Teide in Tenerife and its thirty-kilometre climbs, fifteen minutes seemed an age. To travel to Majorca as a junior was enough of a shock – faster roads, longer drags, the endless switchbacks of Sa Calobra, the snaking descents, quicker than you'd ever been before.

Up to the north-west as part of British Cycling's Olympic programme. Riding out from the city centre through Altrincham with my housemates Cav and Ed Clancy. Climbing the Cat and Fiddle out of Macclesfield, that long haul up to the windswept tops with motorbikes fizzing past and the thump of a lorry's slipstream catching you in the chest as it freewheels down the other way.

The Peaks became our playground. Over Snake Pass to Ladybower Reservoir and Sheffield beyond; Holme Moss, steady rather than brutal unless the wind decided to put its hand on your forehead and push you back; Winnats Pass, short but spectacular, winding through a green cleft valley coming out of Castleton, hard when you're fresh and a heartbreaker when you've been further out and have four hours weighing heavy in your legs.

Steep roads, slow roads. Even downhill you were always on the pedals, pushing gravity for everything it could give you. Shane Sutton knew what I was like, fond of the bigger gears, especially when tired. He'd yell at us to spin it out more to save our legs. 'Knock it down a few, G! Save the legs!' Sitting quite far forward on the saddle, as in the velodrome, searching for those critical few extra watts of power. 'C'mon, G, pedal! Spin it!'

And then came the Tour, and eyes opened afresh to what the big boys could do on the big climbs. We were on the Col de Peyresourde in the Pyrenees. It's long, proper long; steep, proper steep. At the finish, I was in bits. And then I watched the highlights and saw the leaders sprinting up it, racing each other. Jesus, did they actually brake on that bend? I had to slog just to get round it.

You watch it at home as a kid and you think they're flying. You begin alongside them and it brings it home how much better you will have to become. The overall pace is chastening. How can you try to win this thing? It's hard enough to finish a day. And it's not even the overall pace that is most striking. It's the sudden explosions in speed, and the velocity at which the leaders hit the bottom of the climb.

I used to dread every lump in the road. Looking at the race book the night before, plotting how I was going to get through the stage. I was rooming with Robbie Hunter. He would tell me that we had to hang in there until a certain point, because that is where the *gruppetto* would form. As the years went by, I slowly got stronger and lighter, losing my puppy or track fat, but I still feared the climbs. The only thing that makes you feel slightly better about it is having breakfast with a sprinter like Cav. It might be unfair, but watching him sweating doesn't half lift the mood. At least you know you can get through the stage.

Now there are fresh climbs to love and hate. There is one just over the Italian border that Richie Porte calls the Boonen Climb, although the big-boned Belgian has apparently never trained up it, just used it as a descent. It's not that long – four kilometres in total – and at full gas you can knock it off in fifteen minutes. But it's tough: the first 1,000 metres really steep, a brief levelling-off to lull you into comfort, another big kick to slap you across the chops. You're going at 300 watts just to get up it.

Froomey took me up it for the first time in 2013. I had just returned from my mid-season break, head and legs swollen from no riding and a lot of indulging. Perhaps he did it on purpose to kick-start me back into action. I was blowing so much afterwards I needed a full coffee stop – piadina, Coke, the works. A few months later I did the same to Luke Rowe, a couple of weeks before he was due to ride the Vuelta. He had done the climb once before but didn't know it too well, so when he attacked it hard I let him ride away before catching him a kilometre from the top and dropping him. I don't think it did his morale that much good, especially as I'd been out the night before.

Then there's what we call the Zoo Climb, in Tuscany, near Quarrata, named not because you have to climb it like a caged tiger, but because at the bottom there actually are caged tigers. It's long but not unpleasant, in a still-suffering sort of way: long switchbacks, Tour-style; a gradual gradient; always in the sun, a nice smooth surface to the tarmac. You'll sweat on the way up but in the almost pleasant way of your body working hard and cooling itself with its own efficient mechanisms.

And then there's Tenerife – Teide to the locals, tidy to a Welshman. Twenty per cent and more, on and on for fifteen tongue-hanging-out minutes. It kicks up, and it kicks up again.

That's good. And equally really bad. But that's climbing: the tougher the climb, the more appealing it is. There is no hiding place when you climb, no excuses. Only on the slopes do you truly know if you are in shape. You have to be light. You have to have power. One without the other is useless.

The hardest climb we race up? The Mortirolo Pass in the Italian Alps, a favourite torture rack for the organisers of the Giro d'Italia. Over twelve kilometres you gain 1,300 metres in height, with an average gradient of 10 per cent and ramps of up to 18 per cent. It's a cruel mountain, a wall of pain and self-doubt. The last time I rode it was on the penultimate stage of the Giro in 2008; even though I had a compact chain-set on my bike (thirty-six teeth rather than thirty-nine on the front, twenty-seven on the back rather than twenty-five) to make climbing a little easier, it was a ghastly hour, a relentless slog with minimal respite. Even approaching it made me feel sick. It gets closer, and the road begins to rise. You change down to a smaller gear. The road rises some more, and you try to change down again, only to find there's nowhere left to go. Call it Gear Fear: that lurch in the guts when you realise it's this and your legs and nothing more.

The question appears in your brain: will I make it up this? I can't stop. I won't stop. Your Garmin beeps and flashes 'auto-paused'. It thinks I've stopped, but I haven't, not quite. Come on, keep going.

If you're feeling bad and you're working hard, it nags at you: I can't make it. The others are away. Those self-doubts must be beaten, like the road itself. Because, when you feel good on a mountain it's like no other feeling in cycling – a lightness on the pedals, a dancer's easy rhythm to your feet.

Climbing is a lonely existence. You can be surrounded by twenty other bike riders, but, when you're suffering, you're in your own little world. Just you and your inner voice, telling you to stop, to ease up. If you could pause time and get into the heads of the twenty others, you know that fifteen would be saying exactly the same thing, but it's so hard to remember that when you are on the limit. 'No-one can possibly feel as bad as I do right now . . .'

Some are born to climb. These are the men that weigh sixty-five kilogrammes all year round, even when they have two weeks off cycling and on the lash. Some will always suffer, like Cav, because they're built for different trials. It's like asking Usain Bolt to run a 10,000 metres against Mo Farah. But, even in your darkest hour, know that we all suffer. Mortirolo for me, Caerphilly Mountain or the Cat and Fiddle or Leith Hill for you. We all hurt, we just do so at different speeds.

Nine tips for better climbing

1. Break the climb into chunks – 100-metre sections, or between bends, or minutes.
2. Pace yourself. Don't go at it like a mad dog, but like a wise owl.
3. Use low gears and try to stay in the saddle rather than standing.
4. Sit further forward than you would on the flat.
5. Keep your hands on the top of the bars rather than the drops.
6. Relax your grip.
7. Keep your upper body as still as possible, and let your legs do the work.
8. If your heart is thumping, focus on nothing but breathing.
9. The bottom line: if you want to be better at it, do it more.

Cobbles

The Challenge

There are those who hate cobbles. Why wouldn't you? When it's wet they're a death slide. When it's dry they're a dust storm. They shake you like an earthquake, rattle your bones, loosen your eyes from their sockets.

And there are those who love them. The cruel examination of nerve and skill. Their heroic history. The whole tension of it – here we go, death or glory, someone's going down, will it be me?

There are no maybes when you race over cobbles. You have to want to be there. It is too hard and too intense and too crazy to think you can just make up the numbers. You can see it in the eyes of your rivals when a race comes towards a *secteur*: you take the lead, I'll hang on, after you. In the Spanish and Italian teams, that attitude is representative of half the riders.

The ordeal of it is what draws me in. There is nothing that truly compares at home – not the cobbled back streets in Cardiff, not the old industrial areas of east Manchester towards the velodrome where our Olympic assaults were planned. In Alderley Edge, just south of Manchester, there is a cobbled drag called Swiss Hill. That was our Tour of

Flanders as young lads on the Olympic Academy – up that, rattling back down, race further out along the Congleton Road and then chase up another lumpy climb called Bradford Lane. Up and down we would go, working the technique, yelling our own race commentary, knowing that northern France and Belgium were a new magnitude of challenge: cobbles like babies' heads rather than kiwi fruit, random gaps and holes to flip you up or stop you dead, cobbles at weird angles that would have you on the deck before your brain had the chance to react.

Watching on television or seeing still shots of the cobbles can give you only a limited understanding of what it will be like. It's similar to when I watch a top snooker player in action. Not only do they make each shot look easy, they have already planned out their next six shots and found the perfect positioning to do so. That's us on the cobbles: not just getting over one, but already having worked out the angle at which to attack the next six. When I play snooker on a full-sized table, it takes me two hours to get through a frame. The winner is not the one who pots the most balls but the one who concedes the fewest expensive fouls. The first time you hit proper cobbles it's the same sensation – that 'Whoah! I'm out of my depth here.' On my Roubaix debut it felt like I was holding a jackhammer and trying to break the road beneath me. I loved it.

Each legendary race throws up its own threats. The E3 Harelbeke: long sections of flat to lull the unwary before bone-shaking interludes and fierce little climbs like the Paterberg. Gent–Wevelgem: forcing you up over the 22 per cent Kemmelberg, the descent a continuation of the torment rather than any sort of release. The Tour of Flanders: seventeen times up cobbled hills. And the evil daddy of them all, Paris–Roubaix. The two decisive sections are usually the Forest of Arenberg, about 100 kilometres from the finish, and Le Carrefour de l'Arbre, but that's a little like saying Mike Tyson's middle and ring fingers are particularly nasty. It's not the discrete parts that do the damage, it's the collective fist in the face, the relentless punches. The roads you ride during the Tour of Flanders you'll cover at other times. Paris–Roubaix is a one-off, and that's what gives it its edge. It's the Alpe d'Huez of the flat, the iconic and the brutal all rolled into one. Nothing can prepare you for it. When it comes to Roubaix, you recon it and then you race it. That's all you can do.

The Tactics and Technique

Cobbles test you like nothing else. It's not just about being strong. It is not just about fitness, or power; if you can ride at 550 watts for three minutes, somehow recover while riding at 45 kph and then repeat that for another fifty kilometres you'll go well, but if you can't handle your bike, or position yourself in the peloton correctly, then you have no chance of winning. That is why cyclo-cross riders like Lars Boom or Zdeněk Štybar have been so successful over the lumps and bumps: they can ride flat out, react, recover and go again. Power can get you a decent result. To win you have to be there in the front all day.

If the test is unique, so should your equipment be. Twenty-eight-millimetre tyres rather than twenty-three, at a lower pressure than normal. Double-tape on handlebars for cushioning. Gel inserts for the slim-wristed.

Try to float rather than bounce. Pedal over the cobbles rather than at them or into the gaps. Keep your cadence high and your legs loose.

Look far ahead and plan your line. There will be an optimum route, no matter how intimidating it might look. Again, although it might feel counter-intuitive in such testing conditions, try to relax.

Hands on the hoods rather than the drops. There will be crashes, punctures, bottles flying out of cages and under your wheels. You need to be able to brake rapidly or dive off quickly to the side. If you're on top of the bars by your stem, you're in trouble.

Keep your momentum. Hit a cobble hard and it can knock your speed. If you can't get that back sharpish, you're dead in the sand. The race will have gone.

Accept that crashes will happen. Don't fear them, or worry where they might come. They are part of this racing. Zen it.

Don't speak on the cobbles. Even if you can get the words out, no-one can hear you. They're in their own world of concentration and pain.

Never eat on the cobbles. At the risk of being patronising, taking your hands off the bars is like shouldering arms to a Mitchell Johnson inswinger.

Stay away from the scared. The riders who hate the cobbles are the most dangerous ones to be riding close to. They'll be tense, jerky and prone to spills. Let them stay at the back and not get involved.

The Aftermath

It's not pretty. All around you are panda eyes and thousand-yard stares, mouths hanging open, clothes mangled. There is always someone badly cut up.

In the old days at Roubaix they'd get changed in the showers under the velodrome. I've ventured down there after a sportive we do from Dunkerque, and it still has the old atmosphere. On each cubicle is the name of a different year's winner. The riders would stand there under the hot water in their ruined kit, trying to wash the grime out of red eyes, scrubbing at their grey legs and arms while assistants scurried around with bars of white soap and towels. I say stand. Roubaix is the sort of race that leaves you crouched on the floor, or showering with your backside on the tiles. Wash me, water, I'm too spent to do it myself. It's almost a shame we do it all now on a bus that looks like a boutique hotel on wheels.

It's one thing riding 260 kilometres in a day. It's another racing it, and something else again having to soak up that pummelling. Not until the Wednesday morning, three days after the race, will your legs again feel as if they're made of muscle and tendon rather than tree trunk. At least your legs are accustomed to you taking it out on them. Your neck, arms and arse are not. And your knuckles – so tight and sore are they that you can't clench and unclench them for at least a week.

And that, perversely, is why I love the cobbles. It's the hardest days that you remember the most, not a flat fifth stage of the Tour when you average 28 mph. It's the extremes that you relish, even if at the time you would do anything to make it stop. You have a sense, even at your lowest ebb, that you will be telling your kids about it: look what I used to do as a job! You have to be strange to enjoy cobbles, but you have to be even weirder not to.

Descending

Never do you feel more at one with your bike than when you are descending.

When the magic is in the air, there is a beautiful flow to the ride. You are water curving through a hose. There is no conscious steering, just a lean with the road, the wind in your face, a roaring in your ears.

Sometimes you just seem to have extra speed. If you are leading the long line and feeling good, everything happens without trying. There is no tiredness. There is no grabbing the brakes. Concentration without concentrating.

As a pro chasing wins I still get the same excitement and thrill from hammering down hills as I did as a kid. I still have the same occasional existential moment, when you glance down at this skinny front wheel as you're doing more than 100 kph and think: it would take only the slightest twitch or smallest pebble to put me down, and only a thin aero jersey and shorts stand between my skin and that rock-hard road.

When you're young, you don't understand the boundaries. When to risk it? You always risk it.

It is always: Go! Go! Go! John Herety, the former British Olympian-turned-manager for multiple teams and general all-round wise owl, used to tell me, 'G, take your Superman cape off!' I was indestructible. I was a bat out of hell, or at least out of Birchgrove.

Those descents I grew up on were grippy under the tyres because they were rougher. They were used to bad weather. If they were steep they were short. Even the long ones coming out of the valleys were only a couple of per cent.

And then we were sent to Italy with British Cycling's Olympic Academy, and it was a case of starting all over again. We didn't care that when it rained the Tuscany roads had as much grip as a bar of soap. We loved the freedom of those long, sweeping descents, the joy of belting down them full blast. It was disastrous – there was at least one big crash every week – but we wanted to sprint down every one.

We grew up together. You learn quickest by messing about and competing, and that's all we did. Ian Stannard, Ben Swift and I racing each other down the hills, the only rule: pedalling is outlawed. Stannard's size gave him a natural gravitational advantage; the other two of us had to overcome it through skill. We were like rival Moto GP riders, nose on the other's rear wheel, trying to steal a draught off the other and popping out of a corner to nick the better line. All games, all essential when the call comes to join the big boys.

Still the crashes came. With every new rider the injury count mounted. It used to drive our coach Rod Ellingworth spare. What could he do? We were kids dreaming of riding the way the superheroes did on our TVs. We were kids off the leash, and often off the road.

Max Sciandri, who had won road race bronze for Great

Britain at the 1996 Olympics and whose local knowledge led the academy to Quarrata, knew all the hills in a 150-mile radius. He would plot our routes and try to warn us of the challenges that would follow. 'Be careful, lads – on this one it gets really narrow after about four kilometres, so scrub off more speed than you think. Single file, be ready for the unexpected.'

Bats out of hell. We went for it the same as ever. And, coming round a tight corner, on a road built for one, came tyre to headlights with a van coming the other way.

On the bright side I managed to keep my front wheel on the road. Unfortunately the back one was in the gutter going sideways through gravel. I was lying there on my back when Max's face appeared in my vision. I could still hear the engine of his car running after he had chased us down from the summit. 'G! What the hell are you doing? Did you not listen to what I said?'

Reputations blossom in the pro ranks. This guy's good. Follow him. This one's edgy. Get past him fast.

Sometimes the skill can be overhyped. They called Paolo Savoldelli, who won the 2005 Giro with a famous descent of the Colle delle Finestre on the penultimate day, 'The Falcon'. It was a great nickname, but it gave him a fierce standard to live up to or ride down. You want to be known as a good descender – it's a reputation everyone chases – but not only as a good descender. Otherwise you can feel as if you have to show it on every hill. A hundred kilometres from the finish, a breakaway clear with five minutes, forty kilometres of flat into a headwind to come.

Where are you going? Settle down, son, what you trying to prove?

Riders who you imagine are good descenders often aren't. Sometimes it makes logical sense: if you've ridden track, you are used to handling a bike brilliantly at speed, and that translates. Some of the best at getting down are sprinters. Why? Because these are the guys who are the worst climbers. Which leaves them no choice but to risk it all on the way down, because otherwise they would never get back on the *gruppetto* or sneak inside the cut-off time – the percentage of the winner's finish time that you have to be within to continue the race. Necessity is the mother of unimpeachable handling skills, and these are men who fight hip to hip at 60 kph in brutal bunch sprints. Perversely, the great climbers are often average descenders. They have never had to push it beyond their comfort levels, precisely because their skills in ascending have given them so much of a cushion.

Bernie Eisel is a great man to be behind on a big descent. So too is Michał Kwiatkowski. Close up you can see how well they handle their bikes. Stick with them and you'll be chauffeured through the best lines at the optimum speed. Failing that, follow guys riding Continental tyres. They will stick where others will not. And sticking's what you want.

There are no secrets in the peloton. Everyone knows everyone. No-one holds back.

When you're descending in a big group it's a noisy old place. As you're accelerating out of a hairpin at the front, you can hear the angry shouts of the riders behind scrapping for lines and space. Brakes squeal, tyres pop. When everyone brakes on a descent, it's just like being on the motorway when the red lights flash and everyone stamps down on the brake pedal: normality turned into panic, heart jumping out of your chest.

Snatches of swearing carry on the slipstream. With each position further back it becomes more feral: harder braking, harder accelerating out of the corners to make up the metres you've lost, more desperation, more fear.

It's a dangerous dance, a conga of carnage. Lose concentration going uphill and you'll only lose time. Lose concentration in the downhill melee and you could wake up in the back of a wailing ambulance. Bright Italian sunshine into a dark road tunnel; baking July afternoons in the French mountains, bare slopes into dappled forest, light and shade camouflaging everything that lies ahead. Potholes are invisible. Dropped bottles sneak under wheels. Punctures send you sideways.

Even the solid road under your wheels can melt in the extreme heat of a Tour afternoon. Suddenly the grip goes. You slide, straighten up, now heading directly for the metal barrier and the drop beyond. Gravel too can get your heart pumping as you exit a corner and see the stuff all over your racing line.

You never trust an Italian road. The surface can go from dinner plate to sandpit in a few seconds. You dream of Swiss descents, the tarmac carefully manicured perfection. If not Swiss, German. If not German, French. But seldom Spanish, and never Italian.

If a puncture strikes, you pray it's the back. And then you pray again, because while you want to slow down as quickly as possible, you cannot brake too hard, and you can only go in a straight line. Where is the road going next? Have the other riders round me and behind me seen what has happened?

You need to read the body language of those in front of you. Richie Porte gets a little nervous. He likes to leave a gap between his wheel and the one in front. If you know how he rides, you don't worry about it. It's his insurance policy. If you don't, you might think he's losing the wheel and take a crazy risk to get into the gap, and crazy risks draw crazy rewards. Bats don't always get out of hell.

Descents aren't always thrilling and enjoyable. Sometimes you dread them. When you are at the back end of the Tour, tired and weary, descending at over 70 kph can be just as hard as the climb up. Concentration has to be full. A fifteen-kilometre descent at the end of the stage, whether you are at the front of the race following attacks or at the back chasing the time limit, can be exhausting.

And the peloton can be a horrible place when you're struggling. Stories fly around: this bloke's lost his nerve. He's a bottler. He's gone.

When Brad had a couple of crashes on the 2013 Giro, it started with a little media buzz and escalated from there. You hear whispers. Snide comments behind a rider's back like bitchy schoolgirls. Stories appear online on the cycling websites. A few more riders start taking the piss within earshot. Only the Aussies have the balls to say it to some-one's face: 'You all good, mate?'

Because, when someone's nerves go, you can't miss it. The body language on the bike tells its own honest tale. They let a gap grow in front of them. They track through corners as if they are going round a fifty-pence piece.

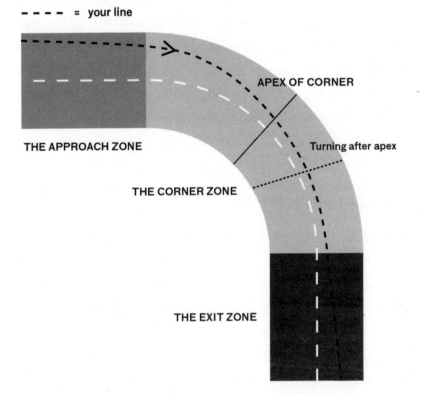

In the wet, the front is the only place to be. Everyone battles for position on the climb, then there's a fierce lead-out-style sprint over the top to be in the best place for the drop,

No-one is immune. When it's wet and the tyres start to go, you can become apprehensive. That only escalates it. The next corner, your front might go a bit more. You get a bit grabby on the brakes on the next one, and the back slides out. Confidence leaches away.

How do you get it back? Just keep doing it. There is no other way. Get stuck in. Focus on what you do naturally. Don't overthink it and let the dark thoughts in.

And learn when not to take risks, even if the headstrong kid still lurks within. If there are 140 kilometres to go in the day's racing, it's not worth the gamble. If it's Milan–San Remo and you're coming down the Poggio with five seconds on the peloton, it doesn't matter that it's tipping it down or that this is a fearsomely technical descent in the best conditions. Now is the time to risk it. Now is the time to throw caution off the side.

Descending with G

1. Always look ahead, never down at your wheel. Look through the corner; your bike will follow where your head goes.
2. Read the road. Use the signs, use your eyes: if you see the outside edge of the road appear to cut off the inside, get on the brakes – there's a sharp corner coming.
3. Never brake in a corner unless you absolutely have to. If you do, squeeze the back brake rather than the front. Enter the corner at the speed you want to leave it, rather than entering it hot and having to brake on the limit.
4. You and your bike should feel like a unified machine. Get your centre of gravity where you want it. You're not sitting on the bike, you're at one with it.

5. Stay loose like the goose. The more tense you become, the more reason you give yourself to get tense.
6. Stay warm. Nothing sucks away your concentration like the cold. And when you can't feel your fingers, you lose feel for the bike.

Escapes

It's not a question of whether there will be an escape on a day's racing. There will always be a break, one or more riders getting away from the peloton and hoping to stay clear until the finish. The only question is whether it succeeds.

A break can go in the very first attack of the day, particularly if the stage is predominantly flat and likely to end in a sprint. Very often it's an easy one to get into, because everyone with any sense knows that it is as likely to stay away as a prop forward making a sprint from beneath his own posts is to reach the opposition try line.

What is most likely to stop it is not a sudden attack of logic from the dreamers but the solid bodies of the workhorses in the sprinters' teams. Why? Because the fewer riders away up the road, the weaker the escape, and the less likely it is to succeed. This means it takes fewer riders from the sprinters' teams to chase, which in turn makes it more likely that the stage will finish in exactly the sort of sweet lead-out that they have been building their entire Tour around. When an escape is made, those same sprinters' teams will work together by sending a rider up to the front of the peloton, with the simple intention of holding the gap between break and peloton at a comfortable margin for the pursuing pack.

Conversely, it's the teams without a star sprinter, or the teams who don't have a rider capable of winning the general classification, who are most keen to send a man away. It's a simple economic sum: the more time they spend away, the more solo screen-time they can bag in the television coverage, the happier their sponsors will be. And happy sponsors reach into their pockets, either for their wallets to send a better class of rider away next time, or for their pens, to sign up for another precious year of financial support for the team. During the early stages of the Tour there might also be a few fourth-category climbs to tackle during the stage, and with them the chance of stepping onto the podium at the end of the day and pulling on the polka dot jersey for a stage or two. And then the wallets come out at the speed of a gunslinger's Colt .45.

There are days when the peloton knows that an escape is likely to succeed, so every team wants someone there. It is like a raging mob trying to break the line of riot police – attack after attack, men throwing themselves into suicidal efforts in doomed attempts to get away. If a posse looks as if it'll break the line and get some distance between itself and the forces of order, there's always one outfit that will miss the move and continue the attacking. It means they won't have to send a rider to the front of the peloton to chase, and it will cover their backsides should the break stay away for good.

Teams who have a rider capable of winning the GC do it differently. On a mountain stage they will always try to infiltrate the breakaway, not only so they have an extra guy in the final kilometres of the stage to act as a launch pad for their leader's final efforts, but so that there will be no pressure to ride on the front of the peloton and chase the break. It forces the other GC teams to use their guys in setting the tempo. On these stages, the pressure falls on the team who has the yellow jersey, and it becomes a matter of fine judgement.

They don't want to chase too hard too early, because it takes an awful lot out of your riders' legs, but that's only the start of it. The escape might not be dangerous to the yellow jersey, so they can let it go – let them have ten minutes and take the stage. But the Tour isn't just about the yellow jersey. Every day is like a world championship. A stage win is massive. Then there are the green, polka dot and white jerseys to chase and defend.

If the stage isn't mountainous, but instead long and lumpy, the team with the yellow jersey may keep the break fairly close. This is to try to hoax a team with a fast finisher into taking up the chase instead. Let the escape go out too far and they may never come to help you, leaving your team a long, hard day of riding on the front. It's a game of chess played at 40 kph.

There are other ruses to try. Limit the gap between peloton and escape just enough to encourage another team to come through and ride for the stage victory or valuable green jersey points. But also let the gap go out enough to encourage the other team to make their move sooner rather than later. A two-minute gap? Not enough. Now the sprinters' teams won't help you until later in the day. 'Ah, that gap is fine. Let's leave the hard work to them for now.'

You realise, when you first look at the route for a Grand Tour, exactly where the best days for a breakaway might be.

Immediately discount the really flat ones and the really mountainous ones. What you're after are the in-betweeners (a little up and down, maybe a second) or first-category climb somewhere along the way to disrupt rhythms and distract attentions, maybe one with a finish up a slight drag to slow up those wolves on your scent. These are days which are hardest to control, which will take a lot out of a team. For some riders – the team leaders who are not in contention for yellow, the ones who need to justify their reputations and salaries – their whole Tour comes down to these stages. Think Frenchman Thomas Voeckler: strong but not indomitable, punchy rather than flat-out fast or a mountain chamois, a romantic who loves the notion of a glorious escape.

Sitting a little further back in the peloton, maybe twentieth or thirtieth wheel, you can watch it all unfurl from afar. The first signals come back to you – a couple of domestiques moving into position to block the road a little for a teammate, a notorious strong man like Tony Gallopin trying to surreptitiously edge his way through the field. You see them going, and you think to yourself: if they get this gap, this break is gone.

Getting in a break during an early stage of the Tour, on a flat day, isn't the hardest escape to make. It's the most straightforward thing you'll do in the entire three weeks, because no-one could care less. The hard part is getting in the right break, the break everyone wants to be in.

These are the periods in the race that you never see on television, yet there is so much action, so much going on.

The racing is intense and can keep ratcheting up for ninety minutes before the escape is finally established. One day during my first Tour, that pre-televised racing went on for ninety kilometres. It was torture. All I wanted was for an escape to go away so I could go easy for a while. When it finally disappeared, the whole peloton celebrated together – riders with both hands off the bars, clapping, cheering, each man shaking his head and laughing, 'Oh man, how hard was that?'

During the later stages of the 2014 Tour, with our leader Chris Froome retired after a series of crashes and our back-up plan not working, the onus shifted towards us to try for a breakaway win. At that point it becomes very much like the lonely single man trying to make good in a nightclub: don't be too keen, everyone will see you coming a mile off; chase too vigorously, and you'll never make it. When you're desperate, you'll try too hard, use up too much energy at the wrong times and ultimately miss the move. It's about being inconspicuous and calm, watching from afar until the time is right.

It's the subtle move that succeeds, the one where no-one even thinks you're trying. There's a bit of luck in there, for sure, but your timing has to be right – maybe an initial move from four or five goes, then three more, the bunch slowing, spreading across the road, mainly those with team-mates up the road, a few shouts of '*Basta!*' ('Enough!'). Now you know riders are tired and have had enough. They want the break to go. And that's the moment – bang! – you sprint across to make it one more in the escape.

There's an etiquette when it comes to attacking in a race. Never attack when the yellow jersey has pulled over for a pee. He will not stop during the heat of battle but after a few minutes of easy pedalling, of watching the escape ride off into the distance. When he swings over it unofficially stops the race and confirms that break as the escape of the day. Young guys can become unstuck, either because they haven't realised that the yellow jersey has stopped or because they're too young to care. Very quickly they are put right.

Sometimes when you're looking to go in the break you will look around you and search for allies. A wink here, a nudge there, the signs in a rider's or team's body language that they too are keen. With experience you can spot the teams that really want a guy in the break. There might be someone you've raced with in the Classics, or a friend of a friend, or a man with a notoriously big engine like German time-trial specialist Tony Martin. One of you will see the possibility of an alliance, and the ice-breaker will follow: 'Come on, shall we go?'

You must also be an instinctive gambler. Willing to gamble that attacks will continue and that it will take a while for the escape to go clear, to gamble that others will soon tire, so you can sit back and save your own legs. If there's a climb coming up, gamble on waiting until the road heads upwards before you make your move. Why? A climb will limit the amount of people able to chase and bring you back.

Study the race book, the official stage-by-stage route guide given to all teams by the organisers. Are there any sections with narrow roads? These are the stretches where it's easier for riders to block the road and shut the race down, so get to the front before and be ready to go. If you're on a slight downhill, wait. The whole bunch will be travelling at 55 kph and more, and trying to get away from the wolf pack at that speed will take so much more out of you.

Should you make that escape, then the real hard work begins. All of you should work hard and do your turns on the front: why else have you bothered making the jump? You are unified by your common aim, and all will roll through for their turn. Once the break is established, a few might try to soft pedal, calculating that they will save their legs for an attack at the death. They might get sworn at, abused, despised. If it means they have a better chance of the win, they will ride it all out.

The bigger the group, the more problems there are. Everyone will look at everyone else. You doing this, or me? Get more than ten riders in an escape and it will be less likely to work. More people will skip turns. There'll be less cohesion. Get six to eight in there and it will be the toughest to chase down, because every one of that group will commit. Two from the same team? It can make a few guys nervous as they know one of them will inevitably be taking it easy.

How much time do you spend on the front, where it's the hardest? As youngsters we were taught to do only as much as the guy doing the least. If you're considered one of the stronger riders, the onus will fall on you. The others will be thinking: why should I burn all my matches when this guy's carrying a flame-thrower? And so, while everyone waits for someone to make a move, another rider can spring a surprise. It's what happened at the end of the one-day Gent–Wevelgem race in 2015. Five of us away, me being watched because I'd won another big race at E3 two days before, me watching the two riders from the Quick Step team. Right under the radar, the outsider Luca Paolini escapes. Everyone looks at everyone else. He rides to victory.

The real world is seldom as amenable to control as the theory. On the seventeenth stage of the 2011 Tour, I got in a break of eight riders with my Sky teammate Edvald Boasson Hagen, with a gap of between twenty and thirty seconds. We all knew the maths: hit this full gas for five kilometres or so and the elastic holding us to the peloton would snap. But there was a complication: at the back of the break was a German rider called Linus Gerdemann, riding for Leopard Trek. His outfit was in contention for the team general classification, and that meant that the others chasing that prize, like Garmin, did not want him to stay away. So they were chasing from behind as hard as they could, even as the rest of us were yelling at him: 'Get back, clear off, or we're all doomed.' Instead, he sat there in the slipstreams, doing not a single turn, pointing at his ear as if to say, sorry lads, my directeur sportif is telling me to do this.

It carried on like that for fifteen kilometres, like two time trials running simultaneously, until eventually the inevitable happened and it all came back together. In that moment of mass relaxation, another break went. Seven riders, Eddie among them. And that one made it, catching all unawares: Eddie riding beautifully on the final treacherous descent to make his own escape from the escape and bag his second stage win of the race.

People watching at home might wonder why most escapes are caught within the final few kilometres. Why not earlier, to leave a little more leeway? Is it not like a cricket team dawdling their way through the chase in a fifty-over match before frantically swinging the bat to overhaul the opposition tally in the last few overs?

It is not by chance. Pursuits are a matter of fine calculation. Catching a break more than twenty or thirty kilometres out from the finish is counter-productive, because you will simply leave enough time and opportunity for another attack to break away. This time it will be from a rider who has been drifting in the slipstream of others for the last 100 miles, so is fresher and stronger and will be a whole lot harder to bring back.

Time checks will come through on the race radio in your earpiece. The directeur sportif will suggest a suitable time gap between the break and you pursuers when there will be fifty kilometres to go. At thirty kilometres, it should be down to x minutes, at twenty kilometres, x seconds. If it's a tough day and you're halfway through the Tour, you might let the elastic out a little further, knowing that the group out front will tire more dramatically; if it's a shorter stage, or a flatter one, you tighten the leash. Catch it with ten kilometres left and the sprinters' teams can keep the pace high enough to hold any other devil-may-care dashers at a strong arm's length.

It's a game of cat and mouse between the escape and peloton. The escape rides 'easy' for the initial half of the stage, thus forcing the peloton to slow because they don't want to catch the escape too soon. That in turn saves the escaped riders' legs for the final frantic forty-kilometre push to the line. There will be times in the peloton when you are dawdling along at 30 kph just to keep the gap at a reasonable distance. Long days, counter-intuitive days. A race to see who can go slower than their rivals.

The solo break is another beast again – rarer, more starry-eyed still, much more likely to die a glorious death. Not many fancy it, because the odds are so stacked against success. When it happens, you've bought your ticket. There is no alternative course of action: you are out there, now lump it. If you do it on a sprinters' day, when all are certain in the knowledge that it can only end in failure, it can only be for self-promotion. Self-preservation would tell you to stay put. The ego can do curious things.

It is harder now than it used to be. Some of those classic breakaway stages have been neutralised by the skillsets of riders like Peter Sagan, John Degenkolb and Michael Matthews, guys who can both sprint and get over the lumpy stuff to win. It means you must plot your big move with more craftiness and care than ever before. When you're young, all you want to do some days is make the break. Instead you must learn your timings from the past masters like David Millar. It is not by chance that the same names always appear in the right moves.

If you are away, if the pack is closing in, it is like being chased by wolves. Do not waste time looking back, do not waste energy wondering. Get your head down and go as hard as you can for as long as is possible.

When you are swallowed up, you are a goner. There is no coming back, no second escape. There is only one rule: get out of the way. Get out to the side, or the gutter, but do not stay where you are. Because the differential in speed between the lonely soloist and the rampaging peloton is so great that you become a human bollard in the road. Some riders make it back through the eye of that storm. But most become blockages, with other riders swerving to get round them, the swear words and insults spewing out. You are not just a crash waiting to happen: you are several crashes.

And then there is the other form of escape, the one you will know all about. Even when cycling is your job, that sense of release when you climb on your bike and pedal away from the mundane real world is still the same.

As a kid, bound by others' rules, it's your adventure, a way to expand your universe. Aged ten I would cycle the two miles from Birchgrove in Cardiff to Whitchurch and feel like I was in another country. As an adult, no matter how banal the worries – a bill to pay, a room to decorate, an argument to forget – it wipes the mental slate clean in the same way. Two wheels and a triangle of metal to some, an escape chute to all us riders.

When the Wind Blows

Wind? What can mere wind do that mountains, freezing rain, flat-out sprints and blazing heat can't?

Don't believe it. When you open the curtains on the morning of a stage race and see the trees outside leaning sideways, your guts lurch. It means the day ahead will be one of great stress, and no-one knows quite what will happen.

If you were riding by yourself there would be no problem. If it was a headwind you might swear at it. If a tailwind decided to help you along, you might say a little thankful prayer. When your job is to shelter someone else from its capricious kicks and the chaos that follows, you feel as happy as the bachelor suddenly given his mate's unruly kids to look after all day. How the hell am I supposed to do this?

You give different weather conditions human characteristics. Rain is cruel. Sun is all smiles but slowly stitches you up. Cold keeps digging away at you with a hard-hearted persistence.

Wind is sly. It pretends it's not there, and then you turn a corner or pedal past a building and – slap! It blows the race and all your careful plans apart.

On the first few days of a Grand Tour the entire peloton is already on edge, spooked by the slightest noise or unexpected incident. And if, just when it is starting to settle down, the wind kicks up, the fragile truce is shattered in seconds.

It doesn't need to be strong; 20 mph will do it, it's the direction. Tailwinds shorten the stage. Headwinds lengthen it. Crosswinds drop a grenade.

Sometimes the waiting can be the hardest part, when the wind is strong enough to stress everyone out but still too weak to do any real damage. Every team's directeur sportif will be on the race radio, inadvertently tightening the tension with every word. 'To the front, boys! Don't sit back. We turn slightly left soon. Get ready for this . . .' And so we do, in panicky bursts. Guys moving up in the grass along-side the road. Guys fighting through the dirt, crashing into each other.

When the wind is strong enough to split the group and a team go for it, within moments the peloton explodes. Half the riders sprint for the front, desperate to find protection in the echelons that form like streams of rain on a windscreen. In theory, they are simple shapes: a diagonal pattern of riders that constantly rotates so that the front man is taking the full force of the wind for only a moment or two before the next rider comes past and he moves back. In practice, they are brutal battles for survival, a constantly shifting formation that must adjust to every bend in the road or slight swing in wind speed and direction.

Forget the great bond of empathy that supposedly unites the peloton. When echelons form, it is war. As soon you see three or more men get together and move to the front, you have to move with them. And, when a team hits it, you almost see a countdown clock in the top right of your vision, as if you were Kiefer Sutherland in *24*. Only rather than having twenty-four hours to save the day, you have an absolute maximum of thirty seconds.

Or you are gone, lost to that lead group, heading backwards at speed. So rapid is the rotation, so limited the room and so tooth-and-nail the fight, that if you don't get in straight away you will be spat out of the back, out of the protection of those tightly packed bodies and into a wall of wind that will stop one man on his own as effectively as a stick through the spokes. Before you can recover, you will have gone backwards into the next echelon, and the same thing will happen again – a brief struggle to keep your head above water, a boot in the chops and out the back you go.

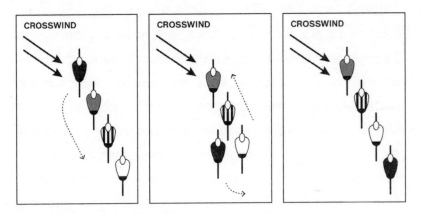

Everyone is shouting at everyone else. 'Out of the fucking way!' 'Hey! What you doing?' You sprint to squeeze into the tiniest gap, force your wheel in and make that next link in the chain shift over, regardless of what filth it will trigger into your ear or ribs.

If you get dropped from the group there are tactics you can try. You can deliberately ride in the middle of the road so that the echelon behind has to separate to move past, giving you the chance to get into the line. It's not considered the most gentlemanly thing to do, but being polite won't get you anywhere in crosswinds. You also have to be going fast enough, otherwise, in the blink of an eye, they'll be round and past you before you can react. And you can be the victim too of a similar sort of sneaky trick: when a team attacks in crosswinds they will ride what's known as 'half road', leaving only enough room for their teammates rather than riding right over in the gutter and taking extra guys with them.

Teammates will try to help each other. If you are rotating through the back and you see a familiar face in trouble, you will try to pause for a moment to let them in. But only a moment, or you too will join the dispossessed in the gutter. If there is no-one from your team, you search frantically for someone to whom you're connected by some other thread – a mate in common, a fellow fan of the Classics, a rider you once duelled with for a win, the time you once helped them out with a spare energy bar or helped out someone in their team. Who cares how thin that thread is as long as it binds you together. In a predatory pack, the outsider will be torn to pieces.

Once you are in an echelon it is almost easy. When they work they are supremely efficient systems. You become one cog in a smooth machine. But, when they are forming, they are malicious and impossible to resist. It is like being a novice surfer thrown into storm waves, climbing aboard only to be thrown off, coming up for air only to be held down by the next rolling wave, getting weaker with every dismissive slap.

When you are looking after a star name, the margins

shrink and the anxieties grow. You can't just sprint up the outside of a group to get into the lead echelon, because someone like Chris Froome or Richie Porte is not as punchy with their accelerations; you must tailor your support to the specifics of their abilities. You have to take them up at a steadier pace, but with the speed things are changing all around you and creating fresh dangers.

And there can be no relaxing. You can be lulled into a sense of comfort by a soft tailwind, leave the shelter of a town for an exposed road through open fields and look up to see the race splintered. Sean Yates, our former directeur sportif at Sky and a grizzled old pro from the 1980s and '90s, would be at us from the breakfast table onwards. 'Right, boys, you've got four hours of total concentration. I don't care what you do after that. You can go back to your hotel room and think about nothing or watch *Game of Thrones* or knock one out. Whatever you want. But for the next four hours, this is work. Never switch off. Never think of anything else.'

It makes windy races some of those most feared in the year. Nowhere is worse than the Tour of Qatar, where the wind is so nasty that every rider is lined up on the start line with half an hour to go, like keen juniors at their first event, because they understand what will follow as soon as the racing officially begins. The neutral zones are not neutral. They are full-on battles for position.

As soon as the flag drops it all shatters. Within five kilometres you can have five echelons. Fifty kilometres later, when you make a ninety-degree turn left and suddenly have a tailwind, it calms down again. Then, another fifty kilometres later, when you make a second ninety-degree turn left, the crosswinds smash it to pieces all over again.

Ben Swift's very first pro race was Qatar. He simply wasn't built for it. In ten kilometres he went from the first echelon to the back. And that was his day, fighting to get in, finding all the doors locked. A lonely, exhausting baptism: no friends, no warning, no idea what you are doing wrong.

I knew how he felt. Deep into my first Tour de France, back in 2007, I thought I might be through the worst: a flat day, the break gone, the bunch chilled out after a nervous start. I was in the back quarter of the peloton, chatting to Brad Wiggins, enjoying a drink having just gone through a feed zone, when, from out of nowhere, order became chaos: crosswinds had struck and the Astana team had attacked.

Panic on the streets of France. The first group went. Then the second. I managed to get into the third, got spat out and tried to hang on in the fourth. I was legless, destroyed. I just wanted the group to slow down and ride into the finish. But Christophe Moreau was in the group, and he was the big French hope. He had a chance of getting on the podium. So the group kept riding full gas for the next eighty kilometres, and I died a long-drawn-out death. There was even a moment when I just stopped pedalling, only for half a revolution. Then I grabbed myself by the lapels. What am I doing? I can't give up. Back onto the wheel. I eventually got through the stage, to find out that my team- and roommate Robbie Hunter had won it. I certainly enjoyed the champagne that night, not for my contribution to the win, purely just for still being in the race.

Where Qatar's crosswinds are predictable, Europe's are

not. The roads aren't as long and straight. There's more street furniture to deal with, more vegetation. What you lose in intensity you make up for in unpredictability.

Sometimes you can hear a gust coming, through the grass in the field beside you or in the trees that line the road. At other times it's like being blindsided by a right hook. You will see riders suddenly slapped across a two-lane road and disappearing over the verge.

Never has it been as bad as in 2015 at Gent–Wevelgem, the one-day cobbled Classic. They are used to the winds in Flanders. Everyone in the race can handle their bikes. Despite that, almost no-one thought the race should have gone ahead.

It was like a war zone. I saw local man Gert Steegmans – six foot three inches, twelve stones twelve pounds, a super-heavy-weight by cycling's skewed scales – blown straight off the road into a canal. Edvald Boasson Hagen was hit by a gust, slammed into a wooden post and broke his collarbone. Around eighty kilometres later, when we thought the race and wind had settled slightly, I was hit in the same way. Round a slight corner, a thump in the side as effective as a Sam Warburton tackle, right leg up in the air above my shoulder, desperately trying to stay on, into the verge and down into the wet turf.

It is an enemy to be feared but also confronted. You cannot ride easy in the wind, just as you could not attempt to ride out a Warburton tackle by jogging rather than running. In a time trial it even gets inside your head. How to pace this? Ride too hard into a headwind and you will have too little left for the climbs. Go too easy and your chance has gone anyway.

You begin to hate it. One year after the Tour Down Under, Sky teammate Salvatore Puccio and I stayed out in Adelaide for an extra week of warm-weather training. Every day, six-hour rides, wind all the way. Headwinds for thirty kilometres, each taking their turn in its teeth, each in their own world of pain and anger. When you cannot ride two abreast there cannot be conversation. Conversation is what gets you through those long rides. Boredom mixes with resentment and exhaustion.

And yet, just a few degrees of difference gives you a tail-wind, the sweetest gift nature can offer up. Those feel like payback for all the times you've suffered, particularly if you plan it so that you head out on your training ride into the wind, when muscles are fresh, in order to be blown home when the legs are weary. In a race it means a shorter stage, extra time in the hotel that night.

Only when you fail to acknowledge it can a tailwind cause problems – heading out with it at your back and thinking: blimey, I feel sensational today, I could ride for ever; and then turning to discover it was all a cruel deception. Then there are the days when the wind seems to know what you've got planned, when it stays in your face on the outward leg of the ride and then suddenly switches direction at exactly the same point as you do.

The wind is your enemy once again. You can swear into a headwind all you like. It will snatch the words away and tear them up before anyone can hear. Hunker down. Make yourself small. Resistance is futile.

Lead Out

You'll know the image: from the pell-mell madness of a bunch sprint, from a crazy conga of hammer-down riders, one man will emerge, as if perfectly choreographed, head down and flat-out, to sprint across the line with arms outstretched and mouth roaring.

How does it happen? As soon as the route of the Tour is announced in the previous November, riders will spot the sprint stages and mentally ring them in highlighter pen. The climbers will earmark the mountain stages, the team principals the grand classification days. The sprinters want the flat ones, the otherwise dull ones, the ones that take nothing from the tank or legs.

Preparation starts in the hills. Get through those mountains with minimal effort. The phoney war continues in the neutral zone at the start, no matter that there are still 200 kilometres of racing to go until any weapons will be deployed. 'Yeah, we're not going to ride hard today, Kristoff's been sick . . .' 'No, you get stuck in, we're focused on tomorrow.' Riders will pretend to be tired, to be struggling to even get in the saddle. Then, with three kilometres to go, they'll come past you like superheroes, teeth grinning, capes flapping.

Sprinters have egos. There are tales of Linford Christie walking round the call room before big 100m finals, stripped to the waist, as if to say to his rivals: this is what I've got, what about you? Cyclists can't do the same. Our upper bodies are too pale and skinny. But the metaphorical chest-thumping and teeth-baring goes on all the same.

It might come through the media – a comment made to a journalist in the knowledge that a rival will hear it and growl. It might be a look on the start line: what are you doing here? It might be a barbed comment yelled in the ear fifty miles in: watch yourself out there, you don't want to crash again like you did last time we came here . . .

Sprinters will rise to it. They are emotional men, their hearts on their sleeves, insults on their lips. You can see it explode out of them when they cross the line – all that pent-up anxiety and fury coming out of them, in the words of my old friend Mark Cavendish, like a fireball.

Their lead-out men – the last link in the chain that flings them clear – have almost exactly the same set of physical skills, but they can be quite different personalities. Cav's long-time partner, Mark Renshaw, is the chalk to his chilli. Cav is all sparks and flames, Renshaw as cool as the Kwaremont in Febuary. The testosterone is there all the same. When two lead-out trains get going, duelling it out drag-race style through the final kilometres, it is alpha male following alpha male in a long-drawn-out line.

You ready yourself for the showdown. A caffeine gel around twenty-five kilometres to go, no closer or you'll be on the bus when it kicks in rather than at the beating heart of the sprint.

At twenty kilometres the real business starts, any escape closed down, the scrap for the front warming up. Cav's train will take it up early, not least because they are allowed to; their displays over the years have bought them that respect. The fight will be for the key slots next to them. With every kilometre that ticks by, the speed and tension build. There will always be one train that tries to leave it late, sheltering in the wheels, letting the others do the hard yards, but this is also a gamble. On your own you can move to the front in the last minute. Doing it efficiently with three teammates on your wheel is a whole heap tougher.

In these minutes there will still be GC contenders lurking, nervous that a crash or puncture will harm their overall chances, the peloton feeling that anxiety and returning it with interest. Lead-out trains and sprinters are shouting at the small climbers, who look anything but comfortable in the mess of a bunch sprint. Your directeur sportif will be in your earpiece. 'Left-hander coming up, guys, then cross-winds from the right.' Riders will rip into that corner, a mini bunch sprint in itself, everyone wanting to be in the best position possible. The kilometres will fly past. That jump from twenty-five to go to ten disappears before you can look around. In my first Tour de France, the pure speed of the peloton in those closing stages left me shell-shocked.

Each man in the team has his role. No longer are you a rider on your own. You are a truck and trailer, making space, not only for yourself, but for the man on your wheel. If you see a gap, it must either already be big enough for two or you must use your shoulders and elbows to make it so.

When Cav was with Sky in 2012, I was his lead-out man at the Giro, a responsibility and experience I relished. If Ben

Swift was around, he would take the second slot and I'd move third, but the enjoyment was still there. I was raised a track rider, and this is what we do – right in the guts of it, men on our wheels, another man an inch away and all of us at 60 kph. To have one of the world's greatest sprinters on your wheel is a glorious honour, even if leading out Cav meant we could make a couple of mistakes and he could still finish the job.

In a sprint lead-out train, that order of riders will never vary. Now, at Sky, on a climb, where two or three of us will be leading out Chris Froome, it can. Who feels good? Who's on fire? When you're towing a sprinter, only the length of turn you take on the front might change. Because, a lot of the time, it won't go perfectly. Perfection is hitting the front with five kilometres left, and then dropping your star off with 200 metres to go. If something happens – you lose the wheel in front, or you get blocked off, or someone hits the deck – you think in the saddle. Your sprinter might go freelance, hopping around other wheels until he finds a superior spontaneous express to climb aboard, or you might have to drop back, find him again in the melee and reignite your charge.

If your legs are feeling good, you can step out of the protection of others and take him back up. If there is a head-wind, that gamble will make even more sense, because your rivals can't get away as far or fast. Through the chaos you try to keep communication simple. Cav's train use only five words: Left. Right. Go. Stop. Easy. It has to be 'stop' and not 'whoah', because in all that noise and breathlessness, 'whoah' could be confused with 'go'. In a team time trial we use something similar: Left. Right. Hold. Change. Hold means: hold your speed, you're going too fast. Change means: next man through.

And it can be chaos. There will always be some guys who don't have lead-outs, bouncing round trying to squeeze into trains, others trying to freelance, all shouting at each other. Many riders know how to swear in six major European languages. Those who don't still understand the tone and implication.

Four kilometres to go. There will be three men, plus the lead-out guy and the sprinter. If you don't have to hit the front yet you will leave it longer, sitting at the side of the big group, biding your time, surfing that wave without being swamped. You position yourselves at the front for corners and roundabouts, for they will string the whole peloton out. Rather than having ten guys around you, you will have them in one long line behind. You can afford to take it steady for the next 100 metres or so, saving your legs, enabling you to get your sprinter that much closer to the finish.

You have to relish the madness of it all – the pressure, the speed, the total reliance on your teammates. Never lose the wheel in front, even if it means shouting at someone, leaning on them, elbowing them. There will be scares. Spokes will ting-ting-ting on the back of other riders' rear mechs. Front wheels will hit the feet of riders in front, leaving you teetering on that ridge of no return. Another couple of degrees leaning to the right and you are down. It doesn't only happen in the big races. The most anxious race all year might even be the charity criterium before the Tour Down

Under in January. It's meaningless, but it's the first event of the year. New riders in new teams, itching to impress their new employers. Riders off the leash after a long winter. Chaos on the calm streets of Adelaide.

Who goes when? You work it back from the finish. Your sprinter wants to hit the front with just under 200 metres to go. That means the lead-out starts at 500 metres. The third man will do his final pull from one kilometre to 500 metres, the fourth from 1.5 kilometres to one kilometre.

If it's not in your legs, if you can't do your turn, it's too late now. Your last chance to let everyone know is five kilometres. If you do lose a man – to a puncture, to a crash – the next guy back in the train must sort it out. Use another team's pull. Sit behind a stranger for a moment or two to save the legs. Ride the wave, floating from one wheel to the next. If you're feeling heroic, hit the front and do a full 1,000-metre pull rather than the usual 500 metres. If there are a few corners or roundabouts, use them to prolong your turn, because you will get a little rest into and out of each: the line strings out, and as you exit the bends you have a precious couple of seconds before the other teams will be back up to speed and alongside you again. Use the weather conditions: if the wind is coming from the right, ride in the left-hand-side gutter, leaving enough room for your team-mates. And this means too that the other teams have to move up past you in the wind, the hardest place to be.

If the rider behind you loses your wheel, if you glance back and the third man, lead-out and sprinter are all trailing, wait for them. Freewheel for two seconds and they'll be back on. Sometimes just trust the superstar. At the World Road Race Championship in 2011, when it was my job in the British team to lead out Cav, I glanced over my shoulder with 800 metres to go and couldn't see him. Oh, crap. Where's Cav?

Then I spotted him, on Aussie rider Matt Goss's wheel, with three other Aussies leading them out. Perfect. Cav's gone freelance. Let's leave him to it.

As they go past you, as you are swarmed by the hangers-on, you have no idea at all what is happening up ahead. Then you look down the road and see a familiar figure with his arms out. It's Cav! Never a doubt, never a doubt.

That moment is a wonderful feeling. You might think that you're giving someone else the glory, that you're sacrificing yourself for another rider. You are, but in doing so you become part of the win. That afternoon in Copenhagen I was disappointed that I didn't get to perform a true lead-out. But we had all been working for Cav all day, all ridden at the front, all dictated the pace. The fact I was there if needed gave all the boys confidence. It felt more glorious still when we helped take Chris Froome to the yellow jersey in 2013 and 2015, but that was because it built and built over three weeks. In that time you go through so much together that it binds you tight. But both felt great. Both felt like shared wins.

And you will be rewarded as such too. Cav, in keeping with his well-deserved reputation for generosity, gave each of us GB teammates a luxury Swiss watch, made by IWC, the rainbow bands of the world champion's jersey across the face, our names and dates inscribed on the casing. That's a special gift, something to cherish. Something to always remind me of the day Great Britain dominated the World Road Race Championships, a dream beyond anything this kid from Cardiff could ever have imagined.

Velodrome

My first emotion when I hear that word: nervousness.

Those beeps, counting down. The crowds, gone from wild cheering to sudden silence. A knowledge of the savage pain that is coming. Beep. Beep. Beep. Legs tensing. Beep. Beep . . . and Go! Go! Shoved along by a mighty back-draught of noise, aiming at the onrushing banking, throwing yourself headlong into the fight.

I can never forget the first time I walked out into the velodrome at Manchester. This was the hothouse where British cycling grew from an unnoticed child into a beautiful medal-swallowing monster, the wooden oval that would be my office for much of the next seven years. We had arrived from Cardiff in a minibus, and as soon as the domed roof appeared in the distance my nerves kicked in. It was both intimidating and inspiring. Inside, whispering as if we were in church, we went to the top of the banking and looked down. 'Man, how steep is that?' Out onto the track for the first time, its contours scaring you then setting you free – sprinting around the bottom to make sure you didn't slide down, then going higher up the track with each lap, up and up to the fence, then throwing the bike down the steep wooden cliffs, the speed thrilling.

For a cathedral of sport, what we did there was mundane. Every morning, in at 8 a.m. Up much earlier to beat the traffic in from the suburbs of south Manchester to the fast-developing east of the inner city. Lap after lap, drill after drill. Double sessions, never an easy one. Team pursuit, madison, points racing, 'go 'til you blow' sessions behind the motorbike. Lap after lap, staring at the hub of your front wheel, unwavering between the lines; drill after drill, doing your turn; back to the back, lap after lap.

I had trained and raced on the roads, with all the variety and natural stimuli that brings. Track was a job, in a building stripped of comforts, designed for hard work. That dull light of the corridors. Grey paint on the walls; artificial lighting. Into the track centre, a circle of cheap plastic chairs. Pulling on shoes, click-clacking over to your bike to change your own gears, no mechanics, no help, just you and the coaches and a distant dream.

You had to be ready to hit every effort. Because every effort is scrutinised, calculated, put on a graph. Everything is intensified on the track. Everything matters. Straight after rolling off the track you will be shown if you've slowed up a tenth of a second. In normal life, a tenth of a second is nothing. But on the bike you ride so hard and so often that you can feel it. And you will be told, without drama, without room to wriggle: 'You slowed up a tenth there on your second half, you should have done more.'

Every velodrome feels different, smells different, sounds different. The London 2012 arena had an aura about it, months before the Olympics began. It glistened. It was huge. Newport, our regular pre-Games training venue, felt in comparison like a friend's front room: smaller and cosier, practical and sheltered rather than the stage for the greatest few weeks British sport would ever see. At Newport, the echoes came back fast, coaches yelling at the sprinters, the boards rumbling as they thundered past. Shouts of encouragement were never lost. When you were training in London, sound disappeared in the space. The deep stands absorbed the background hum even as we emptied ourselves in flat-out efforts.

Some tracks carry bad reputations. Some are known for being heavy under the wheel or a slog to get round. The slow ones, like Los Angeles or Apeldoorn in the Netherlands, have longer straights and tighter bends. Tracks that instinctively feel fast are shaped more like bowls than canoes, so the longer bends give you that sweet slingshot as you fizz round into the straights. Some are faster simply because they're warmer. It can mess with your head. You can leave Manchester doing 14.2-second laps, get to Apeldoorn and find 14.5 secs feeling like a brutal struggle. At least Los Angeles brings back good memories for me; it was where I won my Junior Track World Title in 2004, only to return less than a year later, minus a spleen and a good few kilos.

Laoshan in Beijing, for all the success Great Britain enjoyed there, lacked a celebratory atmosphere. The stands were virtually full but all the magic happened on the boards down below. But that was a dream compared to Moscow: 333 metres long, the surroundings grimly austere, the local riders all hard guys pedalling round for hour after hour, sweating blood, the toilets just holes in the ground. It is also nine metres wide. By comparison, Manchester is 7.2 metres, which doesn't seem a great deal less, but it makes a hell of a difference. It's like an extra stump on a cricket wicket, a tennis racquet with a sweet spot an inch larger. If you start a team pursuit from man four, it's like facing a Belgian berg when the banking rises up in front of you. Sprinters love it there. The huge bankings give them extra speed. If you want to break the world 200-metre record, head east.

Then there are the tiny, tight tracks where the six-day races take place. Ghent: 166 metres long. Bremen: 180 metres.

I rode in Bremen with Cav, as under-23s, before the pros. (We won every night, but on the final night the organisers wanted to put on a demonstration race. It was a derny race, where one rider from each team rides behind a big motor-bike on the track. It was purely for the fans. The organisers wanted a home win, so one of the German lads got the nod. Cav was to finish fifth of six, and he was devastated. 'Why? That's ridiculous! We've pissed it every night!') Then there's Calshot in Southampton: 160 metres. It is a challenge to ride flat out round that wall of death while staying on the black line. The tighter the track, the steeper the banking, the bigger the thrill.

Sometimes your favourites are less about the glamour than the sense of speed. In Melbourne, a sensational city for sport, it is not the big racing venue at the Hisense Arena that we all love but the much more basic DISC Velodrome in the north-west of the city, where Jack Bobridge made his attempt on the hour record. It is just a tin shed, in many ways, but it is warm and fast, and we were in good shape, flying round in a way we seldom did at Newport in a frozen

Welsh winter. It was the same at the local training track in Perth, en route from the UK to Victoria – warm outside, fast inside, a lovely effortlessness to the big numbers coming up on the analysts' screens.

As a kid it was all outdoor tracks, each of them with their own idiosyncrasies. My local track in Maindy has a pronounced dip in its back straight. I threw up my dinner before my first race, a combination of nerves and the fact I'd eaten a ton of pasta sauce only an hour before.

Training at Maindy had its challenges, not only because of the cold nights but also the local kids. Claiming to be bored, some found it amusing to throw stones at us as we went past. Around Bonfire Night the stakes got higher. Compared to dodging a fizzing firework, ducking a rock is relatively straightforward.

The old stager in Brighton's Preston Park runs noticeably downhill in the last 100 metres. It also has a ten-metre section where there is no barrier at the top of the track, just a two-metre drop-off to the walkway below. Travelling to race at Herne Hill, a classic cycling venue but also home to old rivals of ours, was like going to an away ground in the Six Nations; a warm welcome, but also a sense of: this is our territory, we will make it hard for you.

Scunthorpe's Quibell Park is a huge old oval with a full eight-lane running track inside it. You would travel as a team in the minibus, standing up and peering out of the windows to get the first glimpse, grabbing your bike to ride round a leg-loosening lap and get a feel for the concrete under your tyres.

Back then, all your racing was over the omnium: a 500-metre time trial, the elimination race, points, scratch for the sprinters, pursuit for the proto endurance athletes. Each rider had their preferred format, but we all had to learn the lot.

For me, nothing could beat the elimination, a devil-takes-the-hindmost contest, with its mad panics and desperate dashes. Always the same stress: I can't be the first to go, I can't be the first. The points race: fun if you're going well, hard if you're struggling. I used to dread it. I knew even then that I wasn't a sprinter. Too skinny, not big enough to be that explosive. That should have made me perfectly suited to the points, but it magnified my nerves like nothing else. If the weather started to turn with me leading the overall standings I would desperately hope for rain so that it would be cancelled. When I finally held my nerve, and the lead, the mental barrier went with it. I was away. Under-16s national champion, as beautiful in its own way as anything that was to follow on other velodromes, on other days.

Team Pursuit

H ere is the contradiction at the heart of the team pursuit: it is so horribly hard, but when it is done well, it is one of the most effortless-looking pieces of perfection in sport. And it looks so beautiful – four discrete characters merged into one stretched-out seamless unit, like identical robots running exactly the same update of the same programme.

The team pursuit is easy mentally. You line up on the boards knowing that you don't have to give a moment's thought to the opposition. All you can do is worry about how fast you can go for four kilometres. If the other team happen to go faster, there's nothing you can do. No tactics, no psychological games. Just get out there and ride as hard as you can.

In that way it's the most controllable of all cycling events. You can turn up, as we did in Beijing and London, and know that you have a very good chance of leaving with gold. Equally, you can flip that around: if it starts badly, or it goes wrong somewhere, then nothing can save you. There is no margin for a moment of inspiration or tactical genius. And when that happens, as it did to the Great Britain quartet at the European Championships in 2011, it is a helpless sort of despair: fighting, recovering, hurting, man down, hurting, going flat out but going nowhere.

Who is the perfect team pursuit rider? Ed Clancy. Gold in Beijing, gold in London. The strength and power for a huge start, the ability to soak up a load of lactic and searing lungs and yet still be able to come through to do perfect turns at the front. Acceleration plus endurance. If you had four Eds, they'd call off the competition.

It is the blend between your four men that is the key. At the London Olympics, we had Ed and Steven Burke on turns one and two, the big explosive men to get us up to speed and soak up the hammer and grind of the start, with Pete Kennaugh and me back-ending the ride by pulling the longer turns in the third and fourth kilometres to drive us to the finish.

But there must be a balance. If Ed went off full gas he could do the first half-lap in 11.4 seconds. Yet he won't, because no-one else can match that. My full gas is 12.2 seconds, and it's no good me doing that, because I would have emptied the tank long before my big push was required. So, instead – blend and balance – we aim to hit the first half-lap in 12.5 seconds dead. For Ed that feels easy, so he can do another few sprinter's turns before his engine blows. For me, tucked in as third or fourth man, it clocks as 12.7 seconds, because I lose a couple of bike lengths as man one and two pass me and I get on the wheel. Starting three or four also means I start higher up the track, and so get a little help from the banking as I glide onto the wheel in front.

There is such responsibility in that chain, such total dependency, that you can become a very tight unit off the bike. It is like being part of the front row of a rugby team – physically linked, unable to achieve anything without your comrades next to you.

You don't have to be best mates, but there has to be a chemistry there. In the year before the London Olympics I spent more nights in the same room as Ed than I did with Sara. Three of the four getting on can be enough, as long as they *really* get on. But you still need to be able to work with the fourth. There must be a unity of purpose, a shared level of effort apparent. If one guy is even slightly off-message one of the others will soon be all over them. Because you cannot win it with just three riders.

A few months out from the 2012 Games, one of the key men in our Australian rivals' quartet, Jack Bobridge, made the headlines for crashing his car after an evening out and spending the rest of the night in jail. For the others in that team, some of whom would have been training hard on the road, you could understand if that felt like betrayal. Here I am killing myself every day, and you've got time to do that?

You won't all be identical characters but, just as your physical strengths are contrasting yet complementary, you need to understand what makes the other three tick and how to get the best out of them. There is nothing to be gained from slowly taking an immense dislike to someone or trying to put one over on them every time you're in the velodrome together. Allow even a little of that attitude to creep in and you will arrive at the Olympics to discover that bloke will be a critical couple of per cent below his best, worn away by the needless friction between the two of you. The team pursuit is about utilising every joule of energy you have, not burning it off in a heated argument. We were fortunate going into London that we were all genuinely good mates.

All of us having lived together at some point, we knew each other inside out.

It isn't easy, not with the physical and mental strain you all put yourself under. You go through a lot of emotions together, and seldom the same ones at the same time. With experience, you learn to smooth the graph: don't be too up on a good day, don't crash too low on a bad one. By the end of our Olympic tilt we had become proficient at it, but we had our moments along the way.

The most intense period came early in my career, in Perth, back in 2005. I was there with the senior boys, on the track five days a week, some days double sessions, some days with track-league races in the evening and morning rides on the road. It was man-breaking training, yet the most testing element came off the bikes. There were almost as many hours in front of the analysts' computers as in the saddle. It got to the point where we had lines on the screen illustrating every single change in formation on every single effort, how long and high each rider's arch was from the front of the line to the back, a different colour for each rider. For some guys, like Steve Cummings, it was too much – death by analysis, strangulation by statistic.

The toughest days – mentally as well as physically – are the ones where you're trying your best but you just can't hold the pace. There is no hiding from it. You hit the front and have to do at least half a lap. Everyone will know if you're slowing. The performance analysts will be recording every revolution, every pedal stroke, every watt of power. You feel as if you are not only blowing your own chances but letting everyone else down too, which is the worst feeling a team athlete can have. If a teammate is enduring such a day, you have to put an arm around their shoulder and help them through it. You need them as much as they need you. Then, when the same thing happens to you a few weeks later, remember the words you said to them, and remember that you meant it.

To the race itself. You establish a schedule for the perfect team pursuit. Within that you must be both foolhardy and rational. You must gauge your efforts down to the last tenth of a second, which equates to only the most infinitesimal difference in force through the pedals or position on your tri-bars. Lift your head to see how far off the bend is and you've blown that margin without even trying. The great jeopardy is that everything you do is for the team, so your own desires must be ignored.

If you have to go 100 per cent on your first turn to hold the team's overall speed, you've just got to do it. Equally, even if the strategy is for you to do three turns of a lap and a half in each, it's not set in stone. If you have any fears that you could slow down, change it. Chuck in a lap or a half instead and let another rider take over. A shorter turn is bad, but it is always better than dropping the speed – because you are then asking for a monstrous effort from the next guy to pick it back up. That will put him deeper in the red than he needs to be, and in turn destroy his abilities for his next turn. Round and round in vicious circles.

You must know both your body and your mind, their fortes and foibles. Can I squeeze out another half? Can I do another seven seconds at this pace? This is where all those hard yards at 8.30 a.m. in an empty Manchester velodrome must come into play. Do I have it in the tank?

If you feel bad, you need to get as deep into the race as you can. Nine times out of ten you know if the magic is in your legs before the race begins, but every now and then you will hit that one time when you might suffer a bad change and miss the back. Even a bike length will do it. You miss the suck of the wheel in front, chase it desperately for half a lap. Those extra seven seconds of effort can be enough – fail to recover, bail out the back.

So much to calculate, so little room to manoeuvre. At the London World Cup event, some six months out from the Olympics, Steven Burke was on the front for a lap turn, and he was in trouble. In that scenario he should have thrown in a half-lap, but he didn't. Disaster.

It wasn't a slow death either. It was like he'd pulled the rip cord on a parachute. Coming out of the bend, which is usually the faster part of the track, that drop in speed kicked back up the line. In an instant, my front wheel was underneath Pete Kennaugh's back wheel, grinding rubber to rubber, the track equivalent of pressing the ejector seat button. Am I down, can I save it?

Somehow I stayed upright, but with all my weight leaning over his wheel, I shot up the track, almost into the fencing separating us from the grandstands. Behind me, Ed didn't have a clue what was happening. A rider never bails mid-line. Never. How to deal with it? Protocol. He closed the gap to Peter, me swinging back down to join at the back. Disaster swerved. This isn't to single Burkey out. But that's the team pursuit: always riding that fine line between perfection and calamity.

The next time we raced was at the Track World Championships. Because of what had happened in London, all the lead rider could think was: can't slow down, can't drop the pace. He also had that magic feeling of fire in the legs. How to use it? Instead of doing a longer turn on the scheduled pace, he did one huge lap at a crazy pace and then bailed. That left the remaining three of us on our own for the final couple of laps, deep into the red, as disastrous in its own way as going too slow. We could see him in our peripheral vision, going round the top of the track at the same speed as us down below.

Tiny margins, huge consequences. There is no worse feeling than being in that line and knowing you are not recovering; being incapable of doing more than a half-lap on your turn, knowing that the other guys are relying on you and that you are letting them down. Losing the wheel mid-line is almost as humiliating. It rarely happens in racing, but in training, when everyone is on the limit, day after day, a gap can suddenly appear. And when it does, with three laps to go, 750 metres can feel like a five-kilometre climb.

What pulls you through is repetition. Work it, work it, work it. You finesse through so many hours in training, following that wheel, that it becomes second nature. The judgements required are ridiculous, if you allow yourself to dwell on it: four of you, flat out at 63 kph, each tyre an inch from the one in front. Try walking that way with three friends at 5 kph and you'll be stumbling all over each other's heels like you're being thrown out of a boozer at closing time. In training, Shane Sutton would push us to the limit. Making us ride in the red, hoping someone would crack – not to break them, but to see if they could make the right decisions under such intensity.

And yet. When it is working, it feels so smooth. There is no fluctuation in pace. No-one ever drops it, not even by 0.05 seconds. When everyone is on song, all flowing together, it is almost easier riding at a pace of three minutes fifty-one seconds than four minutes, because the sacred sense of momentum, that sweet sling off the banking, carries you through.

How do you nail every change like that? We obsess about what we call good deliveries. Just before your turn calls, you begin the process of thinking about speeding up, knowing that you will actually be maintaining the pace and that the thought gets your legs turning at just the right rate. And, because you obsess about it, you feel like you hardly ever do a perfect one. You are always tinkering with it, over so many hours and hard yards – doing five kilometres in really low gears, pedalling your arses off, the gearing amplifying any mistake you might make, struggling so much that it replicates that race pressure.

As cyclists going into the London Olympics, we were aware that we were considered the engine room of the Team GB medal assault. As a member of the team pursuit quartet I was aware that I was part of the engine room of the cycling squad.

If you allowed that sort of pressure to affect you it would

Team pursuit gold at the World Track Championships in Majorca, 2007: Brad, Paul Manning, Ed Clancy and a rounder-faced me. The moment we realised Olympic gold was a real possibility.

In Beijing, winning was the most glorious contagious disease, running unchecked through the British cycling squad. The night out afterwards was pretty special.

Ed and me at the World Cup in Manchester, 2008. As the look between us indicates, I shared a room with him on more nights that year than I did with the woman who is now my wife.

My first Tour de France, 2007. I know you can't see my jaw, let alone my cheekbones, but as a 21-year-old Tour novice, I had much to learn and less to eat.

A chinwag with race leader Fabian Cancellara on the 2010 Tour, proudly wearing the white jersey for leading young rider. "Nice shades, they match your jersey." "Yeah, strong look".

Retaining our team pursuit Olympic title, London 2012. Four discrete characters merged into one stretched-out seamless unit, like identical robots running exactly the same update of the same programme.

Ed Clancy, Steven Burke, Pete Kennaugh and me on the podium in London. The night out after that one was even better than 2008.

Closing ceremony, London 2012. 'Hey Chris, there's a bar in town that's giving out free cocktails to Olympic gold medallists. You might be alright'.

Showing Cav the love after he wins the World Road Race title in 2011. It was one of the great thrills of my career: leading out my old housemate and friend, a long way from messing about as teenagers in the Manchester Velodrome canteen.

'G is someone you can always count on to be at your side – though that can quickly mean danger on a night out drinking.' Mark Cavendish

Tactical and motivational chat, midway through the Tour, 2013. Froomey's only just got back from his podium/media duties. I'm already in my lounge wear.

Warming up for the individual time trial, Tour 2013. Note state-of-the-art skinsuit, expensive headphones and two bits of cotton wool shoved up my nostrils. The Olbas oil on them opens the airwaves. Old and new school.

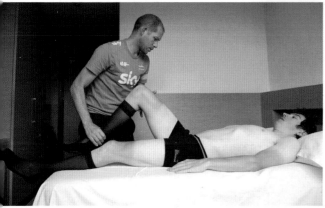

An example of a typical cyclist's tan: Sky physio Dan Guillemette can't help but grab a handful before Milan-San Remo, 2014.

The best meal of the day: breakfast before stage seven of the 2014 Tour with Richie Porte. Important rule at the breakfast table: no second helpings of smoothie until everyone has had a glass.

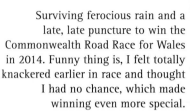

2014 Tour, stage 10. A mere flesh wound. There is only one thing that helps you deal with crashing, and that's crashing. It is as inevitable to a cyclist as losing your wicket is to a Test batsman.

Surviving ferocious rain and a late, late puncture to win the Commonwealth Road Race for Wales in 2014. Funny thing is, I felt totally knackered earlier in race and thought I had no chance, which made winning even more special.

Winning the Classic E3 in 2015, by now with the lean face of a proper road cyclist. You also win your own weight in beer if you are victorious at E3, although it's a lot harder to hoist aloft on the podium.

The evening of the penultimate stage, 2013 Tour. Froomey's in yellow and he's staying there. My first beer for a couple of months is tasting every bit as good as I'd imagined.

Between the gutter and the stars: the 2015 Tour, stage four, having my teeth rattled by the brutal cobbles but determined not to let Vincenzo Nibali get away this time. Note: sometimes the gutter is the best place to be.

Stage 12. Race leader Froome, biggest danger Nairo Quintana on his shoulder. Hence my race-face. Attacks came from everywhere that day, but we made it through the Pyrenees with yellow jersey intact.

Finishing stage 16, having earlier been rammed into a telegraph pole and fallen down a ravine. It was like real life Mario Karts. As if that wasn't bad enough, I lost my favourite shades in the scramble

Champs-Elysees, Paris, July 26 2015. Three weeks of pain, tension, pressure and intense effort end in the perfect way. All for one, one for all.

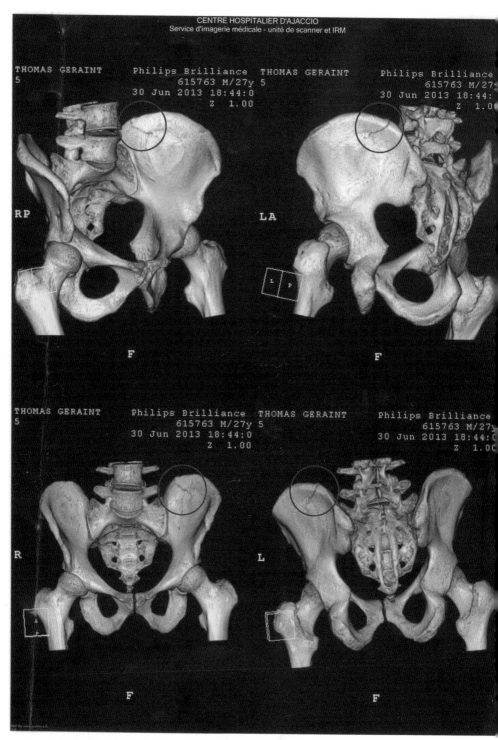

Not a set of fossilised elephant ears, but a 3D scan of my fractured pelvis at the start of the 2013 Tour. The good news from our medics was that it would heal okay if I rode, with no long-term damage. The bad news was that the pain would be intense. They were absolutely right on both counts. I insisted I carried on; their brilliant medical treatment helped me make it to Paris.

destroy you. How to keep it at bay? You try to focus on the process rather than the outcome, that hoary old truth for all sportsmen. You turn the television or radio off any time cycling is mentioned. And you lean on the character of Shane, our own personal Mr Motivator, a driving force with few equals.

There will come a magic day when you know that the blend is right. Before both Beijing and London that revelation came in the humdrum surrounds of the velodrome in Newport: a session where hard suddenly felt easy, an effort when we could feel the extra pace, the sensation of, whoah, we've got something good here now. You will do an effort which is only a couple of laps shy of full distance, which is a lot in training, and absolutely nail the schedule. Everyone coming off saying how we could go faster, the coaches trying to control that raging bull. You feel invincible. Let's go faster. Let's do more.

As Beijing approached, the coaches wanted to try out another guy in the potential pursuit line-up team. So to prove my form I did a solo four kilometres against the clock, as did Brad Wiggins – reigning Olympic champion in the individual pursuit, less than a month off retaining his title.

We both did a sub four minutes seventeen. I was only a second down on Brad. And I remember thinking: bloody hell, I can't believe I've just gone round so fast.

The coaches rethought again. G, you can ride the IP as well as the TP? Yes, I could. But the final of the individual pursuit is the day before. I've been training with these guys for three years. What if I race in the IP and then feel even marginally tired, and we miss out on gold in the TP by 0.2 seconds?

As it turned out, we won by almost six. I could have raced both. But I've never worried about it, just as I only very seldom wondered how the Aussies were getting on while we were hitting our peak in Newport. You would tell yourself you couldn't think about it. But you'd also think: they can't be going this quick . . .

PLACES

Majorca

A gorgeous island, and one that reminds me of feeling fat.

It's to do with the timing. Our training camp in Majorca does not come in March or April, when so many other Brits are charging around its lovely long climbs in the Tramuntana mountains or sprinting along flat coastal roads. It comes in the month before Christmas, when we have all had a good few months away from long rides and small portions. Majorca is when the Team Sky training gear feels a little more snug than you remember it, when the chefs cut back on the servings dished out at dinner and your pleasantly relaxed body is rudely reminded that it is supposed to be a bones-and-muscle racing-machine.

It wasn't always this way. When I first travelled to Majorca, as a first-year junior on the Welsh squad, it seemed so glamorous: eye-candy climbs like Sa Calobra, rolling spins out to the lighthouse at Formentor with the sea crashing down below you, little hilltop villages that look deserted until you turn a corner into the main square to find five cafes with tables and chairs full of bikes and riders, coffee and fresh orange juice and baguettes being thrown down throats. You could dream of being a pro: time-trialling along the coast road from Alcudia to Pollensa, flying down the descent of the Puig Major, hammering through the Orient Valley.

And then you become a pro, and it's all about the routine. Long rides, massage, food, sleep and repeat. There will be rain, there will be hailstorms. You complain about neither because the rain back home will be heavier and the hail far harder.

Only twice since those junior days have I been back in summer. On both occasions there was a higher calling to the routine, an urgency otherwise absent in the prosaic winter months: we had an Olympic Games less than a month away.

We stayed in our usual hotel in Port Pollensa. We almost failed to recognise it. In place of the quiet promenade and occasional old boy sucking on a pipe, thousands of holiday-makers in shorts and shades, the smell of chips, kids licking ice creams. As men who dream of licking ice creams, it could easily have gone wrong, but the Olympics brings a sharper focus to everything you do.

Our final training day before Beijing in 2008 could not have been further from the idea of a sun-tickled, feet-up beach holiday. It was supposed to be a split day: morning session on the time-trial bikes up along the flat road on the approaches to Lluc Major; afternoon on the turbo. Except I was so spent from being hammered into the ground over the past three months that I couldn't finish the last effort before lunch. I stopped by the side of the road, slumped over my TT bars, drenched in sweat. I couldn't face the ten-kilometre ride back to the hotel, let alone the afternoon session.

Our coach Matt Parker tried his best. 'Come on, G, how much do you want this?' So much, more than anything else, but there's nothing left in me. Desire alone cannot power an engine drained of fuel.

How did I get home? By pretending that I wasn't trying, by pretending that I was only riding to the next corner. Four hours later, I was on a turbo on the roof of our hotel; Pollensa and its oblivious chip-eaters down below, Brad on one side of me, Shane Sutton on the other. Neither moved as the next hour pushed me to the sort of dark, decrepit places I never knew existed. Shane the sentinel, pointing at the computer readings: 'Come on, G! Keep that cadence up! One minute left. Push, push, push!'

Four years later, Majorca became an escape pod rather than a house of pain. At twenty-six I was the experienced Olympic athlete rather than the pale-faced rookie of 2008, but with the pressures of London building, the team pursuit squad needed to get away. While we were a tight unit, we had different strengths: Pete Kennaugh and me the endurance boys, Ed Clancy and Steven Burke the fast-twitch sprinters.

Those distinctions powered our competitive natures and thus our incremental improvements. Our start-gate sessions in London had seen Ed and Steven hurting me and Pete, throwing in some insults as they went away. Majorca was our territory: one of us sticking the wheel on them every day, going away on the longer efforts to leave them thrashing away in our wake. In our final block we went further still, on a rise we named Mont Muro. It was more of a slight incline to a roundabout, just outside the little village of the same name, but the plan was simple rather than subtle: Pete and me, third and fourth wheel, onto the slope, flat-out attack. Within 500 metres we had twenty seconds on them. 'Not so fast and twitchy now, eh, boys?' Those games, those friendly battles, were what took us to gold.

With Pete and the rest of the Sky squad, the winter mood is equally sociable. Towards the end of the camp, when reserve has been broken down by weariness, you find the different nationalities coming together. Over five-hour rides with new teammates, for whom English is often a second language, the conversation is always the same. 'Have a good off season?' 'Where'd you go on holiday?' 'What's your first race?' 'Want to ride the Tour?'

In the evening there are bar games, although because of the five-hour rides the standards are seldom up to those one might expect from international sportsmen. The pool table is fine. Get down properly over a shot and you are virtually lying down, which makes it the ideal evening activity for a cyclist. Sadly the standard is so poor (two consecutive pots brings cheers, three, whistles of amazement) that you are never in your seat for more than a few seconds, which is a frankly horrific scenario.

The darts is barely any better. No-one wants to stand, so the usual formats – 301, Round the Clock – are eschewed in favour of something shorter and sweeter: best of three darts, sit down, let five other blokes have a go while trying to nick their chair for a footrest. I can't pretend that it doesn't make me proud that I'm the only rider to have notched over 100 in one visit, and thus have my name on the honours board. I'm also realistic: if the cycling goes wrong, pro darts is not going to keep me in carbon frames. As for the table tennis – in theory we're all up for it, in reality walking to fetch the ball every few seconds is far too much effort. And in any case, no-one can match our combative Norwegian Lars Petter Nordhaug or teenage Czech ping pong champion Leopold König, both of whom favour the pen grip and destroy us bumbling amateurs with a volley of wristy flicks.

If those sorry potterings help to bond us as a team, team management like to aid the process in more bullish fashion. You will be wearily pushing open the restaurant door to be confronted by a big poster proclaiming '2016 STARTS HERE!' or leaning up against the wall while waiting for a lift to find that they've stuck Team Sky-style blue lines by the light switches. Does it make a difference? It certainly makes management feel better. Will 2016 start in a deserted restaurant? For some, for sure.

Competition, as always, fires up our engines. With an hour of a ride to go, we'll set up a race for home: Commonwealth vs Rest of the World. It has to be complicated. Four of the Commonwealth compadres in a break, thirty seconds in front of the RotW group, which also includes four from the Commonwealth. How are we Commonwealth braves going to play this? A plan is hatched: we will hold the chasers back until five kilomeres to go, when the gap will hopefully be around ten seconds. Then, on a slight rise: bam! Two more of our guys will jump across.

It works a treat, not just in this particular contest but as a way of sneaking a big effort into training without actually noticing. Because these sorts of efforts at this time of year are far from the traditional approach. The old school can be summarised in an aphorism: never go hard before Christmas. At Sky, our Spanish riders will grumble. To them, riding faster than 35 kph, even in the sweet scenery of their homeland, is tantamount to pulling a parachute. 'This does not make sense! This hurts!' Bernie Eisel is invariably infuriated if the coaches suggest a two-up time trial. 'Come on, guys, it is December!'

It can make for an interesting team dynamic. Because in my track days we would ride hard all winter, I'm happy to push it. I also want to be in shape for the spring Classics. But you find that there is a collective pull that will carry everyone along. I will sit down for lunch next to Nicolas Roche, see him nudging a small piece of fish around his plate and think: ooof, maybe I should surreptitiously slip these extra potatoes back in the pot. By the end of the four weeks, what began as a loose group of disparate characters will be operating with the same mindset.

Never has that been better illustrated than at our Christmas dinner in 2014. It was decided that we should come in fancy dress, which was fine until Santa after Santa kept filing in. There must have been a good twenty of them by the time the doors stopped swinging. Only David López (Mrs Claus), Mikel Nieve (Frosty the Snowman) and Bernie (a cracker, complete with 'pull my cracker' label) broke the team unity. I think Dave B loved it. Look how the lads have come together!

We enjoyed ourselves, despite repeatedly freaking out at the cloned Clauses; to be served the full Christmas works –

three meats, gravy, sprouts, apple and blackberry crumble for pudding – after ten days of nothing but rice and salad is the sort of treat that can make you a little tearful with gratitude. Particularly in my case, as when I got back to Cardiff the traditional Thomas family Christmas pud never happened. My mum is usually well on it, but this time we were all too hammered to remember both that we had bought one and that we had not eaten it. We discovered the pudding twenty-four hours later, unwrapped but untouched, listing slightly in the microwave, as lonely as the cyclist who orders a knickerbocker glory in sight of his team director.

Belgium

You want to know what Belgium is like? Before one race over there when I was a teenager, rather than putting the riders up in a hotel, they stuck us in a barn. With stretchers for beds.

That's Belgium.

Belgium, for the professional cyclist, means the end of winter and the slow start of spring. So, when I shut my eyes, I see this: rows of dark, bent trees; narrow, wet roads; grey skies overhead with rain on the way or just passed through; barren ploughed fields; and cold-looking cows. Plus the occasional knocking shop.

In some ways, the country seems frozen in time. It's a place where the wind blows hard and the droopy moustache rules uncontested. The main squares of the towns where we race and stay seem so familiar from films that you half expect to hear a heavy, clunking sound and see a tank roll round the corner, gun barrel swinging round towards the clock tower.

It's a nation in love with cycling, a nation in love with the strange, the unpronounceable and the almost unrideable: Omloop Het Nieuwsblad, E3 Harelbeke, La Flèche Wallonne.

Racing there as a junior was a significant culture shock. We'd pile over the Channel and come up against traditions that were entirely alien to a lad from Cardiff. You would go down for breakfast, starving hungry as always, to find only black, chewy bread, slices of meat and hunks of cheese. For a while I couldn't work it out. Had I come to the wrong room, or had I slept in and come down instead for lunch?

Everything was fried. Everything had meat in it. Particularly popular was meat that had been fried.

Before races we would always be served the same dish: a watery spag bol, with cheese on top that had the appearance and taste of stale straw. To this day it brings back awful memories. My wife, Sara, makes a cracking spag bol, but I simply can't handle it. Too many mental scars.

I'm aware that the Belgian tradition of mayonnaise on their chips is frowned upon by many British visitors. With repeated trips and tastings it grows on you; I now view it as a good thing. The beer is a different story. You need to remember that cyclists are very poor drinkers. We don't have the build for it. If ever we could handle it, long spells of abstinence have turned us back into teenage novices.

It's a dangerous game. In Belgium, every beer is an exponential version of what we might taste at home. Their session lager is equivalent to our man-killer. If they just want a light ale, perhaps something around midday on a hot afternoon, they'll still start off on something coming in at 9 per cent.

That's a problem for anyone, let alone a cyclist at racing weight with the sort of thirst 220 kilometres of hard riding brings on. Every year after Paris–Roubaix, the longest and hardest of the spring Classics, the chef at our usual hotel will celebrate the end of the misery by bringing out a tasting menu of local beers. It never ends well. In fact, it always ends the same way, with one of the riders being sick on a rug. But they keep putting on the party, and they keep putting out the rugs, so they can't mind that much.

Usually, of course, we avoid beer. It's not a good drink when your job depends on keeping the weight off. The preferred tipple, because it carries the fewest calories, is a G&T or a vodka and slimline tonic. Unfortunately, ordering that in a pub in Cardiff, as a man, doesn't tend to go down particularly well.

In many ways we're similar to jockeys. Always watching the weight, always counting the calories. I'm told that if you go out in Newmarket it's the same sort of vibe – lots of small, lean men with small, feminine drinks. At least the British riders have their teenage escapades to fall back on. The French riders, despite coming from a culture that allows children to enjoy a watered-down glass of wine with their lunch, are notorious lightweights. There's an annual criterium in Japan where the booze tends to flow afterwards. Within a few half-cut hours the French are transformed from stylish iconoclasts into weak-kneed eighteen-year-olds.

I digress. Belgium is special for cyclists, its races as redolent of spring as the Tour is of high summer. The Classics build from late February onwards, Omloop and Kuurne–Brussels–Kuurne on the opening weekend, the excitement and profile increasing with every race that goes by, the coverage in the newspapers spreading across more and more pages, the talk, everywhere you go, only of cycling.

That first weekend always follows the same plot lines. The

significant riders testing each other out, the weather always rotten, snow frequently in the air. These were always races traditionally dominated by the natives, but the Brits have been coming hard, just as we have on the track and in the Grand Tours – my Sky teammate Ian Stannard winning Omloop two years in a row, my old mate Mark Cavendish sprinting to the win in Kuurne in 2015.

Belgium is a place to rug up, to pull on as many layers as you can. Cobbles, mud, crosswinds and short, vertical climbs. You're glad the descents are equally short, because it keeps you from freezing solid. You see your name in the papers in previews of the big showdowns, which feels encouraging until you realise that you cannot read Flemish and that the words 'Geraint Thomas' may be followed by 'does not look to have the legs and will struggle badly on the Kemmelberg'.

It's not always great racing there. It's a country I rarely visit after April. The races are always stressful, always dangerous. Street furniture everywhere; riders on the pavements and bike paths trying to move to the front of the group; having to dodge kids, dogs, cars, people in wheelchairs. Out-of-control bunch sprints, a few too-keen guys from smaller teams taking big risks to impress the bigger teams. In the Classics you deal with it: it's the Classics. Afterwards, you don't want to deal with that any more. The Belgians? They love it. It's what they know.

E3 Harelbeke holds fond memories for me. It was where I won in 2015. I've always enjoyed the race (I was third and fourth in the preceding two years) because it tries to lull you into a false sense of comfort, staying relatively flat over the first 100 kilometres before throwing in a dozen nasty climbs in the second half. On the fateful day, Zdeněk Štybar, Peter Sagan and I rode away on the Kwaremont, the most famous climb in the region. The other two were looking tired coming into the final twenty kilometres, pulling the odd face, making the odd noise. I thought they might be bluffing, but decided in my head that I was going to have a go. Pick my moment in the final kilometres and just go. Štybar looked the stronger of the two, so I tried to catch him off-guard. Only one way to find out. Big effort, big effort, glance back under my armpit . . . not bluffing.

That's the Friday. Two days later comes Gent–Wevelgem, through western Flanders and up and over the 22 per cent punch in the guts that is the Kemmelberg. And still they come – the Tour of Flanders, with its seventeen climbs, up and over the cobbled hills of Oude Kwaremont, Paterberg and Koppenberg, desperately trying to save some juice over the first 150 kilometres for the pell-mell madness of the last hundred; La Flèche Wallonne, taking you three times over the Mur de Huy, only 1,300 metres long but averaging almost 10 per cent and kicking up to a cruel 26 per cent, the Amstel Gold race still in your legs from three days before; Liège–Bastogne–Liège, the oldest of the Classics, won and lost on its long hills.

Of them all it's Flanders that I love the most. It suits me down to the rubber on my tyres. This was where I came of age as a teenage wannabe, and it feels both familiar and thrilling – the narrow roads and the kicking climbs, the *secteurs* of cobbles, the smell of embrocation, the discussion beforehand in every restaurant and hotel you go into and the level of detail in which the ordinary fan can analyse a race. There is a museum in Oudenarde, where the Tour of Flanders now finishes. Memorabilia from all the iconic races, pictures of snow, mud, destroyed riders. Heroes of the sport hanging on the walls. Mangled bikes. This is Belgium's history, and it is cycling's history. To pay homage by riding through it feels wonderful.

There are skills required for these one-day trials that are like nothing else in cycling. Never can you rest easy. Six or seven hours of unbroken concentration. The race can blow wide open in an instant, and if you're not at the front with antennae twitching, fighting your way through the *secteurs* with spider-sense on full alert, it'll be gone and away from you. The old pros know every corner and cobble. 'Watch out for the house with the red door – there's a sharp left, into a narrow road, immediately afterwards.' 'Here there's always wind, so be near the front just in case.'

It's often not the climbs themselves that are the worst part. It's the race into them. They're so narrow and rough that, once you're on them, you're log-jammed where you are. So the approach to each one becomes like a mini bunch sprint, almost like a points race on the track compared to the longer, more infamous Alpine climbs, where at least you can settle into your rhythm and pick your rivals off.

It makes the anticipation and the wait the worst part of all. My fellow Olympic team pursuit gold medallist from Beijing, Paul Manning, used to say to us: 'Don't go looking for the pain, boys, it'll come to you.' Never is that truer than in Belgium. On or off the bike, some might say.

In the team pursuit it's actually harder to ride at 95 per cent of your absolute maximum than it is to go flat out. It's the equivalent of a long-drawn-out Chinese burn that you cannot escape from rather than a sudden cut. So it is in the Belgian Classics. Holding it fractionally back. Keeping that last burst of acceleration in the tank, but still going so hard that the pain is hunting you down.

On every nasty climb you assess your legs. How am I feeling? What has that taken from me? It's horribly easy to talk yourself out of carrying on, to forget that everyone else is being drained in exactly the same remorseless way. When the final break happens, it's almost a sweet relief, even though the sudden effort – out of the saddle, head down, breath rasping into lungs – hurts even more. Now it switches to the pain of a deep but quick cut instead of the endless burn. The intensity is horrible, but you know it cannot last for ever.

It shapes the characters of the men who grow up riding this landscape. Belgian riders never complain. They barely talk. They look forward to crosswinds. The worse the weather gets, the happier they become. The Italians don't even train in bad weather, let alone enjoy racing in it. They don't have to. If it rains, they can take a rest day, safe in the knowledge that the next will be perfect for riding. Try that in Belgium and you'd never get on your bike.

And Belgian riders are big. As a kid I was average height. When I raced in Belgium I was suddenly a midget. I've often thought that Ian Stannard should be Belgian rather than

English: tall, big legs, big head, strong like an ox but fortunately much faster.

They can suffer like few others. Which is rather handy, bearing in mind the problems they have with fashion. You know when you used to visit your gran's house, and everything felt fifteen years ago? That's Belgian riders. Clothes that went out of style years ago. Haircuts that Premiership footballers had last decade, that even League Two defenders would turn their noses up at.

The French cannot drink like the Belgians. The Belgians cannot dress like the French.

The French rider thinks: 'Does this coat look good on me?' The Belgian rider thinks: 'That anorak will do.' The Belgian fan thinks: 'Those waterproof trousers are perfect, because it's definitely going to rain.'

What you appreciate about the Belgian cycling fan is their knowledge. Stick your head into a pub full of old men and they'll all be sitting around the television watching a race you've never heard of.

As a cyclist you become obsessed with not getting ill. At Team Sky we carry a small bottle of hand sanitiser wherever we go, so we can avoid germs and illness as much as possible. So, when you are stopped by a fan carrying ten identical cards for you to autograph, who sneezes across all of them, wipes his nose on the palm of his hand and then offers you the pen which he's had in his mouth, the alarm bells start to go off. Particularly when you sign the lot and then they stare into your face and ask, 'Who are you, please?'

Possibly as a result of that, possibly because we get bored, possibly because Wiggo was born in Belgium and has picked up some of the language, we are all able to swear in Flemish. I shan't repeat any of it. It probably doesn't make grammatical sense anyway. There's one about being the father of some rather badly behaved women. There's another that calls into question the target of your deepest affections. And then there's one about being naked in the kitchen, which makes no sense at all but is Brad's clear favourite. I'd rather not delve into it.

Italy

Is Italy the spiritual home of cycling? I think so. But then I consider France, and I hesitate. What's that? Belgium? Well, thanks. Hmm. Perhaps I can propose a curving land corridor that starts in Belgium, heads south-west, straightens south until the Med and then bends down the boot. Not so much a spiritual home as a spiritual large landmass containing a significant number of disparate cultures and languages.

But still. While the French and Belgians also all seem to grow up racing bikes and watching bikes racing, and all seem to have great heroes going back through cycling's ages, there is something special and distinct about the Italian cycling aesthetic.

They love the flashy rider. They adore the flamboyant attack. If you combine the two and a flashy rider makes a flamboyant attack, the nation falls to its knees. It doesn't matter if the attack is doomed. In fact, it's considered almost ideal if the attack is doomed. It gives it an even more alluringly romantic hue. The further out from the finish the glorious kamikaze move is, the wilder the reception will be. Think Gino Bartali, Paolo Bettini. Not so much death or glory as death and glory.

The tradition lives on. In the 2014 Milan–San Remo, Vincenzo Nibali attacked on the climb of the Cipressa. That's never worked. Nibali knew that. He knew too that he didn't have the legs to do anything else in the race, so he made his grand, futile gesture. And the *tifosi* loved it.

Four key characteristics of an Italian rider

1. Overflowing emotions when crossing the finish line, whether as winner or buried in the *gruppetto*.
2. Talking about your mother, family or fan club in post-race interviews.
3. Milking it a bit after crashes, if not quite as flagrantly as their footballing compatriots after a stout tackle.
4. Off the bike, favouring coloured jeans and puffa jackets.

I served my apprenticeship on an Italian team. There were many cultural surprises for a young lad from South Wales, but none came close to the first time a chap I had never met before came over and kissed me on the cheek. Twice.

I grew up nodding at people. Even people I am related to were generally loath to go beyond a handshake. In Britain I often find myself torn when introduced to women I have never met before: should I go for a kiss, offer my hand or just fall back on the good old reliable G nod? Let's say you take the kiss option. Which cheek? What are the clues one is supposed to find in that brief window of body language that indicate whether it should be one kiss or two? Should any of these myriad kisses actually be kisses as we defined them at home (lips making contact with opponent's skin) or just a vague squeaking noise aimed somewhere beyond the outer edge of their ear?

Never has the nod seemed a more sensible option than under such duress. But often it's too late. It's out of your hands and coming fast for your face. In which case, my tactics are to roll with it. Let them lead it out – to nominate the cheek, decide whether there will be a second one, choose an order of approach. Simply stay relatively still, smile slightly and let them go to work. Before nodding politely.

There are a few Italians in the peloton that smash the stereotype. Enrico Gasparotto, who was in Barloworld with me, loved a beer or five. Salvatore Puccio, who has been in Team Sky for several years now, is thoroughly anglicised, although he still loves a bright pair of Y-fronts and a plate of pasta the size of a volcano.

But you cannot fight the Italian way. They are wedded to the methods of the past, and great respect is paid to those traditions. Steaks for breakfast, Gianni Bugno style. Campagnolo chainsets. Never a cappuccino after midday – it's a breakfast thing. Strange-shaped jam rolls in their back pockets rather than bars and gels. Recovery shake? No, a tuna panini is fine. Pasta and chicken on the same plate? No chance.

At Barloworld, there were plenty of these idiosyncratic rules. No mushrooms, they're bad for the stomach. No dessert, although a kilo of mozzarella is fine. No beer, but a glass of wine of greater alcoholic strength is encouraged. We even had a rider who was so superstitious that, when a black cat crossed the road in front of him on a training ride, he turned straight around and went home.

When going down for breakfast or dinner at the team hotel, always spruce yourself up. Nine times out of ten, you'll be sharing it with another team. If you look like death warmed up you are handing them an immediate advantage. You don't have to have every strand of hair in place – sometimes there's no hiding the bags under your eyes – but don't just roll out of bed, hair everywhere, clothes looking a state. Never wear flip-flops to dinner, always shoes. All psychological games.

The gatekeepers to this world are their directeur sportifs: often twice as old as those from other nations, former riders themselves, legions of champions having come through their care.

The mentality is very much that Italian is best. You have knee pain? Ah, you must see this man in Pistoia about orthotics – he is the best. And then you arrive at the address you've been given to find some old boy doing it out of his spare bedroom.

The Italian post-ride massage. Is it practical? I'm not sure. Is it theatrical? In a way, yes, but it's also quite orchestral, with the masseur using many of the same hand gestures as a conductor lost in the passions of a Puccini opera. Lots of flicks. Lots of grand flourishes. An enormous amount of oil. A lot of oil means a lot less friction, which in turn can lead to the odd slip of the hand or ball flick, which is rather unsettling. By the end, you're not sure if you're a cyclist or a tossed salad.

They will often have a signature move. One chap who used to massage me liked to spritz your undercarriage with antiseptic spray without any prior warning. Psst, psst – the spray would hit your exposed areas. I'm certain it was meant well. But if you had any sort of cut or nick – well, you just had to hold onto the bench and wait for the smarting to pass.

As you rolled onto your front to allow your calves, hamstrings and glutes to receive the composer's treatment, he would then suddenly whip away the towel that was covering your modesty. Whoah, what's happening now? You'd be lying there, feeling vulnerable and increasingly cold, silently speculating about what other moves he had in his locker. I would try to last for a few minutes but always broke, holding my hand up mid-performance to stop him and grab back the towel.

Training the Italian way is equally idiosyncratic. 'Today, I need an hour behind a scooter.' Off they go behind an old Vespa. 'I need to sweat before this race.' On with the rain jacket, up a tough climb. The reasons were often vague, yet there was a core of logic and science to it. On the track I used to find that eating too much salty pasta made me feel sluggish, and that the way to fix that was a workout where you got a good sweat up. We may not have donned heavy rain jackets, but the principle was the same.

Where Italy definitely shades it from Belgium, and also France, is in the post-training refuelling. The first time I competed there, at a track race in Fiorenzuola, I went down for dinner and hit the salad bar hard, as expected. At which point they brought out pasta that tasted like it had been made by angels. Followed by a steak hewn from the loin of the Archangel Gabriel's own cow. I was still weeping tears of pleasure when the *crostata*, a delightful jam tart, came out to polish me off.

It wasn't a one-off. Lost and hungry on one training ride after that race, we pulled up by a cafe that looked as if it had either been shut for ten years or had just served its last meal. With minimal expectation I ordered the same as the grizzled senior riders: panini and coffee. This was the moment I first truly discovered the joys of proper Parma ham, mozzarella and cappuccino. It was wonderful, at least until I got back to Cardiff and started pestering my mum to get some of this 'weird raw ham stuff' next time she was down at Tesco Extra.

Where I grew up, *Panini* was a sticker album. Coffee came in granules. In Tuscany you could stop at a place which seemed to be someone's garage, find no menu, order what they suggested and find yourself eating *tagliatelle al ragù* so good that the memory of those awful spag bols in Belgium was almost erased.

Italy is a country made for cyclists and cycling. Along with the great weather, the roads in Tuscany are perfect – hundreds of tiny, twisty lanes, little ancient towns on the top of mountains in the middle of nowhere. Why were they there? Heading across the empty plains you'd have the most prosaic thoughts: 'Ooh, imagine going all the way to the supermarket, getting home and realising you've forgotten the milk.'

But Italian races are never dull. The organisers love to keep you on your toes or out of the saddle – a cheeky climb in the last few kilometres, a technical descent just when a big group will have formed. There was barely a race I did as an amateur that was flat.

I will always remember my first ride in Tuscany. I had just ridden the Track Worlds and the Commonwealth Games, so I was a bit porky by road-cycling standards. We rode up a climb to Montecatini Alto, an old medieval village high on a hill. And it was only just a hill, not a mountain, and only a three-kilometre hill at that. But to me – too much muscle, not enough lean – it felt like an Alp, and the 23°C felt like 30°C. I thought my head might explode.

I was young and plump for most of my time at Barloworld, which, because Sky only really race the Giro and Milan–San Remo, represents most of my time racing in Italy. It meant I sometimes struggled to appreciate the landscape. At one race outside Bologna the day finished with three laps up a horrendous climb. My teammate Steve Cummings and I knew that (a) we had no chance of finishing, and (b) the race the next day would suit us much better. Our response was to pull over in the feed station and hide behind a car like two naughty schoolboys until the car with directeur sportif Alberto Volpi in it whizzed past. We thought we'd got away with it. And then the race radio announced '*Thomas e Cummings abandon!*' so loudly that we could hear it from our hiding place.

Riders will moan during Italian races, knowing deep down that they are actually delighted to be tested so hard. The Giro in particular loves a brutal day, ideally something snowy where even people with crampons fear to tread.

Which is ironic, because Italian cyclists hate to ride in anything but ideal weather. They will never train in the rain.

Always the passion is there – in the voice of the race announcer on the start line, shouting for three hours without a break; in the support, banners out on the roadside for any local boy in the same way a football supporter back home has a particular soft spot for a home-town player; old men watching it all in bars; in the newspapers, with a minimum of two pages on each race in *La Gazzetta dello Sport*.

For us racers it makes everything seem that much bigger and more exciting. If that means putting up with Italian teammates who spend most of their time moaning about the quality of the food outside their homeland, insisting that nothing compares to the pasta or coffee or panini they grew up with, that's fine. In any case, most of the time they're absolutely right.

Alpine Adventures

What do you think of when you think of the Alps? Lush green meadows? Ski passes and beers on the slopes? Cowbells and sunburned noses and clean air and snowy peaks?

When I think of the Alps I think of this: sweat in the eyes, burning in the legs, a crowd so deep and so close you can smell the beer and barbecue on their breath. The noise they make is so intense it's like being in the Millennium Stadium as the Welsh team run out to face England: a continuous roar that hurts your ears and rattles your bony chest.

And, as you summit the climb, sudden silence – ears ringing, then breath sucking and sighing, the light fizz of other riders' spinning wheels sounding like champagne settling in a distant glass.

As a kid riding for Maindy Flyers in Cardiff's northern suburbs I would dream of these mountains. Sometimes I was in Heath Park pretending to dive under the posts at the Millennium, or smashing home the winner at Wembley. Most of the time I was sprinting up empty lanes imagining Alpe d'Huez.

Never did I dream of being one of the great climbers, one of the stars who I watched explode up those climbs on television. I dreamed only of being me, attacking them with a few kilometres to go, catapulting away, never to be caught again.

And then I was there, and I dreaded those climbs.

It is one thing riding them in training, sessioning the curves and ramps with teammates all around. It is quite another racing up them in the Tour, 180 kilometres already drained from your legs, fourteen days of hanging on and fighting hard dragging you back.

For the first few years at the Tour you want so desperately to finish the whole race. Your greatest obstacle, both physical and mental, is the Alps.

Over breakfast you study the route maps for each day to try to work out where the *gruppetto* will form and simply try to hang on 'til then. As the mountains come into view there is such fear in your stomach. All that is ahead will be bad. But you've made it this far. You can't fail now.

If the day starts with a climb, it's dread at dawn and every man for himself. Everyone is nervous. The riders chasing the yellow jersey worry about a big rival escaping early, turning the day into a frantic, exhausting chase for their team. The breakaway experts are stressed because this is their big chance. Get in the break, make your name. Miss the break, miss the headlines. And the sprinters – to be out the back of the peloton five kilometres into a 180-kilometre stage is the definition of disheartening. It's a day for an extra coffee, for a warm-up on the turbo, for a glance at the skies and a kiss of your lucky charm.

This is how it happens. At the start the road in front of you is a long, horizontal line of sprinters, a wall of muscle. It should make no sense. These are the men who hate the climbs, whose bodies are built for entirely different tests.

Which is exactly why it does make sense. These are the men who want the race to slow, who want to place the incoming pain on hold for as long as possible.

On a flat stage, the neutral zone is an easy pedal, a social spin of chat and stretching. On a stage where there is a six-kilometre climb starting at kilometre zero, it's manic. Flag drops, road kicks up, race goes. Like a dam slowly filling with water, the barrier of sprinters holds the race together. Climbers are itching to get through the cracks, itching to attack. The unity of the big boys' teams stays strong. 'Watch left!' 'Right!' Shouts to warn the troops on the front line of potential threats to the peace. The pace is slow, but you daren't tempt fate by saying it out loud. Then, bang! An attack, followed by another. Sometimes the dam might hold for another thirty seconds. Then it bends, ruptures, explodes. The pain that has been on hold for the longest six minutes of the Tour so far finally hits.

You hear the first attack before you see it – a panicked crackling on the race radio from a teammate ('It's started – one Quick Step rider') a sudden click, click, click as everyone shifts gears at the same time, the shouts of your directeur sportif in your radio earpiece. The shapes change on the road up ahead – the big guys swamped by the little men, the slim nose of a peloton forming where once was the wall.

What shocks you the first time you live it is the speed. They just go. The rhythm in the legs, the distance they spin out behind them, the way they are actually braking into corners that you are struggling to get round.

Teams battle to put their grand classification men in the best slots for the climbers. The climbers' teams fight to do the same. As the climb gets serious, the lieutenants swing off and away to the side to clear the stage for act two.

Once on the climb you try to concentrate and relax. You find your response. Don't try ticking off the hairpins. The distance between them is too irregular. One will hurt you by not arriving when you want it to or trick you by appearing before you expect it.

But always break it up. No-one can think about climbing those Alpine slopes in their entirety. Split that endless effort into mouthfuls you can swallow. Watch the kilometres turning over on your computer and know that every one that ticks past is another one in your slipstream rather than your eyeline. Every pedal stroke takes you closer.

And pray for cloud cover. I grew up in South Wales and matured in Manchester. In those cities, grown men walk around with their tops off at 20°C. It wasn't just that 35°C never happened. It was unimaginable. To find it on an Alpine climb on my first Tour, back in 2007, almost ended my race. Jersey totally unzipped, sweat dropping into my eyes. My whole body soaked, my head throbbing horribly.

After fifteen kilometres of one climbing stage I was already getting dropped. I emptied one of my bottles over my head. The second would have gone that same way had it not been an electrolyte drink. I drifted back through the convoy of team cars. The Barloworld car pulled up alongside with team manager Claudio Corti leaning out of the passenger seat. 'Claudio, I need a bottle.' 'Tom! You've only done fifteen kilometres. We can't give you a feed until at least forty!' Shit . . .

He undid his seat belt, leant further out and threw a glass of water over my head and back. It was so cold I lost my breath. And then it warmed, and I licked my lips, and rode away into the heat haze.

You don't worry that the massed ranks of supporters will fail to part in front of you like the Red Sea. It always happens. Instead, let those childhood memories power you on. This is what I grew up watching. This is where I want to be. Make that adrenaline your fuel.

You know those names on the road? The flags, the 'Allez G', the half-dried paint and the scrawled chalk? It's all invisible. You see none of it. The only way you might catch the slightest glance is if you are at the very front of a group and, if you're up there, you're not looking around you. Same for the scenery. You might as well be in a tunnel. The only view you're interested in is the wheel in front.

If you want to spur on your rider, wave a banner at face height. I always see the Welsh flags. I always hear the British voices, even when the shouts in your ears seem to assume a solid mass. Every familiar accent kicks you on.

And you can definitely enjoy it. You're climbing with the best riders in the world, setting the tempo, leading the charge. You're hurting, hurting, hurting. But you are where you want to be, in the form you have worked for hours each day to hit. This is your greatest test. Meet it with your best.

Of them all, it's Alpe d'Huez that you love and dread the most. There are longer Alpine climbs and there are steeper ones, but this is the most iconic, the one that lives up to all that teenage expectation.

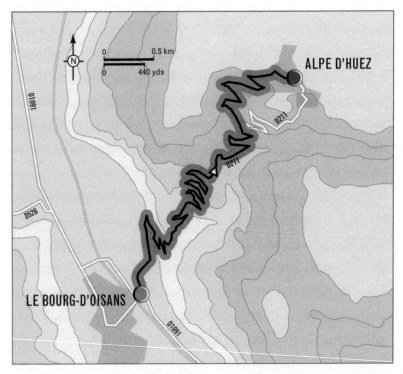

It may appear a benign squiggle on the map, but Alpe d'Huez is just over thirteen kilometres in length, ramping up to 11 per cent, those iconic twenty-one hairpins zigzagging back and forth above you.

All the riders feel the same way. Riding it in the *gruppetto* is a wonderful thrill. Riding it at the front, with the Froomes and Contadors, is even better – leading the way through Dutch Corner, the bedlam of Irish Corner, climbing with the best, leading the charge through more than 100,000 screaming fans.

In the 2013 Tour we rode it twice. A haymaker with the right, a haymaker with the left. As we passed through the village itself, the crowds suddenly disappeared. It was like stepping from the stage at a rock concert into an alleyway outside the venue. Echoes, ears ringing, hearts thumping.

Then you have the double punch of the Col du Télégraphe and Col du Galibier: almost twelve kilometres at just under 8 per cent, a breather on the 4.8-kilometre drop down to Valloire, and then the hard yards – eighteen kilometres of climbing when you're already 1,400 metres up, averaging 7 per cent, leaping up to 12 per cent.

You have to break it down into portions you can manage. Try to enjoy the consistent gradient on the Télégraphe, because the Galibier will hurt – through the altitude, through the barren landscape that height produces.

Towards the top, the road curves sharply right. When you're riding well at the front you can glance back down and see the race strung out below you. A sweet feeling. When you're looking up instead at a long line of cyclists riding away, your heart sinks into your stomach. Those are the days when you pray for bad weather, because heavy cloud and mist obscure that morale-sapping view. If you can't see them out in front, you can kid yourself that they don't exist.

The Col d'Izoard – almost twenty-three kilometres long if you're attacking it from Guillestre in the south, sixteen kilometres of real climbing – can be almost pleasant in training, when you can appreciate the long gorge and the green meadows. The descent to Briançon actually takes you somewhere, rather than being a steep one-way street, as many are. As Ben Swift likes to say, 'Why did they take us up there, just to come back down to the same road?'

Like the Col de la Madeleine, it works for me. I'm lucky; I seem to cope naturally with high altitudes better than others. The scenery? Come race day, it's all just a peripheral blur. What you do notice is the road surface humming under your wheels on the descents – smoother than the Pyrenees, longer runs between the bends.

When the rain comes in, when the temperature drops, the Alps become a cruel place to ride your bike. You might be staying in a nice mountainside chalet rather than the usual Tour tedium of a Novotel or Campanile, but when the cold is such that you would actually rather be going uphill than down, the thought of a wooden roof and softer duvet doesn't even register.

On the way up you sweat. Before the top you drop back to the team car to get more kit. It takes an eternity to get warm gloves over your wet, numb hands. The struggle to get your arms through your jacket and to zip it up is a race against time, because you'll be starting to descend at any moment. Sometimes I've had to stop and, like a toddler, have the team soigneur put my clothes on for me. It's a worthwhile humiliation; being warm, or at least warmer, on the descent is a lot more important than sticking with the group you were in. They can be caught and beaten. The cold in your bones cannot.

When you climb again your legs blow up. They have

already done too much. The cold has already sunk so deep into your muscles. You try to spin your legs on the descent but the speed is too high. You fight on.

This is the Alps. It's a love affair, but one that breaks your heart every time you rekindle it.

Champs Élysées

A memo to anyone thinking of catering for a party attended by a professional cycling team who have been racing themselves into oblivion for three weeks: finger food will not suffice.

Do I even need to explain how hungry you are when you finish the Tour de France? How much you are looking forward to eating like a lardy king after an entire summer of exercising the dietary control of a Hollywood leading lady? Then you will understand how the seven remaining riders of Team Sky felt when we staggered up to the post-race party in our Parisian hotel in 2013, yellow jersey winner Chris Froome in our ranks, to find that the food on offer was the sort of thing you might expect at the opening of a suburban art gallery.

Riding onto the Champs Élysées is our equivalent of the last day of the summer term. There is a sense of happiness and closure, of 'here come the holidays'. You would start throwing eggs and flour if you weren't too exhausted . . . and wondering if someone could possibly use them instead to rattle up some pancakes for the post-race party.

Never do you more appreciate what a challenge it is just to get round the Tour than in those final few hours, when the memories of the horrors are still fresh in your mind and legs. If you are completely spent, you are at the back, wasted. If you are racing at the front, you're still wasted. Imagine taking a dried-out orange and trying to squeeze one last drop of juice from the desiccated flesh. That's how you feel by the Champs Élysées.

You start dreaming about how delightful it will be to wake up when you want, where you want, with whom you want. You dream of showering, of unpinning your race number for a final time. And you dream of food, which is why a member of staff was dispatched to McDonald's with a fork-lift truck while we poured vol-au-vents down our throats by the plateful. *Garcon! Encore, s'il vous plait?*

It begins at the team bus with partners and beers, not always in that order. If you run out of lagers, head to Orica; Australians would never dream of underbeering. If there are pizza boxes, get the sprinter's elbows out and fight your way through. Now is not the time to finish in second place.

In 2015 the bus party was almost the best part. The swannies had handed us all a beer at the finish, and I'd then necked two glasses of champagne while being interviewed by Danish TV, so I was already in the mood. And then everyone piled on – riders, support staff, partners – and the tunes were cranked up.

A yellow jersey win brings a fair few new faces to a party. That's fine – sponsors are part of the win – but, like soldiers returning from a tour of duty, a rider knows that only another rider understands the emotions he is experiencing. You train together. You race together. Through the bad days when Froome is alone in the front group of twenty and there are sixty kilometres to go. To the great days when you deflect every nightmarish arrow slung at you. One by one, you throw yourself onto the pyre so that your leader may be venerated.

So when the opportunity comes to slip away from the suits to a nearby club, you're out of there in one last breakaway group.

As always with a club, everyone gets messy. It's just a question of the order you get messy in. Who is the lead-out man? Who will bail early? Who will drive on the express train when momentum is in danger of stalling?

After some hard races you're too tired to drink. You dream of duvet rather than Duvel. The Tour is different. Even the monks want to party.

Beers slip down as if you were a hollow tube. Enthusiasm is reignited in fried minds. Some ambitious dancefloor moves are attempted with minimal success. Only once – when our Colombian rider Rigoberto Urán pulled off/got away with some extraordinary salsa moves with teammate Xabier Zandio's wife back in 2011 – have I seen anyone dance as if their legs were not made of solid marble.

Inevitably an hour arrives when everything becomes rather vague. All that remains in the memory are fractured snapshots: Richie Porte on the floor, being swung round on his back by one of the swannies; someone throwing a pizza like a frisbee and then realising that they actually quite fancied eating it; Froomey and I hugging each other under the disco ball, all boozy man-love and shouting over the music.

'I love you, man!'

'Yeah! You're a legend!'

'Shall we have a drink you can set fire to?'

'No. Let's have four of them!'

And then, with a ghastly inevitability, it is suddenly morning, and you are in a hotel room that looks like a laundry after an accident with a strimmer. Bags everywhere, all of them upside down and empty. Clothes hanging off the mirror. A sensation in your stomach of both intense hunger and overwhelming sickness.

The usual recriminations. Why didn't I wait until I got home and have a few there? Who thought it would be a good idea to get drinks that you could set fire to? Why did I ask for that early flight?

There are various environmental factors that the man with a monstrous hangover would prefer to avoid. Bright lights. Harsh noise. Unnecessary heat. Being made to stand up. Being told what to do.

All those things coalesce in the departure lounge of an international airport.

Even hearing the words 'Charles de Gaulle' brings an involuntary lurch to the guts. Why are these lights shining in my face? Oh Lord, my back aches. Why is this queue so long? Why has it not moved, and where did I put my passport, bearing in mind I had it in my hand about thirty seconds ago?

You're late for your flight. You're going to miss it. You're going to be sick. No – don't think about being sick. Just concentrate on breathing. Man up. Handle it. You do not feel sick, you do not feel sick. Sick? Did someone mention sick? I have to get out of here. I'm going to be sick! Let me out of this queue! But you can't. I'm late for my flight. I'm going to miss it. And repeat.

Sometimes you can wrestle control of a hangover through sheer resolve. Such resolve does not exist after three weeks of riding the Tour de France. Sometimes you can pull down your sunglasses to help you through it. Sometimes self-esteem stops you. You do not want to look like one of those idiots who wear sunglasses indoors.

At that stage, you are sure of only one thing: this is the single worst day of the Tour. Give me a mountain. Throw me into the middle of a team time trial. Just put me back on my bike.

At home, it all settles. The happy memories: seeing my dad in a tree halfway up the Champs Élysées, frantically waving a Welsh flag. Spotting Sa at the bus, happy to see her, no tension left, no longer thinking of the next day and what's to come. Then you see the tin of Welsh cakes she's brought out with her. Dreamland! Ten minutes and thirty-odd cakes are gone, the finest sprint of the entire three weeks.

Welsh Cake Recipe

450 g (1 lb) self raising flour
1-2 tsp freshly ground nutmeg
200 g (7 oz) soft butter
25 g (1 oz) soft lard
225 g (8 oz) caster sugar
225 g (8 oz) sultanas or currants
2 eggs
Drop of milk to bind if needed

- Mix the nutmeg with the flour, rub in the butter and lard until it resembles breadcrumbs
- Stir in the sugar and dried fruit
- Bind the mixture together with the beaten eggs, add a drop of milk if mixture is too dry - dough needs to be firm
- On a floured surface, roll out dough to a thickness of about 1 cm and cut into 6 cm (2½ inch) rounds
- Cook on a greased griddle (medium heat) for about 3 mins on each side
- Cool on a wire rack and enjoy!

Going through the tunnel on the laps through the capital's streets, watching the boom arm of the crane camera swinging away, just as you saw from the other end of a TV cable as a kid. Your first glimpse of the Eiffel Tower. British voices yelling encouragement. On your first Tour it blows your mind; I was only supposed to do a week, and here I am about to finish the Tour de France, riding round the Arc de Triomphe!

Trying to organise a team photo on the move: 2013, and Froomey's got four minutes over second place for the yellow jersey, let's drop back to do this properly.

Where are the champagne flutes? Whose job was that? Hang on, where's Pete Kennaugh? Bloody hell, have we dropped him? Three kilometres to go, two kilometres, one kilometre . . . ah, here you are, Pete – you look like that last effort almost killed you. Right. Arms round each other's shoulders. Hands off the bars, Richie! Don't fret about the cobbles. Hands off the bars, Richie!

Then, two days on, lying on my sofa in my house in Cardiff: oh, that was it. It's over. I sort of miss the structure. I need to get back into a regime. Man, my legs feel like balloons. I should go out training. How long until my next race?

FEELING IT

Pain

There is the pain of racing hard, your body's rev needle deep into the red and your engine screaming at its limits. There is the pain of training, when you are forcing your body to do things it is not yet capable of doing, neither crowd nor great prize to pull you through. And there is the pain of major trauma: rupturing your spleen, breaking your nose and scaphoid, fracturing your pelvis.

That is not some arbitrary list. The ruptured spleen came in Sydney in 2005, when a piece of metal flicked up from the road into the spokes of my front wheel, sending me down to land on the stem; the nose and scaphoid (plus mangled pelvis) when going over a ravine at the 2009 Tirreno–Adriatico; the pelvis on its own, a mere fractured pelvis, at the start of the 2013 Tour.

It wasn't so much the fracturing of the pelvis that was the problem as the fact that I had twenty days of the hardest bike race in the world to come. Or, rather, twenty days of the hardest bike race in the world to come that I still intended to ride.

Had I watched someone else being lifted over their cross-bar and into their saddle the next morning (I couldn't lift my legs high enough on my own) I would have laughed and asked them why the hell they were bothering. It was without doubt the worst pain I've ever experienced on a bike. Each pedal stroke felt like being jabbed with a burning branch.

Each tiny bump in the road felt like the branch was being rammed in a few twigs further. Trying to get out of the saddle to get over a slight rise was extraordinary. Trying to put some actual power down was like being sawn in half.

So why did I keep going? Because I had trained all year for it. Because my teammate Chris Froome had a great shot of winning the yellow jersey. Because I could get the bike moving forward, and if I could get it moving forward and keep it moving forward then stopping was silly. I've never before or since suffered so badly. But I could feel myself getting better every day, or at least feel that burning branch giving off a little less smoke with every passing stage.

The nose, scaphoid and pelvis together? That was the most frightening, because I knew it was going to be bad. In the crash at the Tour in 2013 there was certainly an 'Ah, shit . . .' moment, but at least the road was flat. At Tirreno–Adriatico there was the 'Ah, shit . . .' followed by a somersault over a metal barrier, an interlude mid-air, going head first into a tree and then an unspecified period bouncing down a ravine. I can remember idly wondering where I might land, and then, having landed, taking my helmet off to find blood all over the place. 'Ah, shit . . .' once again.

At this point you want immediate and unsurpassed medical attention. You want reassurance. What you do not want is to see your Italian directeur sportif running over, staring at your face and body and looking as if he's going to soil himself. Mine was flapping like a panicked old spinster, clutching his own head and wringing his hands. Don't worry about me, mate, you concentrate on your own dismay.

My recollection of the ambulance and hospital is hazy. They may be received memories. They may be from an episode of *ER* I once saw. I do remember returning to the team hotel, because I was carried in on the doctor's back like a kid being piggy-backed round the playground. Carried into the lift, placed on my bed. It was my roommate Steve Cummings who saved me – bringing up food from the restaurant, moving my bed closer to the bathroom so I could crawl to the toilet in under an hour rather than two.

The spleen would get top marks as the one that hurt most in recovery. You're on crutches with a fractured pelvis, but at least you can get on with a limping life. When you have your spleen removed in an emergency theatre – well, they cut your midriff open, slice right through your muscles and move your stomach around to get the offending organ out. You wake up to see a row of staples running down your centre line as if you were a cheap race programme.

I lay there before the op, fresh out of the ambulance, and was asked if I needed morphine. Probably, to be fair, but I've got a race on Sunday, so no thanks. The scans came back. The only racing you will be doing is straight into theatre. Right. Morphine it is, please.

It came on an intravenous drip, with a button to activate it when the pain bit hard. It wasn't quite on tap; you could jab it all you liked, but if you'd already had that half-hour's allowed dose, you weren't getting any more. My teammates at the British Academy – Mark Cavendish, Ed Clancy, Tom White, Matt Brammeier, Matt Crampton – would come to visit me in the shared ward. Unfortunately, visiting hours were at 6 p.m., when you had either been waiting through hours of appalling Australian soaps for *The Simpsons* to come on or were knackered and slightly wonky on morphine, the pain having driven your button strategy over the preceding twelve hours.

There is no dignity at such times. It's not just that you desperately want to be out on your bike with the rest of the lads. It's that, because you're about to have your spleen removed, you require a catheter. (My main feedback on the equipment would be this: the sting of the lubricant being applied is actually slightly worse than the entry itself. Perhaps that's just me.) You've had your spleen removed, and you've woken up in intensive care with a severe fever. You'd like something for the pain? We can offer you a suppository. Oh.

There were some wearisome days and dark nights. You'd hope that the experience of shared pain would have bound us patients together, but instead we turned on each other. Each night someone would have a bad night and keep the rest up. Like a true cyclist, I tried to suffer in silence, but a few of the others wanted you to know every detail of their pain.

One chap on my ward had been building for weeks towards his first solo bowel movement that didn't involve a metal pan. I watched him edging towards the communal toilet, mentally running a book on his chances of making it. Limp, grimace. Limp, grimace. Limp, stagger, into the toilet.

I went in there myself a few minutes later and came out rather faster. He'd come up about a metre short. The floor looked like an accident in a butcher's shop.

* * *

They say that different people have different pain thresholds. Whether we can ever genuinely know if that's true I'm not sure, but I do know that if you bowl about claiming to have a high threshold, then the rest of the peloton will consider you a fool.

In general, cyclists are considered stoical sufferers, if nothing else because we have to learn to be. Everyone crashes. Everyone rides mountains. But it becomes specific to your sport and your experiences. If I was hit with the sort of tackles that Welsh centre Jamie Roberts routinely soaks up, I'd be both outraged at the moment of impact and in small pieces shortly afterwards.

Those that do complain are not forgotten. My Sky teammate Chris Sutton is a good lad, but he does like to share the intensity of his misery with those within earshot. After Gent–Wevelgem a few years ago, Ian Stannard was trussed up in hospital with a broken back after a horrific fall. CJ – Chris – was in there too, despite the extent of his injuries being a cut knee. The doctor was with Stannard when the cry came echoing down the hall. 'Doc! Doc! I need something for this pain!' The doctor shook his head and called back, 'Sir, you have already had something. Your friend here has broken vertebrae. Please keep it in perspective.' Five minutes later, Stannard being ratcheted into a neck brace, the silence was broken again. 'Doc! Doc! Please . . .'

The pain of pure riding should get easier with experience. It doesn't.

Shane Sutton used to enjoy telling us that you can't over-train, you can only under-rest. Such words offer minimal comfort when you have four flat-out twenty-minute efforts to grind out up a mountain in Tenerife 2,000 metres above sea level. The voice in your head urges you to sit up. Okay, I'll just get to fifteen minutes. You get there. Okay, get to sixteen. Now seventeen. Eighteen. Argh, I can do this now. Then the huge sense of satisfaction. I got through it!

Yet pain is not an absolute. If you're on a good day, riding in the front group, the pain feels less intense. Your morale is high, so it doesn't feel so bad. You can deal with it for longer than ever before. When it hurts in training, more than you think it should for that effort, you tell yourself to ignore the numbers appearing on your power meter, because you fear what they will tell you. Then, in the next effort, you glance down to see good numbers appearing. Suddenly it feels as if it's manageable, even though the exertion is exactly the same.

It's that inner voice which is most sensitive to pain. It will whisper in your ear, realise you are trying not to listen and begin to scream: this hurts, this hurts, just sit up.

But the pain will always come to an end. It won't last for ever. So what's another couple of minutes at the end of the day? It's easy to think like that now, while lying in my bed. When you're halfway up a ten-kilometre climb, legs and lungs burning, sweat leaking out of every pore, you listen instead to that inner devil.

Pain can just take over you. It's all you can feel and concentrate on. The outside world is a blur, as if you're in the back of a taxi, half asleep, staring out the window. Subconsciously, you keep the bike going uphill – you hope on the correct side of the road – but, consciously, all you are aware of is the pain. Your own little world of torture.

On stage 19 of the 2015 Tour, when I began the day fourth overall but ended it fifteenth, I knew I was in trouble from the moment I woke up and discovered I was 1.5 kilogrammes lighter than when I had begun. In the saddle it immediately became clear I had nothing in the legs, and that a day of intense physical and mental anguish was coming my way.

You try to pretend it's not happening. You desperately take on loads of extra energy gels and electrolyte drinks. Maybe this will settle down. Maybe I'll recover. When the bluff fails, it's just hell. Out of the back of the main group, still so much of the climb to come, a precious top-ten finish disappearing away from you, the only option to slot into the *grupetto* and save what little you can for the next day.

Then there's emotional pain, which lasts longer, far longer. As a cyclist you lose a lot more than you win. Most of the field is made up of domestiques, workers who help their team leaders, who thus go into each race knowing they won't win. There can only be one winner. This is why, when your opportunity comes but isn't quite finished off, it can hurt more than climbing Alpe d'Huez. When I dropped from fourth to fifteenth overall in the Tour, it hurt, but I could still be happy with my performance. In a way it was always going to happen. It was expected. Yet when I went into the Tour of Flanders in the same year as one of the pre-race favourites only to finish fourteenth, the disappointment was far more intense and lasted much longer. Dealing with these lows is more important than your post-stage food or massage. That top inch is what wins and loses bike races; what brings you through is the knowledge that there is always another race around the corner.

Even though you have to keep going, there are rare times when you just can't. Sometimes it's not the right thing to do. You know deep down when it's right to push on or to stop. Only a couple of times have I missed an effort I had set out to do. Once was in a session outside Adelaide a couple of days before the Tour Down Under. My teammates were relentless afterwards. 'Ah, what's wrong? Can't manage just one more? Want us to give you a backie home?' I stayed strong. I knew one more would have pushed me over the edge. Yet I still felt soft.

Training in a group enables you to ride out more of that pain than you thought possible. You are all in it together. You all push each other. Chase each other. Everyone has their bad days, and you've just got to push through. Because, when you ride on your own, the devil shouts louder.

The Bonk

Can you consider yourself a cyclist if you have never bonked? You can, but not a cyclist who has ever truly pushed themselves.

I'm not saying that bonking is a good thing. It's a miserable process to go through: it's not just the glycogen stores in your liver and muscles running low, it's having the shelves raided until you can barely stand and have lost all sense not only of where you are but also who you are.

Call it hunger knock, if you prefer, or hitting the wall, if you hang about with distance runners. There is still something comical about it, and not only because of its designation.

It's the desperation and confusion it brings. As a teenager on long rides, I was terrible for forgetting to bring any money. When the bonk struck it would therefore turn me into a chocoholic panhandler: excuse me, sir, spare some change for a Chomp bar? Sometimes I'd be so far into the middle of nowhere that there would be no-one to ask. Instead, I'd find myself crawling around on my hands and knees on the pavement outside the village shop, somehow hoping that I'd find enough one-pence pieces to be able to afford a Freddo. Does this shopkeeper look kindly? Perhaps I can stick two Freddos on the counter, look shocked when she says I've only given her money for one and get away with it with a gasp of exhaustion and a dramatic tumble sideways.

Even when you do have cash, you can be so out of it that your mind fails to source the quick fix you need. Aged fourteen, out on a monstrous Five Valleys loop from Cardiff into the Brecon Beacons, my friend Ross and I just about got over the last climb and then bonked for Wales with twenty miles still to go to get us home. Ross, thankfully, had a couple of quid in his back pocket. What he didn't have was the mental fortitude to read the label on the bottles of lemonade he blew the windfall on and notice, in large letters, the words 'SUGAR FREE'.

In that scenario, every slight rise in the road becomes an Alpine col. You have a vague sense of being somewhere familiar, but find it impossible to put the pieces of the puzzle together to make a coherent picture. Did we come through here already? Did I already ask myself if we had come through here already? Oh no, a railway bridge . . . how are we going to get over that? We're in Taff's Well, just outside Cardiff? We might as well be in Abergavenny.

You begin the process of thinking of all the slight rises on the way home, try to select the route with as few as possible and then realise you can't think straight and so can't make a decision anyway. Your arms are like jelly, almost numb. Your legs are empty but have a warm tingle. Your vision blurs, except for the black spots, which you can see very clearly. Every red traffic light comes as sweet relief, until it turns green and you have to try to beat inertia all over again, which is even worse. You think you are riding in a straight line along the kerb. Instead you are more like Leonardo DiCaprio's character in The Wolf of Wall Street,

Jordan Belfort, when he tries to drives his white Lamborghini home from the country club after a punchy night out.

You can sense a bonk coming on, which is when you start to rank the foods that might save you from its black embrace. A Mars bar is always up there, in the main because of its size and solidity. For the opposite reason, a Curly Wurly doesn't get a look-in; it's all holes. Cadbury's Caramel: satisfying in the mouth, a punchy sugar rush. Snickers? More to be savoured than deployed in emergencies, although you wouldn't turn one down if offered.

A KitKat? No. Nothing constructed from wafer, no matter how many fingers. I wouldn't even look at a packet of Maltesers. Who wants a lighter way to enjoy chocolate when you have used up so many calories your stomach is starting to eye up your own internal organs? A Double Decker works because it is a big, lumpy brute of a bar. A Yorkie is too hard. It needs to be melting in the mouth to be enjoyed, and, when you're bonking, there is simply not the time to allow things to melt. Toblerone? Impossible to get down quick enough. You would either serrate the roof of your mouth on its chocolatey peaks or create a distinctive triangular shape in your neck as you attempted to swallow too rapidly. Anyway, you can only buy those in airports, right?

It is the one occasion where the purchase of a full-fat Coke is legitimised. If you do reach for one, it also works as a time machine, taking you back to your childhood: as a professional cyclist, full-fat Coke is as likely to appear on your shopping list as pork scratchings. The same is true for a Freddo. On the rare occasions these days that I splash a spare twenty-two pence on one, it transports me to a lonely Valleys corner shop, a sweaty back and knocking knees.

Occasionally I will wonder: do French riders crave the same foodstuffs when they bonk? I'm aware that my own fantasy list could hardly be more British. I've never seen a Double Decker in a French grocer's. Perhaps they experience a more refined bonk: desperate for a Petit Écolier, craving a packet of *langues du chat*.

My all-time worst bonk came as a kid in Cardiff. I was so mangled I could barely get my house keys out of my pocket. I knew they were in there, and I knew the hand clutching the door belonged to me, but I couldn't make the two things connect. I just kept gently nudging the doorbell with my forehead in the hope that someone inside might hear me. When I got inside I had neither the will nor the ability to get changed. I became a one-function gadget: eat, find more to eat, eat, find more. My stomach a bottomless pit in which no amount of food would register.

At least at my parents' house there was always something in the cupboards. Those first few months on your own are a learning curve in numerous ways, but never more so than when you get in, requiring food to be inhaled rather than chewed, only to find nothing to go for except a chutney left over from Christmas and some expired tea bags.

In a strange way, they were good times. When I jelly-legged my way up the street, safe in the knowledge that my mum's Sunday roast was at that exact moment being transferred from oven to table, it was a magnificent emotion. Shovelling down the food, Grand Prix on the telly in the

The Neutral Zone

One day you are inside the slick heart of the most carefully organised team in professional cycling, the next, back in a flat you haven't seen for weeks and can barely remember the alarm code for.

There is no gentle transition from institutionalised rider to man about town, and it poses its own first-world problems. Taking your dirty washing and absentmindedly leaving it in a bag outside your bedroom door, before being nonplussed to find it still there in the morning rather than returned neatly pressed and smelling of Alpine meadows. Putting it into the washing machine and forgetting it's there; finding it two days later, still damp and smelling worse than before. Stumbling into the bathroom, expecting to see the end of the toilet paper folded into an arrow shape, and then wondering why your soap is neither covered in shrink-wrap nor the size of a box of matches. Pulling back the duvet and assuming there will be a chocolate on your pillow, then realising that it's not the duvet you've pulled back but the fitted sheet, because no-one has picked the duvet up from the floor where you ditched it earlier that day, and that to actually pick up the duvet you'd need to be wearing protective gloves because no-one has changed the cover since the last time you saw one of those chocolates.

It's a wonderful feeling to not receive a WhatsApp message telling you what time to wake up and have breakfast, and a dreadful inconvenience to realise breakfast won't be served to you by a brilliant chef – not a super-smoothie, not a bowl of porridge or a three-egg ham omelette with a double espresso on the side. It can actually be a nice change to make your own omelette, but the opportunity is not open to you – you have no eggs and no ham. Nor is there any milk. You would dash to the corner shop, but suddenly you'd be confronted with all the foods you've been craving, across four crowded aisles. Eighteen different sorts of biscuits. King-sized chocolate bars. Some form of artisan crisp. Which means I either can't go in the first place, or I can try to send Sara, using that excuse. It never works.

Let's say you manage to source some breakfast, probably through a lucky find in a low cupboard. There is then the cultural shift of going from being surrounded only by professional bike riders, completely immersed in a world of cycling, to sitting down opposite your partner and making appropriate conversation. Which, you soon discover, does not include races of the past that have finished in the area or the percentage steepness of nearby hills. Neither does it include off-the-cuff comments about girls who appear on television, not unless you want an elbow in the ribs and a 'You do know you said that out loud, don't you?'

In time, the domestic part of your personality reawakens. Before then it is a minefield. A dropped piece of toast is instinctively followed by a very punchy swear word. 'Did you really just say that? You never used to use that word. You've changed ...' Sometimes it's not even the swearing. Sometimes you've been away so long that you inadvertently call your loved one 'Mate'. It's not a term that implies intimacy, and they will let you know.

I will go round to Sara's mum and dad's for dinner, forget that I am now with civilised people and make the sort of smell that everyone on the Tour does as a matter of routine. On seeing the shocked reaction on the faces around, I panic and reach for emergency tactics. Blame it on the dog. Shake my head in disgust while giving the innocent hound a look which mixes disapproval with apology. Take this one for me, son, and it's dog biscuits all around as soon as their backs are turned.

Later that day I'm in bed and make exactly the same mistake. Again the crisis strategy is employed. If Sara is still brushing her teeth, I keep my backside flat to the mattress, lock the edges of the duvet down with my arms and pray for dissipation. If the issue is audible, I either go for sympathy ('I have got the most dreadful stomach ache from trying to keep these in') or comedy (pulling a little face in the hope it makes it all better).

As a pro cyclist, you come from an environment where it is common practice for half-naked bike riders to wander from room to room, en route for massage or to see the physio. Do not employ the same clothing strategy at your mother-in-law's house, because being caught making a cup of tea wearing nothing but your creased boxers brings awkward silences and downturned eyes.

Total freedom brings as many challenges as strict routine. On that first morning back in your own house you wake up with an unfamiliar thrill: I can do anything I want, whenever I want. An hour later you're unable to remember anything you actually wanted to do.

In the same way that you hear tales of rock stars struggling to cope with domestic life after months on the road, we miss our own kicks. The crowds that swarm around you when you step off the team bus. Hearing British voices roaring you on. The adrenaline that fizzes through you moments before a race, that sense of intense nerves but also unmatchable anticipation. The nonsense chats with teammates in the exhausted aftermath ('Did you see that crash? Ah, man, I was so close to that!' 'How hard was that start? I thought I was bad until I saw you . . .'). The camaraderie of being one cog in a smooth, successful machine.

The frantic thrill of a sprint lead-out, the kick of a caffeine gel. Mark Cavendish glued to your back wheel, you trying desperately to hang on to the wheel an inch in front of yours. Sliding out in corners, tyres gripping at the last moment, heart banging as you escape a crash by a couple of pieces of gravel.

From all that to making a salad for tea in the complete silence of an empty kitchen.

It takes time to make such substantial adjustments. With time you don't so much grow better at it as grow better at understanding it will happen, and giving yourself the leeway to let it.

After the Track World Championships in Melbourne in 2012 – British medals everywhere, world records, an unforgettable atmosphere of celebration and satisfaction – I returned home to Manchester to a cold, empty house and sat in my front room with a cup of tea at 10 p.m. on the Monday night, watching something on TV that I had forgotten by the time the credits rolled.

For months you have been dreaming of this moment: a week to relax and do what you want. And then you realise that watching TV on your own with a cup of tea is a poor substitute for the stuff you were doing before. It's the same when you are injured. Your silver lining is the resolution that you will really use this time to do something genuinely interesting. You will explore and embrace the real world. Instead the real world leaves you depressed. You just want to train hard, to push your body to the limit. You want to race, be fed through the mangle of a hard day with your teammates around you, you lot against the world.

There is the comedy of going to a corner shop in Cardiff and accidentally saying '*Merci*' when the woman behind the counter gives you your change. There is the unfamiliar experience of lying in bed at night unable to fall asleep, because your body has grown accustomed to five-hour hammerings in the saddle before it feels tired. There is waking up the next morning after strangely dreamless nights – in place of the intensely vivid dreams that stage racing seems to bring on – and looking around thinking: where the hell am I, before recognising the curtains and realising: ah, in my own bed.

And it can be mundane. Racing is not the real world. It's only racing, pure and simple. You can deflect the rest of it. 'Ah, I'm racing now, I'll sort it out when I'm back.'

Then you get home, and there are three-month-old bills, and missed birthdays, and bank statements, and a thousand flyers from people wanting to redo your drive, or clean your windows, or trim your herbaceous border. Or a speeding fine from six months ago which you have missed, followed by a letter issuing court proceedings and finally a letter stating your court date, which was unfortunately in the middle of the Tour. And there you were thinking that I missed the 2012 Tour for Olympic prep . . .

That's the ordinary world. And you are an ordinary citizen of it once again.

I Never Take the Stairs

A ka the eternal tiredness of the racing cyclist. And believe me, it is eternal.

There is an ethos among pros: don't stand when you can sit, don't sit when you can lie. If we could get someone else to do the lying down for us, we probably would.

For finely tuned endurance athletes, you can appear to be the laziest men in the world. So weary are you after a day's riding on a Grand Tour that, if you're in your hotel room and you need to get the Wi-Fi code from reception, you'll happily put up with outrageous data charges on your phone rather than have to move. You might be watching the worst programme in the world, but you'll watch it rather than get up to find the remote or change the channel on the television itself. Even talking on the phone can be too much, and I'm aware how ridiculous that sounds.

Your girlfriend wants to talk to you, and yet you can't manage to form complete sentences, let alone engage in witty or interesting conversation. Throughout the hotel the same argument will be playing out with different long-distance couples: the monosyllabic rider, the partner who feels snubbed by a total lack of response about the new curtains they've just ordered.

It can bring its own surprises. I returned from Australia after the Track Worlds to find a dog in the house. Apparently we had discussed it over the phone. Or, rather, it was discussed over the phone – I'll find one that doesn't moult or smell, one small enough to travel round Europe and chilled enough that it doesn't need an exhausted cyclist to take it out for long walks. Okay, Ger?

I must have grunted. Maybe I just heard the bit about no long walks. Either way, I got home to find Blanche had moved in. A lesson to you all.

Mind you, there is one thing you can always find the strength to do: eat.

When you come back in from a ride, stomach empty and moaning, your refuelling strategy is reduced to a simple rule: see it, eat it.

Instead of making a sandwich, which would take all of ten seconds, you'll eat all the constituent parts straight in an unconnected blitz – three mouthfuls of cheese, a spoon of pickle directly into the mouth, some bread torn off a load and eaten as you open another cupboard. Some ham rolled up and stuffed in; three handfuls of cereal.

Before you know it you've emptied the fridge. You'll eat something that you would never touch in more sane times because you're too knackered to walk two minutes to the corner shop and buy some pasta. When you do nominally cook something properly, you can be so exhausted that moving it from saucepan to plate before consumption feels a task too far. My Team Sky teammate Ben Swift used to cook ready-meals in the microwave and eat them straight out of the scalded plastic. Tea at the Ritz it was not.

The most tired I've ever been was after my debut Tour de France in 2007. I was twenty-one years old, the youngest man in the race, and I finished 140th out of 141 riders. I only intended to complete one mountain stage, which came on day eight, and yet somehow I made it all the way through. Fun? For most of it I felt ready for a coffin. I was absolutely gone.

That tiredness is total. Always hungry. Always sleepy. Every morning, the biggest battle is just to prepare yourself mentally for the fight ahead, for the pain, for the six hours of grovelling. Still sure you fancy being a pro cyclist?

When you finish a day's hard racing you never take the stairs, not even a flight of them. The hotel lift becomes your best friend. And it's not just your legs. Your arms, and your back, your neck . . . It feels as if you have been broken into pieces and reassembled in the wrong order, like a Lego man in the hands of a bored child.

Sometimes you're brushing your teeth at the end of a long day and you glance up at the mirror to realise you've still got blurred vision. You go to the bathroom for a pee and you sit down on the toilet seat rather than standing up. In the shower, you lean against the wall. I've even had a sitting-down shower. On my backside, unable to move.

Once or twice a year you feel good. You can be riding strong and having a good day, but you'll still feel tired. If you do feel okay, you just do more. You either ride for the team for longer or you try to win, but you're still just as tired. You're just in a different place on the finish list.

So, why do we do it? There is a sweet spot when you are riding hard where it hurts, but not so badly that you can't keep it up. And then, when you go really deep, throwing it all into your attack, it actually feels good.

When you go on holiday, you're aware of a strange sensation after a week or so: your legs don't feel sore. And it can be quite unsettling. You almost pine for the sore legs and the lying on the sofa.

You feel yourself getting fatter. Eating and drinking whatever you want and getting up whenever you like is something you dream about for most of the year. And then it happens, and you miss the old routine. Which makes me (a) annoyed, and (b) wonder, how the hell will I cope with it when I retire?

Boredom

To those who believe that the life of a pro cyclist is one long succession of thrilling sprint finishes, freebie £8,000 bikes and pecks on the cheeks from podium girls, let me tell you this: I once did a three-hour turbo session in my conservatory in Newton-le-Willows.

For those who don't know what a turbo is, it's when you park your freebie £8,000 bike on a stationary trainer, start pedalling fast and slowly go out of your mind.

I hadn't planned to do three hours. The normal mental threshold for a turbo session is about an hour, maybe an hour and a half if you're feeling inspired. Otherwise, the tedium is too great: pedalling as hard as you can with the only thing to look at being the wall opposite, or the beads of sweat dripping off the end of your nose and onto your handlebars.

But I was feeling keen, it was only my second training session of the winter and it was snowing outside. At least, it was when I started – within twenty minutes the windows were steamed up, there was a puddle of my sweat on the floor and my hands had started going wrinkly. I was in my own microclimate. Downpours forecast. Heavy depression on the way.

Boredom comes in many forms. The traditional way to combat it on the turbo is to break it up into chunks: twenty minutes' warm-up, deliberately not thinking about it; three chunks of ten-minute intervals and recoveries; a few five- and ten-second sprints; ten minutes easy. Worry only about the block you're doing, not what might be left to do. Before you know it, you're done.

That certainly works. It works even better if you utilise the technology available to you.

You can watch television. The problem is that you can't really concentrate for any extended period of time. The noise of the flywheel on your turbo rotating at speed is like a washing machine with a full load on the 1200 spin cycle, so, unless you're watching something with subtitles – and it's been done – you'll miss critical plot developments. For this reason, anything multilayered or nuanced (*The Wire*, *Game of Thrones*) is a no-no. Chat shows, physical comedy: fine. Sport can work, but you have to be selective. Snooker gives off the wrong vibes and pace. Football works. Some riders watch a bike race from the past and go hard when the attacks are going, which wins bonus points for invention. A buccaneering Welsh rugby win is even more inspiring, although I find myself wishing I was there rather than in a conservatory that is wetter than the street outside.

Because cyclists spend such a large proportion of their day training or racing, the rest of the time involves trying to do as little as possible in as prone a position as you can find. This can obviously lead to boredom, unless your hotel-room takes the same approach to informative and educational posters as a dentist's waiting area.

All of which means that we become expert at doing nothing without going insane. In other words: chilling.

I consider myself pretty accomplished at the chill. You might think students were the ones to beat at this game. Well, in some sort of International Chill-Out, all three podium places would be taken by professional cyclists. Especially if alcohol was a banned substance. It's not just the regular practice of having to do nothing at all for extended periods of time. It's not only that we could perform superbly anywhere, home or away, after years of honing our skills across Europe and beyond. It's that we can also suffer. We can absorb pain, for hour after hour. It's a life of extremes. Students? With all respect, they wouldn't stand a chance.

My techniques vary. Watching a DVD is almost the easy way out. The true champion of chill can just lie there, with no external stimulation whatsoever, and exist happily in that motionless, yet fully awake, state for an entire afternoon.

Staying in as a young man can be boring. My solution at one stage was to stay out. In the period after winning my first Olympic gold in Beijing, it went a little bonkers for a while – a combination of being the right age, of having all my friends around, and being fit enough to successfully do a runner from a taxi after I'd missed the last bus back home.

Clearly that solution was incompatible with my ambitions to be a successful cyclist, so I initiated a harsh but effective three-point plan: 1. Move away from Cardiff. 2. Move away from my 'normal' mates. 3. Settle down with my girlfriend.

Living with your partner is undoubtedly very pleasant. It is also undeniably less rock and roll. 'What's on telly tonight?'

'That painting programme on BBC Two.'

'Cracking.'

And so your definition of chill develops. It is realising you've seen the same advert on television every day for a whole year, but you still have no idea what it's for. That's champion chilling.

I find you can have chill form as well as cycling form. If I've been at a Grand Tour or a training camp up on Tenerife, it's hard to snap out of that carefully honed routine. Sometimes, when Sara is chatting away to me, I can allow myself to drift away too far. After a while I'll perk up enough to ask her a question, only to find that she's been answering it in detail for the past forty minutes. It's just as dangerous to always respond with what feels like a safe, non-specific answer: the 'Yeah, know what you mean,' or the 'Mmm, sometimes.' A lot of the time that will suffice, but occasionally it slowly dawns on me from her response that she's asked me if I want a cup of tea, or what time I'm training in the morning.

For that reason it's often tempting to simply grunt, which is neither romantic nor new man but dovetails perfectly with the state of chill. But it should always come with a clear user warning. When my world and that of Sa's family first came together, there were problematic yet inevitable misunderstandings. Her mother would interpret my silence and minimal physical response as illness, anger or distress. 'What awful thing have I done to upset Geraint that much?' Nothing. Quite the opposite. I simply lack the energy to utilise my voice box.

Long stage races can have their moments of tedium. The

first few days of Paris–Nice tend to be long, flat and with no breakaways. You'll be bumbling along at less than 40 kph, desperately trying to stay focused on what might happen later. You torture yourself by watching the kilometres crawl by on your trip computer: 220 kilometres to go, 215, 210. Oh God, I wish I was back on the turbo in my conservatory. Watching snooker.

Travel is supposed to broaden the mind. It can also bore the mind. Hours on the team bus, hundreds of hours in the skies. If you forget to charge your laptop before your flight to Tenerife your heart will sink, because just as you can have bad days on the bike, you can have bad days off it – sitting in the middle seat of a flight to the Canaries, sweating heavily, your backside numb, legs cramped. You are pressed against the guy in front who has reclined his seat into your knees as soon as the wheels have left the runway, your own seat acting as a punch bag for the equally bored five-year-old sat behind you. Close your eyes, dream of better times: future parties, future wins, future plans.

Being bored at the same time as other people seems to help. Even if you're both just lying on your beds, not talking, you can take some comfort that you are in it together.

Sometimes I scare myself by imagining a world without DVDs, smartphones and tablets. If my career had been twenty years earlier, could I have coped? You might well say that people simply used to have the most amazing conversations. You might be right, but not if they were cyclists.

We battle through. You often attempt to read but, after six hours on the bike, the concentration is seldom there. My Sky teammate Ben Swift will always be doing something – stretching, seeing the physio, reorganising his suitcase. You might throw a topic out there: which rider would you sign for next year? Would you rather win three World track gold medals or the World road race? Would you rather have one mega-testicle the size of a spacehopper, or twenty micro-testicles the size of seedless grapes? You can always ask Brad these sorts of random questions. He will entertain such notions.

Ed Clancy might be a little more cerebral. He enjoys telling you that if you took two identical clocks, and sent one of them whizzing around the world's orbit, when you placed them back together they'd be showing different times. Space, relativity, big concepts. Ian Stannard, naturally a listener, will soak it up. Former teammate Matt Hayman enjoys a riddle: a father and son are involved in a car crash and are taken to separate hospitals; the doctor walks into the boy's ward and says, I can't operate on him, that's my son ... How is that possible?

I've seen some awful mistakes. Now the majority of the team is based in the south of France, Swifty decided to buy a book to finally learn the language. It was part one of a three-part plan: French in two months, then 'finishing off' his Italian, which currently stands at twenty words, and then cracking on with Japanese. Ideal for a bloke from Rotherham who mainly hangs out with a bloke from Cardiff and another from Milton Keynes.

Then there was the season Swifty decided to take up the saxophone. What he was thinking, I don't know. Actually I do – he had the delusion common to all adults taking up a musical instrument, and thought he could go from novice to expert in about six weeks.

I'm not sure he even played it six times. He certainly never brought it on the road. In some ways, that's a shame. Imagine kicking back on the team bus after a tough day's racing while he played some melancholic jazz, like some sort of leathery-faced legend in a little underground bar in New Orleans. Instead, of course, it would have been lying awake in an Ibis on an A-road outside Lille while he tried to master 'Twinkle, Twinkle, Little Star'. And failed.

Get Down

The best sorts of crashes are the ones when you're down before you know it.

There's no time to be scared. No time to panic, to think about your ribs cracking or your shoulder separating, or your skin being grated off like stale Parmesan.

That's the good news. The bad is that there is no down slide without a downside. If you're into the tarmac that quickly, it's because you're going fast. And going fast means bigger impacts, and bigger impacts mean less skin and more mess.

The worst? The ones when you don't slide. The ones where your skeleton crumples and your internal organs crash against muscle and cartilage.

Except sliding is bad too. You slide on velodromes, and you pray for polish so that you skid like a puck over ice. I hit the boards once on the old track in Moscow, which had last been sanded before I grew body hair. Slide? I had so many splinters in me I looked like a wooden hedgehog. And sliding means burns, and burns are horrible. Burns never heal. You have to scrub them in the shower. You stick to the bedsheets. You can't sleep. When you climb on the bike, every little motion makes them leak a little more.

Losing both hands off the bars is the most awful feeling in cycling. Sometimes you're down and it's just done. When you lose your hands on the bars, there is a good second or two when you know it's going to go wrong. Those are slow seconds. The inevitability of it, rather than preparing your body and mind for what is to come, seems to amplify the pain that follows. Even if you somehow stay upright, your heart is going crazy afterwards, your hands shaking as if you've just swerved a juggernaut on the motorway.

You try to rationalise it. A few years ago I crashed badly during the time trial on Tirreno–Adriatico – into the roadside barrier at pace, head first into a tree, bouncing down a rocky slope and ending on the road below, looking back up to see my bike swinging from a branch in the tree and a mechanic on tiptoes trying to reach it. I broke my pelvis and scaphoid and was lucky not to do much more. After that I told myself that I was starting to learn when to push it and when not to take my foot off the gas. It took this for me to realise there is a time and a place to take risks. The TT in Tirreno, when you're tired and the best result you can hope for is a top twenty, is not it. Cresting the Poggio climb at the back end of Milan–San Remo with a handful of seconds over the peloton? Then a risk or two is acceptable.

But here's the truth: nothing's good about crashing.

There is only one thing that helps you deal with crashing, and that's crashing. It is inevitable, as unavoidable as losing your wicket is to a Test batsman. You grow up crashing. You race your brother, you crash. You get up, you do it again. You crash on the track, you crash on the road, you crash in the rain and you crash in the dry.

And here's another contradiction for you: despite that, none of us like talking about it. When I was with Barloworld, the riders would insist that when passing the salt it must be placed onto the table, not hand to hand; they were hardly going to be happy to chew over old war stories or work out where the inescapable might happen the next day.

Crashes happen on descents, on corners, on straights, in sprints.

At the Tour Down Under in 2011, I was left as Ben Swift's lead-out man after our Sky teammates Chris Sutton and Greg Henderson had respectively crashed and gone missing in action. All was unfurling beautifully – to the front with 500 metres to go, ready to tow Swift to 200 metres and then watch him catapult past. Except, as I left the door open on the left, he went right. I just had time to think, 'Uh-oh, this could be bad . . .' before I was proved right.

Two guys both tried to get into that one-man gap. One took my left bar. Life in acceleration, I'm in the air, I'm down. Crap. A hundred and fifty other riders are coming at me at 40 mph. Into a ball and pray.

It's little better ten men back. At least you get some reaction time, which makes it slightly safer but a hell of a lot more scary, just as when you're driving at 70 mph on the motorway and suddenly all you can see in front of you is brake lights and swerving cars. You see two men somersault one way, bikes the other. You look for your gap and head for that, at the same time dropping the anchors. Any sudden movement will just cause another crash. Even if you manage to avoid the one in front, you are still in danger of being rear-ended. Waiting for the skid and thump.

When it happens behind it's the sounds that really get to you. Carbon scraping. Mechanical stuff blowing apart. You glance back to see the last two seconds of it – men sliding, heads hitting kerbs. First thought: I'm glad I'm in front of it. Second: I hope they're okay.

Sometimes you get lucky. Sometimes you don't. On stage 16 of the 2015 Tour, coming down the descent of the category-two Col de Manse, French rider Warren Barguil got his line wrong on a corner and blindsided me at pace. Boom – I was sent straight towards a telegraph pole, smacked it with my head and disappeared down the ravine beyond.

It looked pretty spectacular. It felt it too. But having been so unlucky I was also fortunate in other ways. I was able to twist my neck just enough that the side of my head took the impact, rather than my face or neck. The tape barrier beyond snagged me and stopped me going all the way down the mountain. And there were enough spectators around to reach down, haul me up, stick me back on my bike and send me on my way again.

I barely bothered looking down. Jump on board, pedal hard, use the anger and annoyance to fire your engine and take you back towards the lead group. It was far harder for Sara, commentating for S4C. She saw the crash happen but not the recovery. Next thing she knows she's getting a call on her mobile from Sky manager Fran Millar. Oh no. What awful news is she about to tell me?

It can be just as random on the track as on the road. With the team pursuit quartet in Manchester, training for the Worlds in Majorca in 2007, I came round the final bend second in the line and started the usual big finish – second man coming past the first on his outside, third man trying to do the same. What I had failed to remember is that the coaches had asked us to go through the finish line as if we had another lap to do. So when Paul Manning, who was on the front, did his normal team pursuit change – an extreme change of direction up the track – I was down before I knew what was happening.

And you don't always slide on the velodrome. Riding a madison race in Ghent as under-23s, Tom White and I had just lapped the field. I was last in a long line of bike riders, and as I started to make my way back to the front, there was a huge flick up the track from those in front of me – as effective in sending me sideways as the crack of a whip, I had nowhere to go other than the barrier at the top. I hit it and fell to my left. Because the Kuipke Velodrome is just 167 metres long, the bends are like cliffs, so my first contact with the ground was the flat concrete at the bottom of the track. I landed right at the feet of our coach Rod Ellingworth. Okay down there, G?

That's why you always try to rescue a crash. Sometimes on bikes – in cyclo-cross, or out mountain biking – it can be better to hit the deck than hit whatever is coming up. On the road you fight like a cornered dog to stay up.

And, if you somehow keep it up when you were convinced you were down, it's almost as good a feeling as winning a race. Out with Richie Porte doing recon for the Tour in 2014, I glanced down at my Garmin, hit a random bump and was suddenly nose on stem, knees on front forks. It felt like for ever, but I somehow managed to get a hand on the bars and pull myself up. Elation. Absolute elation.

When you can't stay up, work out the best option for crashing. Going down a descent outside Nice in the wet one winter, my rear tyre blew. I was coming into a corner, a waist-high wall directly ahead with a precipitous gorge behind it, and, just to the right, a parked car. I aimed for the car. Why? Because it was better to hit the known danger than launch into God knows what in that ravine. This time I was lucky – my good tyre bit into the road and my cleats found enough traction on the concrete to stop me just before I hit either. But the calculation had been made, and in less time than it takes to read this sentence.

Your brain accelerates ahead of you. Instinct takes over. Like jump jockeys, racing cyclists understand that it is better to roll than to break your fall with outstretched palms and arms. That way leads straight to broken collarbones and wrists. When you roll, sure, you lose skin, but your cycling muscles will work another day.

In a race you get straight to your feet. No thought for your body, only the pack disappearing up the road from you. Where's my bike? Quick, give me that. Chain on? Wheels spinning free? Into the saddle, let's get going. Only then do you start the internal assessment. What hurts? Does this work? Is that sharp pain going to fade or build to a crescendo?

You might ride past some fallen riders and know that they are the ones with a reputation for staying on the floor a long time. Come on, son, what are you doing? Get back on. Get back in it.

Later on, you hear that the one you thought was milking it actually broke his collarbone. Oh, sorry, mate . . .

The same crash is more painful in training. There is no adrenaline to cushion the fall, no frantic rush to remount to keep the shock at bay. Instead there is the more logical response: why has that happened? Am I okay?

In a race there are bodies everywhere, so sometimes you will aim to land on a body rather than a bike. Land, straight up, hope they don't know who it is, get your bike and go. At other times there is no disguising it. Once I jumped up, all my weight through about five millimetres of my left toe, to hear a scream of pain. I was standing on Danish rider Matti Breschel's finger, and he knew it.

Bikes hurt. When I ruptured my spleen it was the stack of spacers on the top of my stem that I landed on, not the road. There wasn't even a break to the skin, just a massive and life-threatening trauma underneath. And not all riders are equal as landing mats. Ian Stannard – six foot two, thirteen stone – is the perfect riding cushion. Chris Froome? You might break him. It would be like landing on a glass bike.

Crash in the cold rather than the warm. You're rugged up, and every layer of clothing is another layer of skin that doesn't get stripped. Although if you're rugged up it may well be icy, and that turns every ride into silent horror. Stick to the main roads, leave the little lanes alone. Ride the

Classics and just accept it will happen. Narrow roads, a brutal pace, slapping winds. It will come.

Me? I'm not superstitious. But I need to get through Saturdays on Paris–Nice. Twice now I've had a 'get down' on that day in that race. It's not that I believe it's fated, but I notice it. Tick it off, G. Prove it wrong. Ride to fall another day.

Form

To riders of old, form was an enigmatic torment – the cyclist's equivalent of the muse, of the mojo.

A sudden feeling of strength in the legs. Boundless energy. A sharpness in the mind. An explosiveness on the hills.

You hoped for it, you prayed for it. When would it come, when would it go? No sooner had you found it than it would desert you. There were ways you could maintain it, tales passed down through the generations, but they were haphazard at best: no hard rides before Christmas; get behind the motorbike for an hour at the end of your ride; when in-between races just do one or two long rides and recovery rides.

You still occasionally get random days when your legs suddenly feel remarkably fresh. After riding hard at Milan–San Remo in 2015, getting away close to the end before being hauled in, I was in pieces for two days. On the Wednesday I went for an easy three-hour ride and felt terrible. On the Thursday I did a gentle couple of hours in Belgium and had all the energy of an aged sloth. On Friday, I won E3 Harelbeke, the first Welshman to win a spring Classic.

But, in a blow for the romantics and a boon for the sports scientists, much of the mystery has been stripped away. If your coach understands your body and how it adapts to the stresses of training, you are halfway there. The other half is understanding you as a rider and an individual. That's not to say the wizards of the past had it completely wrong. Some of those old wives' tales inadvertently had their basis in good science. Have a little sweat, the day before your race, to open up your muscles.

But get the combination right and you can plan form: when it comes, when it peaks. Even that apparently arbitrary magic in the legs at E3 makes logical sense. Riding three hours easy with nothing hanging on it inevitably makes you feel like you're just churning it out. You're ticking off the kilometres. You're bored. Come race day – a race you have been training for all winter, which suits your abilities, in which you get your tactics right – you are motivated and alive. You are knee-deep in racing intrigue. You can tap into your carefully constructed reserve of energy.

It's not only what you do, but how you arrive at that training plan. In the old days a coach would tell a rider what to do, and the rider would do it. For us British riders it's now much more grown up: a discussion about what you think you need, an exploration of different options. When you understand why you're doing something, you buy into it. When you buy into it, you make it work.

And you don't stumble into form. You can feel it coming, happy hints of it in efforts and races, on repetitions in training where a climb that hurt before still hurts but takes ten fewer seconds. In a stage race you can feel yourself getting faster, which is strange as you should be getting gradually worse. It's a happy delusion; you're actually getting slower, but at a more gradual rate than everyone else. And that will do very nicely.

As track cyclists preparing for the Olympics of 2008 and 2012, we experienced the best of the old and new. Our analysts, filming every single lap, recording our heart rate, power output, watts per kilogramme, would spell it out for us with bar charts and graphs. Shane Sutton provided the horse-whisperer stuff: I can see from your pedal stroke, from your demeanour walking to your bike, that you need to rest. Cut the intensity, throw in a few long rides, clear your head. The two schools were seldom out of sync.

You can think yourself out of form. Before a big target you have to fight the urge to analyse every pedal stroke. How was I on that short climb? Hmm, my legs ached a little going over that bridge. Once you're in the contest, those feelings of introspection and insecurity can run away with you. With the denouement still 100 kilometres away you have too much time and mental energy to burn. Should my legs be feeling better? I'm sure that ache in the left hip wasn't there when I started. Am I breathing too heavily for an incline like this?

At the 2014 Commonwealth Games road race I was convinced I was a goner. At one point I turned to my Welsh teammate Luke Rowe and said: 'I feel terrible today. I'm knackered. You push on.' It was the same at Gent–Wevelgem in 2015, where I ended up third. Christian Knees and I were the last two Sky boys in the race. 'Mate, do your own race. I'm done for.'

Instead, I kept going. The final act of the race begins with a few attacks. Ah, I'm not that bad compared to everyone else. Here comes that big hill. Crunch point. That's the move.

You go, without thinking, on instinct. We're away! Now, who's here? Who's looking good?

My gold medal from Glasgow is a reminder of many things. Not least the fact that, in the pithy words of Shane, your head can be a right bastard.

That knowledge should make it easier as you get older. You also gradually realise that there is a world outside bike racing. Your life will not come to an end if today does not work out. Except, you might lose your job at the end of the year. And, if they don't want you, why would anyone else? This might be your one chance. Is your head more of a bastard than the heads of those blokes just ahead of you? Hang on, is that left hip getting worse? And so the paranoia rolls on.

Wisdom comes not only from finding form and believing in it, but in not crushing it with affection. Cycling is about hard work and pain. You push yourself to dark corners of the mind where, in the words of Muhammad Ali, crocodiles roam.

Every athlete wants to keep pushing – for that extra kick, that extra fraction of a per cent, a little more of the mojo. But more is not always better. Longer does not mean faster. Faster does not mean stronger.

Never are you in more danger than when you're feeling good. When you're feeling good, you think you can take more. You are knee-deep in form, and you're loving the feeling. Delusion mixes with delight. I'm sure I can handle one more effort, one more climb, one more hour on this ride.

It's the top inch of your body that makes all the difference. When you're in training and follow three hard days with a rest day, you feel terrible on the day you're doing nothing. If you do a five-day stage race, you're delighted you don't have to race on a sixth, yet on a Grand Tour you'll keep going for twenty-one. When your mind switches off, your body shuts down.

Fight the paranoia. Trust the practice.

At the Olympics in 2012, on the afternoon of the team pursuit gold medal race, we saw our Australian arch-rivals on the rollers two hours before they were due to race. It wasn't a coffee ride. They were going hard. Uh-oh, says the chimp on your shoulder. If they're doing that, why aren't we? Because we are perfectly prepared, says the scientist inside. We climb on board half an hour before the gun goes, work through our tried-and-tested twenty-minute warm-up, step off and race. It works. It wins.

But it's not easy. We trusted our pursuit plan because it had brought us unprecedented success. It had worked before Beijing, at Beijing, at Europeans and Worlds and in training. Neither was it inflexible. It had been tweaked, re-examined, tested under duress.

If you don't have that structure, if you don't have faith in that structure, it's too easy to waver. When you're winning, the confidence flows. When it hasn't quite worked out, the anxiety rises like bile in the throat.

It takes balls to rest. It takes huge belief to do nothing for a whole day, and then take it easy the next, knowing that, by the third, you'll have something that would never have come had you gone hard and hard again. We are mathematicians seeking to balance the most unstable of equations; con artists trying to trick our own bodies and minds.

When you're young and you want to impress, your confidence in those boundaries is weak. You're not even sure where those boundaries lie. If you're young and you're not going well, you train harder. Of course you do. In doing so you dig yourself into a hole. Your next race is worse. You train harder still. The hole gets deeper.

How long does form last? No matter how you plan, it is finite. The more consistent you are off the bike, the smaller the fluctuations. Your diet, your sleep, your flexibility and your core stability all flow into your form. So does your mental approach.

In 2014 I held it well – a start at the Tour Down Under, a build-up to the Classics, third in E3, top ten at the Tour of Flanders and Paris–Roubaix. A breather, then a win at Bayern–Rundfahrt, a decent showing in the Dauphiné and Tour and a win at the Commonwealth Games. Peaks and troughs, but the peaks were in the top 5 per cent of my abilities, just when it was most required.

But it can go quickly. In early August that year, out on my time-trial bike, I hit a stone and went down hard. I was only due to be out for two days, but that wasn't enough for my recovery. It stretched beyond a week.

I had wanted to go the Worlds and ride hard for Ben Swift. I knew I now wouldn't be able to, and that got me down. I started eating a little more, had a few drinks. By the time I got back on the bike, I was two kilos heavier – nothing by the standards of a normal bloke in his late twenties, calamitous by the reckoning of an endurance cyclist. Two kilos isn't an abstract amount when you're a cyclist. It's four full water bottles in your jersey's back pockets. That counts. That's the form gone for another season.

THE RULES

The Rules

You may be aware of a mysterious posse of cycling aficionados who call themselves the Velominati. You may also be aware that they have come up with a set of strictures by which to live your cycling life. I like many of their rules. I also have a code I live by: this is it. Ignore it at your stylistic and practical peril.

On the Bike

Have a decent amount of seat post showing. Simply because it looks more graceful.

The more colourful a training bike, the better. But the colours must work together – you can't pair a Technicolor bike with a similarly bright kit. Similarly for that reason, I have no problem with coloured tyres, provided they don't clash.

Do not angle your brake hoods to look like guns. That just looks wrong.

Technology must be matched to your ability. You might see a ten-year-old kid with a disc wheel. You should walk over and put your foot through it. For that reason, there should be no deep rim-wheels on club runs. Certainly the only occasion you should ever wear a time-trial helmet with visor is a time trial. Quite a few manufacturers are now making helmets with filled-in vents. They look terrible. Only wear one if you genuinely need to make minuscule aero savings.

Socks and shoes have to match. As well as saddle and bar tape. If you are wearing black shoes, then black socks. White shoes, white socks. The only exception is if it's raining, when black socks are acceptable. White can turn to grey pretty quickly.

Your phone is for emergencies, not checking Facebook. Rear pockets should contain a pump, a spare inner or two, tyre levers, your phone and perhaps some cake.

If you're riding in a group, never wear headphones. It's the height of rudeness. If you want to listen to music on your bike and you're alone, use headphones. And then only have one earphone in, so you can hear instructions and traffic.

No whistling. Because that is saying to the other guys you're riding with that they're going too slow for you.

Rule the waves. Always give a polite gesture to fellow riders, or, even better, a 'good morning' or '*bore da*' – whatever floats your boat. Too many guys on their pimped-up bikes think they are above this. Obviously there are times when you don't have to – for example during a three-minute full-gas effort. Also, a polite wave isn't an invitation for people to turn round and ride with you. Plenty of continental guys seem to assume this. If you do end up following someone, be it a pro or someone just a little better than you, don't just sit on their wheel saying nothing. Have a brief 'How you doing?' chat and then crack on with your own thing. I once had someone follow me on a three-hour easy ride – for the entire thing. He stayed a couple of bike lengths behind me the whole time, even stopping ten metres down the road when I stopped for a nature break. That's not cool.

You cannot use someone's nickname unless you personally know them well or have been introduced to them as such. A lot of commentators use nicknames that the rider himself has never heard of. Like 'Eddie the Boss' or 'Mr Mainwaring'. I always introduce myself as Geraint. Although, after their third attempt at pronouncing it, I just say 'G'. But I wouldn't go up to Andrew Flintoff and call him Freddie. Or Aaron Ramsey and call him Rambo.

Never have a squeaky chain. I should say that you should clean your bike all the time, but I can't, as I hardly ever clean mine. You need to keep it maintained so you can always train on it the next day. It can be as dirty as you like, but the chain can never squeak. I've even used olive oil, but that's obviously the last resort.

You can't have three rings on your road bike. They just look wrong. If there's a climb you can't get up in your smallest second ring, keep trying until you can. You'll do it eventually.

You've got to have two bottles and two bottle cages. Otherwise you have to stop more often for refills, putting everyone else out. When out training, a lot of the Italian pros will have one bottle which they fill with their spares and tools, leaving just one with liquid in. Don't they sell saddle bags in Italy? Worse still, as amateurs many Italians would race with only one bottle – for the whole race not just the final hour. I've never understood this.

What to Wear

Be yourself. Wear the jersey you want, and wear it with pride. If you want to show your support for Sky, or GreenEDGE, wear their kit. Don't worry about what anyone might say. They are probably a very average first- or second-cat rider.

Arm yourself properly. I always find it strange when someone has tights or leg warmers on but no arm warmers. At least your legs are moving. Your arms do nothing. So, if you're only going to cover one set of limbs, make it your arms.

Socks over tights or leg warmers is wrong. You wouldn't wear socks over trousers. You're not Superman. Leave it. Arms of sunglasses over the straps of your helmet, not under.

If it's cold, wear the right clothes. Wearing shorts and a jersey when it's freezing is not brave, it's stupid. Having said that, the Italians go over the top. It will be 18°C and they'll be bowling around in down jackets and buffs over their necks. That's weird. It's the opposite to some ex-England rugby boys I know, who wear too little in dreadful weather. They must have suffered too many big hits from the Welsh boys.

Socks should always be worn. The British team pursuit boys no longer wear them. When I first saw that I was severely disappointed. You can't save that many thousandths of a second by not wearing socks.

White shorts should never be worn. Particularly when it rains, because you will appear naked.

Never wear cycling clothing off the bike. When you are out socialising, the only pockets on your garments should be in your trousers. If you're not on a bike, you don't need pockets on the back of your top.

Zip it. If riding in the UK, do not ride with your jersey completely undone. Nobody wants to see your stomach. It is not 35°C and you are not approaching the summit of a brutal Alpine climb.

Hair and Care

Close shaves are a good thing. When shaving your legs, find your natural line, and stick to it. Avoid hair long johns. Avoid hair hotpants. Txema González, the Team Sky soigneur who sadly passed away at the Vuelta in 2010, would berate me for stopping mid- to high-thigh. 'Why aren't you going all the way?' It's also fine to let it grow back during the winter. One: it's extra insulation. Two: you can feel more of a man, at least until January comes and it's time to whip it all off again.

No wax, no women's products. Never use your girlfriend's Ladyshave. Use whatever razor you have to hand, and use shower gel or shampoo rather than shaving foam or oil – they're uneconomical, for starters. Waxing is forbidden, because it will take you too long. Leg shaving should never take more than five minutes. Get in there, get it done. If you sustain nicks and bloody cuts, good. They're battle wounds.

Beards are acceptable until the Classics are done. You cannot sport a beard in a Grand Tour. The Classics are dirty, scruffy, get-stuck-in races. The beard can act as a natural buff. Come May, you would in effect be wearing a hair scarf. This is both impractical and unpleasant on the eye. Sorry, Brad, it's only because I can't grow one.

Sideburns should only be worn if you can pull them off. Wispiness is out. Someone who does not know you has to be able to look at your face and know instantly what you're attempting. If they are unsure, you have failed.

Beware the moustache. US rider Dave Zabriskie had one a few years ago, but the danger is that you look like a traffic cop or porn star. Turning up at the start of a season with something under your nose is not advised. One year Sky took our official publicity photos during the first training camp in December. For most of us this was preferable to the usual time at the end of the off season, when all the riders are pale and chubby, but not for all. December follows Movember, and Luke Rowe still had an ugly-looking slug across his upper lip. That will be forever with him now.

Every team should have at least one rider who has a mullet. It doesn't have to be Mick Jagger-style, but it has to be flapping out the back. Mine got pretty long at one point, but Rigo Urán had an authentic head of hair on him. Too many cyclists are simply having buzz-cuts.

Do not shave your arms. This may surprise you, but plenty of cyclists shave their arms. I had to shave mine for the Olympics in London, when we wore short-sleeved skinsuits. That felt extremely weird. It just looked wrong when you looked down, like you'd borrowed someone else's arms. The biggest price was paid by Steven Burke, who had the most to lose. Pete Kennaugh has only a light covering of hair, while the hairs of Ed Clancy, being ginger, are almost invisible to the casual eye. It probably made as much difference as wearing no socks.

Jewellery should start and finish with a wedding ring. Having a chain hanging out of your half-zipped jersey brings back bad memories of Lance Armstrong and Tyler Hamilton. Earrings are too Jan Ullrich. Before you race you should both mentally and physically be stripping down for battle. Every last thing you don't need should be removed.

Tattoos are a good thing, but they should be for your enjoyment only. If you choose to get the Olympic rings, it has to be somewhere discreet. On no account get 'San Remo' on your leg or 'Liège–Bastogne–Liège' across your shoulder blades. There is more to life than cycling. If it's something to do with your family, by all means have it somewhere public. If your tattoos clash with your team kit, you shouldn't sign with that team.

When Recovering

Button it. You can say how tired you are, but don't bang on about it. Everyone is tired. A single mention of it at the dinner table should suffice. Don't try to milk it – no ostentatious noises of weariness while sitting down. Be positive, talk about other things.

Don't hog the massage. The good rider rotates. Each soigneur will be looking after two to three riders, so you take it in turns. The leader might get priority a few times, particularly if he's been on the podium or been with the media for a long time – but you should take no longer than an hour, unless you are a real mess. And, if someone's waiting, you shouldn't ask for any extras, like a scalp massage.

Mind your manners at the dinner table. There's no need to wait until everyone is seated. You all filter in at different times. But, if someone is still in massage, you should be judicious about taking too many seconds too many times. Don't take all the steak or the last bit of fish. Team Sky nutritionists like us to have vegetable smoothies – make sure everyone has had one before dipping back for a second glass. There should also be no messing about with your phone at the dinner table. Use it if you have to, but don't let it dominate the vibe.

Stop the flip-flop. It's a bit of an Italian thing, and something I must have picked up during my time at Barloworld, but wearing flip-flops at the dinner table is a no-no. Caps should not be worn at the table, although Americans do get a little leeway here. Compression socks and shorts should not be seen in public, especially airports. Wearing them while walking from room to room is fine. At other times, the combination of long socks and shorts reflects badly on all us cyclists. Don't do it.

Racing and Training

Always finish. Never stop during a race. Even if it's cold and wet, always complete the task you have been set. Never give up. I managed to complete the 2013 Tour de France with a fractured pelvis. And ended up riding down the Champs Élysées with Chris Froome in our yellow Oakleys. I'll always have them now.

Skin is waterproof. Never let bad weather put you off training. British Cycling's mind guru Steve Peters used to tell us that motivation can be really high or really low but, if you're committed, you'll always go out there and do it. Even when you don't want to, you'll still do it. Just get out there. It's only three or four hours of suffering. You've got the rest of the day to warm up and recover.

Train to the weather. Be sensible. There is no point in going out and doing six hours steady if it's lashing it down. Get out and do a shorter, faster, more intense session instead. If you're out and it is horrible, another rule: do an extra effort, and come back an hour earlier.

In a breakaway, do as much as the guy who is doing the least. Turns in a small group are never a straightforward affair. You want the lot of you to stay away, but you want to be the least tired in the group. You might think that everyone ending up doing very little would have a cumulative effect, but you always have at least one guy who wants to show you how strong he is, because he's feeling great. On a club run, you'd usually take ten-minute turns at the front. But, because you get a bigger variety in ability, it's not a problem for some riders to get a tow. And some will be stronger, so they can sit at the front, thus earning the right to boast about their deeds later.

Everybody hurts. If you're out in it and it's miserable, know that there are 80 per cent who aren't even out. You're out and proud. Personally, I suffer most when my hands get cold. But there's not a lot you can do. Shake them and do windmills with your arms. Stick them under your armpits at traffic lights. Know it will eventually end.

Use your brain. Don't look at an intimidating training session as six different efforts; think only about the first one. And break that first one down into little chunks.

Work first, drink later. Don't stop for a coffee until you've done the hard work. Otherwise you'll get warm and comfy and it'll only be worse. Reach for a caffeine gel if you're struggling, but don't think too far ahead – get the next hard bit done; relax when you deserve to.

The Necessary Small Details

Watch where the wind blows. Sports nutrition is a fine thing, but it can be a little tough on the guts. We have a protein drink at Team Sky that has an active ingredient designed to clean you out, and that can lead to issues with smells. If you feel something brewing, peloton etiquette is to move to one side of the bunch so that no rider is directly behind you. In a race scenario, where there are four of you battling for the win, that protocol still stands. You need to have some principles that are inviolable.

Wee wide. If you're peeing off the bike, and have spotted that other riders have stopped by the side of the road, be sure to give them a sufficiently wide berth. The way to do it is not to unclip a pedal and roll up a short, but to shift slightly off the saddle so there is no pressure on your behind and then pull down the front of your bib shorts. Some struggle with it. It takes a lot of practice. I weed myself a few times before I learned how to pee off the bike. Only when it was raining, mind, and when I was on the back of the group. But when I won the Flèche de la Sud in 2006, in a break of three or four of us hammering down a hill, I just had to go. It was such a sweet relief to get it out after holding it in for so long that it was close to jubilation. Then I attacked on the next climb and won the stage. I was racing for the Great Britain national team at the time, meaning I was wearing shorts that were red, white and blue. Or grey and smelly, by the end.

If you are stopping for a pee, look before you swing off the road. In Amstel 2014, one of the Astana riders spotted a little gap on the pavement and made a sharp turn right. Just as I was coming past. The next thing you know, I'm on the floor, which wasn't ideal.

Spit socially. The same principles apply as when struggling with wind. Make it obvious what you are about to do, perhaps with an audible hawking sound. It is the same when clearing your nose. Clear both nostrils to the same side, away from the direction of other rivals. Lift the elbow high to clear your own sleeve from the path. Should you misread the flow of riders around you, or inadvertently hit a rider who has accelerated up on your outside, you must wipe it off with your own glove after apologising profusely.

Pooh-pooh the poo. Should you need a number two, your first sensation will be one of slight surprise. I have never needed one in a race, through a combination of the fight-or-flight instinct kicking in pre-ride and also simple luck that I have never been hit by the runs as many are. Riders have lost races through needing to clear out their pipes but being unable to stop, and thus being unable to give their maximum. Address the issue before it becomes mission critical.

Food and Drink

There is no point in the cycling year at which ordering an ice cream while out on your bike becomes acceptable. You can eat ice cream only when wearing ordinary clothes. When I was on a T-Mobile training camp as a junior with fellow Team Sky man Ian Stannard, we stopped on a long training ride. While all the grizzled pros ordered the de rigueur espressos, Stannard got himself an ice cream. The look on the faces of the pros told you everything you needed to know. Huge error.

You should never look at the nutritional information on food packaging. Up until Christmas, that is. Just enjoy it. After Christmas, either look at it and feel guilty, or don't eat it at all.

Do not use chewing gum on a ride. At some point you are going to need to spit it out, and it will inevitably end up in someone's shorts or in their rear mech. At some point too you are likely to crash, and swallowing chewing gum is no-one's idea of a medical good time.

You should not be eating on a ride until you have completed a minimum of two hours. Unless you're in the middle of a Grand Tour, in which case you should be grazing throughout.

Justify your gels. It's not like they are the tastiest things in the world. If you're training for two hours, to warrant a gel you either have to be doing an effort, or five or more sprints. If you are doing three nasty sprints, you can have a caffeine gel as a little lift, but no second gel.

Water only, if riding for two hours or less. On club runs of three to four hours, with two bottles on your bike, it's more than fine to have a carbohydrate or electrolyte drink, but certainly not a Coke. To ride with two big bidons of Coke or another soft drink full of sugar is self-defeating. Don't do it.

BOSSING IT

This is to Certify that

Geraint Thomas of Maindy Flyers Cycle Racing Team

Set a Newcomers Track Record

in a time of _47·00 seconds_

for the distance of _1 LAP (460 metres)_

on _5th September 1996_

Signed _Debbie Wharton_   Date _5th October 1996_

British Revolutions

There are different ways you could gauge the transformation of British cycling from niche leisure pursuit to the Olympic-conquering mass-participation machine that it is today. You could tot up all those Olympic golds, from Athens onwards – or, should you want to save energy, add up the few events Britain didn't win gold in, because it'll be quicker. You could think about Brad standing on top of a car on the Champs Élysées, yellow jersey hanging off his lean frame, toasting an impossible moment in true Wiggo fashion: 'We're just going to draw the raffle numbers ...' You could think about Cav, with his head down and mouth wide open as he sprinted to the World road race title, or those homecoming parades through the streets of London, or three cyclists winning BBC Sports Personality of the Year in five years, or the knighthoods tossed around like empty bidons.

Having ridden through it all, I prefer something more down to earth. When I was a kid, pedalling round the lanes outside Cardiff, a car parping its horn at you was followed by a snarling face at a rolled-down window and a mouthful of abuse. Get off the road! Pay your road tax! Piss off out of my way! These days, after everything that's happened, you still get honked. But now it precedes a big grin, a thumbs-up and a clenched fist of encouragement. That's what the revolution has done.

Looking back, it might all seem preordained. I can tell you it wasn't. What is now commonplace once seemed impossible. We were tilting at distant targets or lost in the daily detail. We were a team but also competing individuals. We were cogs but also free to make our own mistakes.

A Briton winning the Tour? As a kid I got excited if there was a British rider in the field. When I dreamed about taking part, it was with a German or Spanish team. I thought I'd have to emigrate to France or Belgium. Winning the Tour, in a British team, and living in Cardiff?

The miracles happened because of the people who came together. First there was Peter Keen and his marginal gains. Then there was his star pupil, Chris Boardman, the godfather of the British scene, the brains, the attitude, the obsession.

I'm at my first ever senior Track World Championships, Bordeaux, 2006. My God, I'm nervous. Steve Peters is barely a name in Dave Brailsford's mobile, still working with the mentally ill at Rampton Secure Hospital. I'm on my own with the chimp. Chris spots it, and strolls over.

'When I was racing, I had a little habit,' murmurs the former Olympic pursuit champion, the world record holder for the hour, the former wearer of the Tour's yellow jersey, a man defined by the detail and scientific precision of everything he did.

'I used to write "Fuck It" on the back of my hand. When I felt tense, when I felt the pressure, I could glance down and remind myself: at the end of the day, fuck it.'

There you go. For all the space-age skinsuits and the magic wheels, it came down to a cheap insult. It's stayed with me to this day. Convince yourself that none of it matters, even when it matters more than anything you will ever know.

My role in it all began in my late teens, when I'd won the Junior Worlds and Junior Paris–Roubaix. A national under-23 programme had been started; among its first intake were Mark Cavendish, Ed Clancy and Matt Brammeier. The word comes in from Shane Sutton, who had been Welsh national coach: don't go near that academy, G, they're not up to scratch. Get yourself on a nice continental team and crack on.

Two months later, I get another call from Shane. Get yourself on that academy. Rod Ellingworth's in charge. It's going great guns. Don't mess about.

I joined that November. Farewell, Cardiff; hello, a very bad part of Manchester. Two tiny houses in Fallowfields. In one you had Cav, Ed and me. In the other, Matt and Tom White. That was how it started: being burgled in the rain.

The advances came in leaps. First, the arrival of good bikes. Not just nice bikes, but head-turners. Signals of intent. A change in personnel – sessions at the velodrome with Chris Hoy and Vicky Pendleton for company. Then attitude. To ride team pursuit we thought you had to have the build of a Belgian: big, tall, strong. Instead, a call-up to the senior squad at the 2006 Worlds in Bordeaux at the age of nineteen.

I blew it. Man three of the four, I came off my pull at the front with three quarters of a lap to go, missed jumping back on the express train by half a bike length and couldn't get back on. The Aussies beat us by 0.004 seconds, basically because I missed the last wheel. That was my first taste – a hard one to swallow, but one that made me desperate to come back for more.

The momentum had begun at the Sydney Olympics with a gold, silver and a couple of bronzes. In Athens, the acceleration was undeniable – golds for Brad and Chris Hoy, the team pursuit climbing to silver, another bronze in the madison.

At the Worlds in 2007, a year out from Beijing, we were flying. Pursuit riders, sprinters, coaches, all bouncing off each other. We were a collective yet also fierce competitors. Medals for another rider were greeted with delight but also a pang of something else: I want a bit of that too. Twelve months on, at our home track in Manchester, you could look around and see a new sort of confidence; if you wore a GB jersey, you would medal. Nine golds, three world records, Hoy and Wiggins out on their own, Vicky unstoppable.

On the team pursuit we made it our aim to set the standard. 2007 was the first time anyone had clocked two sub-four-minute rides, in the same day, first in qualifying and then the final. In Manchester we smashed the world record. It wasn't that we felt invincible, but you knew that if you rode as well as you could, then no other team could touch you. Six riders competing for four places, pushing each other in every session.

It was a wonderful feeling to have, the sense of constant improvement. It's the secret dream of every sportsman. You would walk into the velodrome knowing that you had what you believed was the best bike, the best wheels, the best

coaches and the best nutrition. You would walk into breakfast and meet marginal gains on the tablecloth: not just
glasses of cherry juice, because of its high levels of antioxi-
dants, but juice only from Montmorency cherries, because
they were found to be slightly superior to any others. On the
track, you could sense the jealous eyes of the French and
Italians on you, and you loved it. We're Great Britain. We're
here to do a job.

What happened in Beijing was no surprise. To win seven
track golds from the ten on offer was unprecedented. But we
had built a supreme confidence over the previous twenty-
four months. I'm sure it drove some other nations on, but it
intimidated even more.

Certainty in sport is a rare thing. There are too many vari-
ables at play, too narrow a margin between the top three or
ten or twenty in the world. That's what makes that domination
so remarkable. Every time a rider in a white skinsuit climbed
on their bike, you knew they had a great shot at winning.

We had planned for every eventuality except the reaction
back home. We had no access to British media or websites
out in China. We were in our Beijing bubble. In training, all
you think about is the gold medal and how you can win it.
You have no thought for what happens next.

And then you land in London, and workmen in hard hats
are cheering you rather than giving you the finger. You are
on the back of a lorry parading through Trafalgar Square,
and it seems as if the whole of the city has come out to
celebrate with you. Hang on, we're only cyclists. No-one
knows what the team pursuit is, do they? They do?

The strange thing about dream-like success is how quickly it becomes matter of fact. Cav wins San Remo. Cav wins the world title. Brad wins the Tour. All impossible to imagine before they happened, all seeming like nailed-on certs once achieved.

So it was at London 2012. The public expectation was enormous. We'll cruise it again. We won seven on the track and one on the road through Nicole Cook last time – and this time, we're at home.

The hidden story of London was that it was miraculous. Rule changes, injury, pressure, distractions. If Britain had won three golds it would have been remarkable. To win seven on the track again, to break world records nine times (against all the odds rather than with them) only those on the inside understand how extraordinary it was.

Of those men and women who drove it on, Shane Sutton was the one with the closest bond to the riders. We all loved him, because he was on our side. I'm not saying he was soft. No-one could ever describe Shane as soft. This is a man who will be the first to tell you you're being a twat, in exactly that language. He also scares the staff, because he's black and white: this is right, that's wrong, let's sort it out now. But, if he thinks you've got a point, he will back you all the way. At our pre-London boot camp, the coaches wanted all the riders to stay in a hotel. Focus the mind, tighten the bond. I had a house just down the road and had been away with Sky for six months. I'd barely slept in my own bed or had an evening with Sara. Shane understood. G, you stay at home. It wasn't me messing with the team ethic. It was Shane realising that I would perform better that way.

He is old school. He would advise us like the former rider he is: get out each morning this week for a long ride, lads, and then throw in some big-gear stuff to keep you strong. Alongside him he had Matt Parker, who came at things from a more scientific approach: chaps, work in four or five over-geared efforts to recruit additional fast-twitch fibres. The balance of the old and new, the marriage of instinct and proof, was what drove the endurance squad to new heights.

You want Shane in your corner. You want Shane at your dinner table, because his stories are better than anyone else's. Proper riders' stories from a proper riders' coach. But you don't want to upset him.

Shane's bollockings are probably the most frightening of all the coaches'. In fact, of anyone I've ever met. I should know; I've experienced the full range. At an end-of-season British Cycling dinner a few years ago some of us younger riders decided to enjoy a glass of wine before getting there. We envisioned it as a sophisticated touch, but before we could take stock we were three bottles in and fuses lit. By the time we went up on stage to collect an award we were in the perfect mood to celebrate, but not for a public inter-view. Dave B spotted us, and launched into that truly scary thing: a double-bollocking. And it escalated while he failed to spot that Pete Kennaugh's mother was there. She quickly took umbrage at Dave's punchy response and language. 'You can't speak to the boys like that! Who do you think you are?'

Unfortunately, one of the iconic coaches in British sporting history. With a Rottweiler of an assistant to back him up. So it was that the next morning's hangover was detonated by a phone call from Shane. The exact words are hazy – disgrace, lucky to still be on programme, one last chance, etc. – but the message was clear. And scary.

That was how the two of them worked. Dave would be at the top looking down; Shane would run the day-to-day. The brains and the brawn.

The two of them have had some dust-ups down the years. They still have the occasional big barney. In between, mediating and ameliorating, was Steve Peters. He is able to both keep them in check and show them how to communicate those passions in the most effective way.

Steve has been essential to many. In the team pursuit environment he was hugely useful, not least in keeping Ed Clancy (a little bit bonkers as a character) on a level, rather than being constantly too high or too low. The pressures within a small squad like that can be intense, much greater than within a football team. Perhaps the most accurate comparison is with a foursome in rowing. All dependent on each other, all competing, all living in each others' back pockets for month after month after month.

On a personal level, I was one of the riders who didn't rely on Steve quite so much. His talks made sense to me. It was just that I was already familiar with his themes, because it was exactly the same stuff my dad had brought me up on. Try your best, don't worry about the outcome. Don't worry about losing, no-one ever tries to lose. You've done all your training, there's nothing you can do now. Just go out there and enjoy it.

But it was a team effort, and we all took what we could from each other. As members of the endurance squad, we would watch the sprinters destroying themselves in training sessions and shout encouragement from inside the track. You could spot if someone was having a bad day or a horrible session and give them the clenched fist or look in the eye to show them you were with them.

And that work ethos became infectious. You would see Chris Hoy coming out for the next flat-out 500-metre effort, still in bits from the last one, and it would drive your own attitude in training. We were divergent personalities, just as we were contrasting athletes. Vicky could be up and down, Chris was laid-back and chatty, Jason Kenny was quiet and watchful. But we felt like a team.

Essential to it all was Rod Ellingworth: founder of the academy, instiller of good habits, both a visionary and a man who can work out the detail to make that dream reality.

His academy changed us not only as riders but as young men. It wasn't just about winning bike races, although that was obviously important. It was about learning to be a good pro, about organisation, hygiene, diet and attitude.

In training we did drill after drill, in format after format – team pursuit, the madison, the Keirin – not just getting fitter but developing skills and racing nous, not just strong bike riders but ones that wanted to race and knew how to do it. We would race everywhere and anything – track leagues, handicaps, points races – always full gas, always competing as if it were the world championships, carrying on even after brutal crashes. Rod loved it. He wanted us racing. He wanted the competition and the rivalry, along with the teamwork and unity when we came together to race abroad against the rest of the world.

He was harsh but fair. He wasn't a barker like Shane. He was the silent type, which was almost worse. He could give you the cold shoulder and be disappointed in you for a full two days, rather than the intense yet brief bollocking that Shane would hand out.

Punctuality was a big thing for him with us young lads: up at 6 a.m. to ride into the track for double sessions plus a French lesson; food for the day planned and sorted the night before; days filled with schedules of food shopping, bike and kit washing, a timetable for recovery too.

It was hard, especially when you were eighteen and away from home for the first time. Rod would be stricter than necessary at times just to make it harder. He didn't want soft people around. I'm sure he did a little rain dance every time we had a ride over three hours, which since we were living in Manchester was not strictly necessary. You had to want to be there and want to improve, want to overcome the challenges he'd set.

We would have random house inspections. Rod would arrive, clearly not for a social call, and start looking round. If the kitchen was dirty or your bike in a state, you'd be asked why and told to sort it out yourself. This is essential to your job. Make sure it works.

He was a constant presence. Checking we were out on our bikes when we should be. Checking we weren't out on the lash when we shouldn't be. We were like his kids. He'd look after us, but only after we'd learned a lesson, usually the hard way. In return he had our full respect, because we knew he was fully committed to his job.

One time, not long after I'd recovered from my splenectomy, we were doing a race that took in the Col du Glandon – a twenty-one-kilometre climb at up to 12 per cent. On the previous day's stage I had crashed badly in the team time trial and taken all the skin off my palms. I assumed I was out. Rod had other ideas. 'We'll patch you up.'

It was five hours of hell. I could barely hold the bars on the ascents. The heat was brutal. The descents were even worse. It was almost impossible to corner or brake. But the challenge had been set by Rod, and I wasn't going to fail.

Because he did care for us. Everything he did was in our own interests, to help us improve. He had two favourite phrases: 'Go out and earn your pennies,' and, 'It's all time in the saddle.' Both as relevant to a Tour veteran today as a young rider then.

That World road race win for Cav was the perfect example of his talents. He thought it was possible. He worked out where it was most likely to happen, put the team and tactics together and created both a programme and intense team spirit. And it all paid off. We dictated the race from start to finish.

Through all the years, as a British cyclist, you felt backed up by a group of specialists that no-one else in the world could match. They were all essential: Rob Hayles and Chris Boardman, researching every tiny possible improvement in our kit; the sports scientists and kings of marginal gains like Matt Parker, who worked out exactly how and where we should peak; the analysts who would film every lap of the velodrome we rode and break it down into mountains of critical data. That was where the extra 0.01 seconds were saved. That was where the revolution was won.

Obsession gets a bad name in the ordinary world. In sport, it's what turns you from outstanding to unbeatable.

You could see it in each one of the personalities who changed British cycling for ever. Hayles, obsessed with carbon, obsessed with taking broken kit away to remake it into something space age. Hoy, obsessed with coffee, obsessed with the nuances of espresso. Boardman, so obsessive about detail and material that when he built his kids a tree house it was made from specially imported rare wood and featured zip wires, annexes and running water.

Weirdos in any other world. In sport: revolutionaries.

Olympics

For many athletes, the Olympics is the peak of their sport. For me, it came early.

I was nineteen years old when the announcement came that London would host the 2012 Games. We were out on a training camp with British Cycling's academy, all the riders and coach Rod Ellingworth huddled around the television. In that moment, there was actually disappointment. Having no inkling what a home Olympics would turn out to mean, a part of me wanted it to be in New York. To a Welsh teenager, the idea of a free trip to America easily trumps London, and, while selection per Beijing felt like a long shot, 2012 – when I would be twenty-six – seemed realistic. Suddenly, a year on, I was called into the senior track squad, and then, two years out, into the team. Aged twenty-two, I'd made the cut.

The Olympics are like nothing else on earth, and not only for the reasons you imagine. The athletes' village is a combination between backstage at a circus, the world's biggest restaurant and an elite breeding zone. Tens of tower blocks spread over a vast area to house all the competitors. Nations' flags hanging out of windows. Athletes and staff everywhere. There is every imaginable shape and size of human, but extrapolated to the nth degree – the enormously tall and thin, the short and squat, those with huge legs and tiny arms, those with matchstick legs and huge arms. You can play a little game as you walk around, if you're interested: match the sport to the body. High jumper, weight-lifter, cyclist, kayaker.

I say walk. Cyclists never walk. You certainly never attempt it at an athletes' village, where the distance between your dormitory and the canteen is so great you actually get on our bikes and pedal there.

For some, it's an overwhelming experience. So many other sportspeople to talk to. Global superstars to gawp at. In the canteen there is every kind of food anyone could ever want, healthy sportsman or not. And it's all free – McDonald's, pizzas, Indian, fried chicken.

Us? We saw none of it. Not the opening ceremony (too much time on our feet), not the socialising, not the golds going down elsewhere. Not Beijing's *hutongs*, not Tiananmen Square, not the Great Wall.

And I have no regrets. We went there to win gold. We thought of nothing else except our race, and staying in the perfect shape to win it.

We even missed our kit collection and fitting in Loughborough. Training and rest took precedence over everything else, especially a couple of months out from competition, so driving a couple of hours to make sure you have the right-sized T-shirt doesn't make the cut. The downside, predictably, was that when the kit arrived, some of it didn't fit. I know. But, by that stage, we were suddenly kids again, ripping open bags and trying on tracksuits, Ed Clancy and me, surrounded by cardboard boxes and cellophane wrappers in our hotel room in Newport, suddenly aware that this thing was real, and we were part of it.

Our last training session had been at the velodrome in Newport. We flew from London to China in a party consisting only of cyclists. We got there and saw no-one else. The notion of Team GB as one big happy family didn't register. We watched a little of it on TV, but only if we could sit down or lie in bed as we did so. Going out and meeting people? We were too obsessed with not catching something to risk shaking hands. Everywhere we went we carried little bottles of hand sanitiser. Surgeons have performed open-heart surgery with fewer precautions.

For me, it was very simple: did I want to return to South Wales telling everyone I'd had a great ten days in the village, or with an Olympic gold round my neck? Would I swap that gold for meeting an interesting hockey player over a free coffee? No.

My first Olympic memories had been of Barcelona 1992, watching Linford Christie win 100-metres gold, as gutted as every other Welshman that Colin Jackson could never add an Olympic hurdles gold to his many World and European titles. That gave me a solid dream with vague detail; while I could see myself standing on a podium, I never knew which sport I would be competing in. But I knew the colour of the medal, and in Beijing that ambition was realised.

Remarkably, we barely felt any pressure in Beijing. From the moment we entered the velodrome in Laoshan, it seemed so simple: do the ride we were capable of and we would take some beating.

All these years on, I can still remember the exact sensations of the team pursuit final. I could hear my breathing in my aero helmet, the noise of the crowd just a distant murmur. Everything almost easy. Everything in slow motion. Waiting to hit the front for my turns seemed to take an age. Each change up and down the banking of the track was nailed. If a slight adjustment was required, we did it straight away, without dramas.

In the team pursuit, we always rode to our pre-arranged schedule. Even with another team racing us, we stuck to our plan: a consistently fast pace designed to get the best time out of us. It took away any emotion. Other teams race their opponents. Their coach stands by the finish line and takes a step to indicate who has the lead: one pace towards them if they are 0.1 seconds down, one pace away from them if they are 0.1 seconds in front. Ours was different: Shane Sutton would take that pace according to where we were against our schedule, not our opponents.

Shane kept walking away from us. Okay. We're up on schedule.

I was on the front coming around with two laps to go and caught a glimpse of the Danes, who we were racing for gold. In that moment I knew we had it. The fact we could see them meant we had at least a three-second advantage.

Suddenly, some emotion hit me. 'Come on, we've got this, finish it . . .' I started to empty the tank, chasing them down all the way to the line. Then, necks craning up at the scoreboard to see the time. Up it flashed: 'Olympic Champions and new World Record.' Only then comes the elation.

Once the medal has been won you can let your hair down. Four years of monastic existence builds its own pressures. Letting go is always easy.

The swimmers are traditionally known as the party squad. They are among the first to get their events out of the way, and so the first to kick back and enjoy the good times. It doesn't always go down well with the other athletes who are still awaiting their moment of truth, and who are thus cast in the role of angry parents with the carousers their half-cut teenage kids. 'What time do you call this? Keep the noise down. And what on earth has happened in the downstairs bathroom?'

We toasted our own medals in unfettered fashion. At the Commonwealth Games in 2006 it was the lawn bowls lot who got in a stink with us after some late-night banging and crashing. We apologised, silently thinking, come on . . .

In Beijing we began at Team GB House, which serves as official social headquarters during the games. Most major nations have one – temporarily taking over a building so they can host functions, welcome dignitaries and promote their national culture. Dutch House, for example, is always a popular destination: there's free Heineken on tap. Literally.

On this particular night we had been celebrating in style. British cyclists had won eight golds in the preceding week, an unprecedented run of success that helped propel the country to fourth in the overall medal table, another staggering result. So there were lots of beers, after years without, some indulgent food and a certain amount of high jinks.

We had all finished – sprinters, pursuit riders and coaches – and had stumbled into the street outside to find a cab to take us back to the village when we heard a bang behind us.

We spun round to see Brad doing a neat commando roll across a taxi's bonnet.

The driver wasn't happy. Like a sprinter from the gate he was out of his seat and into the road in a small angry blur, screaming about how his car had been dented, and about how much he wanted in damages. By this stage, Brad was already gone – he'd hopped in another taxi and was on his way home. Out came some Team GB bigwigs, all charm and calm. It's not a problem, sir. Your car is fine. Look, there's not even a dent. What they could have added, had the bloke been an aficionado of the velodrome, was that he should have been thankful that it was a lean pursuiter rather than an outhouse-built sprinter in the collision. Had it been Chris Hoy dipping a shoulder, his bonnet would have needed more than a brush down with the back of a blazered sleeve. There were also weightlifters out that night. A Beijing taxi versus one of those boys would not end well for their crumple zone.

I was brought back down to earth when I landed in Heathrow. My dad's car had broken down en route from Cardiff. Time to get the train home. Fine. I lugged my huge bag and bike all the way to Paddington, catching some strange looks, only to find my bank card had stopped working. Sod it, I thought. There's a gold medal in my luggage. Could I gamble it?

My Beijing luck was still with me. On the train I bumped into a cycling journalist who was also homeward-bound from the Olympics, and he kindly bailed me out. I forgot to ever pay him back. Sorry, Will.

The celebrations continued in South Wales. Whether it was because I was the only man at Cardiff Central with a track bike and GB tracksuit I don't know, but for the first time in my life I was signing autographs outside a velodrome.

The partying began punchily and kicked on from there. Every morning one of my friends had to phone in sick, only for us to do it all over again the next night. It was like the greatest lads' holiday of all time, except the only sand was in the playground in Heath Park and I went home every night to my mum and dad's house.

By London, I was four years older and wiser. I both knew what to expect and was more ready to take it in, more open to the wider experience. In the run-up to an Olympics it is easy to get lost in hype and hoopla. Medals are won in the years of hard work beforehand, but they can easily be lost in the week leading up to the Games.

Compared to London, the build-up to Beijing could barely have been more relaxed. We trained in Newport, ignored by the wider world. On the one media open day that was organised, only the established stars – Hoy, Wiggins and Pendleton – were needed. The rest of the time we chilled in the hotel, addicted to *MotoGP* on my Xbox. There were many times when Paul Manning would knock on our door on the way to lunch to find Ed and me, still in our sweaty kit, racing each other, lap after lap. There were definite roles in the team: us the little kids, Paul the big brother keeping it all in check.

London? London was everywhere. It was impossible to ignore. In the quiet back lanes around Knutsford, where we'd train on the road, there were Olympic decorations in people's gardens, straw men on bikes, homemade banners supporting Team GB. Every night the television was dominated by it – items on the news, documentaries on athletes, shows about sport. I loved it. It was what we had missed in Beijing. Not everyone felt the same way. My room-mate Ed saw it only as pressure. 'Argh, another one? Just stick *Bargain Hunt* on, please . . .'

I understood that an elite sportsman should always focus on the process rather than the outcome, which allowed me to ride some of the waves that could have capsized my younger self – getting food poisoning the week before, having a room right on the edge of the athletes' village that was so close to the main stadium that you could lie awake at night with the roars and gasps rolling around your ears. You knew to stay off Twitter, to ignore the huge crowds pouring in and out of the Olympic Park just outside your window, to not make a fuss when you queued up near Usain Bolt in the canteen.

Not all Olympic athletes are created equal. There is a pecking order of excellence and ambition. Some will want autographs and selfies from others. Keeping your head down might look antisocial, but sometimes it is the only way.

The worst part of it all for me was the night before our first qualification ride. I knew that we were in good shape, but I couldn't help thinking how fast the Australians or the Danes might go. It was the fear of the unknown. You just want to get out there and race, but we were doing less cycling than we had in months. Fewer and fewer hard sessions, more and more lying around, resting up. More and more time to think. More time to mess it all up.

It builds through the week, up to the night before the race. You start thinking about how your legs feel, how they are going to feel, how the other boys will feel. What if something goes wrong? It will all come down to less than three minutes fifty-five seconds. The margins for error are minuscule. In a Grand Tour you have twenty-one stages to put things right. On the track, if it goes wrong, that's it. Dream over.

So how do you handle it? I revert back to the computer in my head. Steve Peters has programmed it with the answers to all your worries. You visualise your ride again and again. From the beeps at the start to your first turns of the pedals, getting on the wheel, your position, your first turn. The noise, the physical sensations, your changes, all the way through until the finish line.

Qualification brings its own calm. That first ride blows the nerves away. You get a sense for the atmosphere in the velodrome. If your legs feel good and you qualify fastest, all the better.

In the twenty-four hours of rest before qualification and the second round and final, you go back through that initial ride. Watching it back, studying the graphs, making any fine tweaks.

The trick is to not read too much into it. It's awfully easy to talk yourself out of a good ride. I was generally okay, just looking forward to getting back out there the next day. Ed would go the other way. He would always try to analyse how the other teams were doing. 'Maybe the Aussies are bluffing. Were they holding back? What if they come out and ride five seconds faster tomorrow?'

I would be in the adjacent bed. 'What does it matter? We're flying. We can't affect their ride.' Straight off to sleep. Only in the morning would I find out that Ed had managed just a few broken hours, and that the fact he could hear me snoozing untroubled served only to make it worse. The irony of it? Come race time, Ed was the strongest guy on the track. Always.

The nerves only returned for me when we sat on the chairs a couple of minutes before the start. Just thinking about those plastic chairs gets my palms sweaty and my throat dry. During the warm-up you could concentrate on what you were doing. You visualise the race. Doing something keeps you occupied. When you're sitting in the chairs, the minutes slow down. Block it out. Chalk on the hands. There is nothing around you but this ride. Up to the bikes on the start line. Climb on, feet in. As soon as the beeps sound, a sudden calm. This is autopilot. And autopilot cannot feel emotion.

In the moment of triumph it is all worth it, even if the feeling in London was not the surge of ecstasy we felt in Beijing but more a sense of relief. We did what we should have done. No-one messed up.

For the next twenty-four hours your world changes. Interviews everywhere. Driven around in a gold BMW. Watching the men's 100-metres final in the Team GB marquee in Hyde Park with a glass of champagne. Then the next British gold medal happens, and the tornado moves on.

You imagine that an Olympic gold medal is the sporting equivalent of a Wonka golden ticket. Get into any stadium, sit where you want, watch what you choose. It isn't, not even in the velodrome. Ed was on the point of winning his bronze in the omnium when I tried to get trackside to see him. An official stood in the way.

'You can't come in here, Olympic family only.'

'But he's one of my best mates. I'll miss his moment if I go that way.'

A shrug.

After being turned away again, further around the velodrome, I finally got in. But I'd missed Ed's final event. I saw him receive his bronze medal, and then I hit the same issue trying to get into the track centre to congratulate him. It ended in a Mexican stand-off with the same steward.

'No? I'll just run across the track, then.'

At last a reaction. 'Do that and I'll call security. You'll be thrown out.'

It was a risk worth taking. Across the track, a bellow for Ed, an apologetic thumbs-up to my adversary.

It feels good to wear normal clothes, to take off the GB tracksuit after two weeks of wearing nothing else. Dave Brailsford liked us to look coordinated. He would designate certain days a red-polo-shirt day, others a blue or white. For the staff, organised and into detail, that was fine. For us riders, good on the bike but short of attention off it, it was a nightmare. My tactic was to wear my tracksuit top at all times. If I had happened to fluke the right colour T-shirt underneath, I would wait until I'd run a visible cross-check on the staff around me and unzip it. If I'd got it wrong, I'd just keep it on. Tactics.

Those days afterwards are a curious limbo, a surreal blend

of weariness, celebrity and sauce. At one point I was watching the Olympics in a pub with Sara, in normal clothes, outside the bubble. On the big screen, Andy Murray was winning another gold for us. No-one in the bar cared about anything else.

Later in the week, Team GB had a big congratulatory party. It was near the launch for the second *Expendables* film; a few of the stars were there, and we ended up having photos taken with Stallone and Arnie. Stallone, close up, looked like an overused chamois – wrinkled, puffy in the wrong places, an unsavoury shade of brown. Then handshakes with David Cameron, who had only a limited idea who we were but was polite enough. Small talk. Too much small talk for a lad from Cardiff.

And then the closing ceremony, wandering round the middle of this vast stadium, unable to hear any of the music because all the speakers are pointed towards the crowd. Who's that singing? Ah, the Spice Girls. Shall we move on?

The destination of choice was China White. We headed there, still in our official ceremony gear: rather fetching red trousers, white T-shirts and blue blazers. Ed and I would end up giving our outfits to my brother-in-law Rhys and his mate Eddie. The non-Olympic Eddie was so proud of his new look that he wore it the next day for his easyJet flight to Ibiza for his summer holiday, which worked out rather well: when the stewardess spotted his blazer, she called him to the front of queue. Then, when he boarded the plane, he did so to a round of applause from his fellow passengers and several rounds of free drinks. Well played, sir.

It had been rather messier the night of the gold medal win. A huge gang of us piled over to Mahiki, the upmarket cocktail bar in Mayfair, which had made the mistake of underestimating the level of home success at those Games by offering British gold medallists free drinks all night. Seeing us arrive – me and Sa, the riders, my parents, brother, best mate and his wife, parents-in-laws, brother-in-law, his girlfriend and cousins – the manager almost passed out. We certainly didn't get any free drinks, but that didn't stop us.

It was some night. I say that as if I can recall it. Apparently I was thrown out of a taxi, merely for admitting I felt a bit sick. That left Sara and me in the pouring rain, stranded somewhere in the West End, me frantically searching for a toilet. Eventually, we had to get a bike rickshaw back to the hotel, which took almost 'til dawn. I can safely say that at no stage was I tempted to give our driver a break and do a bit of pedalling myself.

In the morning I woke to a vague recollection of our journey back, and something to do with the concierge helping me to our room. Then I turned to my phone, and saw six missed calls from the press officer at British Cycling. I looked at Sa. She looked back. 'You're supposed to be on *BBC Breakfast*, aren't you?'

Balls. Where are my clothes?

'Ger, stop. Look at the time.'

It was 10.15 a.m.

I texted the other boys. Nobody had made it.

Faster, higher, stronger. But not after a night on the cocktails.

Sky

What's it like being on the most high-profile outfit in cycling? I was in the Team Sky car once when a chap alongside on a motorbike started waving frantically. We slowed down a little, and his waving became an exaggerated pull-over motion. I stopped by the side of the road. Had we dropped an essential piece of kit off the roof rack? Were we heading the wrong way? Was he an obsessive fan, after one last autograph?

I unwound the window as he strode over. 'You Sky? You Sky?' Here it comes. He wants one of Brad's yellow jerseys for a school raffle. He's got an idea for a climber-specific bike made out of balsa wood. He wants Steve Peters to silence the angry voices in his head. 'Yes, but we're running late, so . . .' A dismissive wave. 'Great. I've been trying to get through on the phone all morning – my telly's stopped working. Can you come over?'

There was something very familiar about being there at the start of it all, back in 2010, for a very simple reason: Sky felt exactly like a road version of the Great Britain track team. Dave Brailsford conducting the orchestra. Coaches coming up with inspired training sessions or locations. Every rider obsessed with improvement. Nutritionists finding new ways riders could fuel pre-race or recover after brutal days. Head mechanics working with sports scientists to come up with new pieces of equipment or entire avant-garde bikes. An unspoken motto: never be satisfied with what you've got.

It sounds like every rider's wildest dream, but not everyone can handle it. Some riders struggle with change, struggle to break the mould. It's the old-school approach, the 'Well, it worked well enough for them, why are we different?'

Because we want to be better.

If you are used to being told what to do, in the classic way of an old-fashioned team, you might struggle to understand how the future feels. You need to truly love riding and want to perform, rather than simply turn up because you have to and want to get your pay cheque at the end of each month. It can be too intense otherwise. You need to take ownership of your own performance. If, when the intensity ramps up in January – much earlier than many teams are used to – you don't understand that the coaching is a two-way process and, instead of talking about it, end up burning yourself out, the year will feel long and fruitless. Everyone challenges each other, asking, why this? And why that? It's supposed to be like training with a carrot rather than a stick, but some guys just prefer a stick.

One of the few demands is that each rider uses a power meter in training and downloads the information from it each night for the coaches. Yet some guys don't buy into the new age of training to your box. Too many numbers cause some to crack. They can't deal with the detailed, rigorous feedback, day after day, the feeling of a benign Big Brother watching over them.

Nowhere is the team's ethos more graphically illustrated than in the Team Sky bus. To even call it a bus is like describing Frank Sinatra as a singer of cover versions. The team transport when I was with Barloworld – now that really felt like a bus: benches, a couple of seats, everything but a driver behind security glass and a bell to ring when you wanted it to stop. I half expected to have to pay £1.20 every time I stepped on.

The Sky bus is black, with dark windows and an air of intimidation. For this reason it has been dubbed the *Death Star*. On board it has two washing machines. Did the actual *Death Star* have two washing machines? Probably, on reflection – you try putting black cloaks and white stormtroopers' uniforms on the same wash and see how far it gets you.

Inside it is less utilitarian mode of transport, more business-class lounge. Huge reclining chairs, one on each side of the aisle; leg rests, each man with his own private area; Wi-Fi and DVD player; showers and a couple of fridges full of fresh, healthy food like chicken and rice salads, yoghurts and, erm, ProPeptide recovery drinks.

The showers never run out of hot water. The only toilet rules are to not hog them. After a tough day in the saddle, it's very hard not to make a loud 'Aaahhh . . .' noise as you sit down. Even if you hadn't been near a bike it would be a pleasure to spend a few hours on these thrones.

It makes a genuine difference to you as a rider, particularly at a Grand Tour. But the biggest single advance the team has made over the previous gold standard is in training. It seems obvious now it has become standard best practice, but Sky were the first to develop bespoke programmes for individuals rather than take a blanket approach across the whole team. They were also the first to tailor sessions to specific goals. If you are taking aim at the Tour of Flanders, doing twenty-minute threshold efforts on climbs will get you fit, but not the precise type of fit you need for that race. Flanders is about short, punchy efforts. Why train for a different test when you know exactly what will be demanded of you come race day?

Our rivals sometimes misinterpret what we do. When we became known for going on pre-Tour training camps to Tenerife, suddenly everyone started going to Tenerife. But it's not the going to Tenerife that matters, it's the training you do there. It's not the altitude; we're only there for two weeks. It's the specificity of the sessions, the fact you watch your food like a ballerina, that you do nothing but rest when you're not riding, as there is nothing else to do, that you sleep so well because the air is so clean and fresh. It's everything *but* just going to the Canaries and riding your bike.

At the start, Dave B and his secret squirrels hit it hard. Everything had to be an innovation. Skinsuits rather than separate jersey and shorts, helmets with no vents, portable sauna tents, warm-downs after fierce mountain stages. A lot of that has been absorbed by cycling as a whole. When we first jumped back on our bikes after forty-five minutes flat-out climbing we were literally laughed at. Then the comedians woke up the next day with legs as stiff and responsive as tree trunks, and they realised that stopping dead from your maximum and then sitting down for four hours was a far bigger joke.

A lot has also been stripped back. At first we tried to do too much, too soon. During the Tour in 2010 it felt as if we were hardly ever in our beds resting. Dave recognised this pretty soon, went back to basics and then slowly started to drip-feed us with improvements.

We have compression boots to wear on the bus now after stages, but it is the simple stuff that has proven the most enduring. During stage races we have to stay in the same hotels as other teams. There is no alternative; those are the organisers' rules. At best you might get a Campanile; at worst you might find yourself in the sort of place that feels familiar from school trips – you open the wardrobe to find the sink, sit down to see ants raiding your washbag, pull back the sheets to see not monogrammed mints on your pillow, but small hairs that are not your own. To have your own mattress topper and sheets placed on there for you by the team each night is not only reassuring, it means you sleep better, and sleeping better is an essential component of racing better.

People in general don't like change. In a sport as competitive as cycling, it's far worse. And so the whispers started up quickly: do they think they're better than the rest of us?

We were also perceived by some rivals as being like robots. All living in this strict, structured environment, not allowed to do anything other than rest, or exactly what you're told. At times, the way we raced didn't help our case. It was seen as boring, too structured – team time-trialling up a mountain, focused on outputting a certain amount of watts. We didn't care: it worked.

The detail matters. Our nutritionists work closely with a chef who travels with us to most of the World Tour races. There is no more hoping you get enough food, or get it at the right time, or gambling your body will get the exact nutrients you require in a form that you can digest and absorb. Good riders are powered by great food. When you're racing there is so little to look forward to, so few pleasures permitted, that your meal times are almost the only thing you anticipate with excitement. Rice every night for three weeks can bring even a strong man to his knees. Variety is key. Some sushi as a starter? A piece of grilled salmon cooked to perfection, still nice and pink in the middle? These are the great thrills of a racing cyclist's day.

Our kit on the bike benefits from being made by a small company who love innovation. A lot of it is exactly what you want when every part of your body is crying out for comfort: soft fabrics, slim stitching, subtle branding. Our kit off the bike benefits from not looking too obvious. There is great pride in wearing a Great Britain tracksuit, but it is not built for passing unnoticed in public spaces.

Team Sky are not always the easiest team to ride for. When Brad was at Garmin and keen for a move across, he made that famous remark comparing his old team to Wigan and his suitors to Manchester United. It encapsulated why a lot of people didn't seem to like us: a perceived arrogance, a bunch of newbies who were too brash for their own good. It didn't matter that we weren't, or that the investment from

Sky not only allowed the creation of a British team based on a core of British talent, but also hopefully helped encourage mass participation too. Critics heard Dave predicting in 2010 that a British rider would win the Tour within five years and found reason to hate. That we had two British riders win it in four almost made it worse.

There are cycling fans who don't like Sky. That is their prerogative, but it does filter down to us. As a rider, you are aware that you are a mere cog, a flywheel in a far larger machine. We ride. Beyond that, we have no power. What you may or may not like about the parent company is not something we can influence.

The team keeps moving on, just as everyone else tries to catch up. The end of 2014 saw an influx of new staff. New ideas, fresh approaches.

One perk hasn't changed: all riders get a free Sky Sports package at home. It's a nice bonus. But, just in case you were wondering, I still don't know how to fix the reception on a TV. Have you tried turning it off and then on again?

Tenerife

A sun-tickled holiday island. Sun loungers and parasols. Cold beers, hot nightclubs. Wet T-shirt competitions, full English breakfasts, duty-free cigarettes.

I think of none of these things when I think of Tenerife. I think instead of a barren volcano, of being hungry, of riding the equivalent of four times the height of Snowdon every day, of teammates cracking, and of being so exhausted that getting up in the night to go to the bathroom takes half an hour of psyching yourself up.

This is our Tenerife – the hardest two weeks of training we do, a fortnight of pain and starvation 2,100 metres up Mount Teide, fifteen miles from the nearest village and just six weeks out from the Tour.

There is only one hotel on Teide, up above the clouds in those black and boiled lava fields. The only guests they used to get at the Parador de las Cañadas del Teide were astronomers working at the observatory on the peak and the occasional holidaymaker running scared of the mayhem on Veronica's Strip down at Playa de las Américas. I imagine it like the hotel in *The Shining*, empty save for ghosts every winter until, one day, the call comes from Dave Brailsford. 'Hello, I'm looking to book in a party of twenty for fourteen days. Do you have any availability?' 'Have we ever . . .'

There is no phone signal and the Internet doesn't work. You're not allowed to eat very much. There is no pool, no games room and the only television channel in English is BBC World. You'd call it a monastic existence, except even monks get to knit cassocks or brew their own potent booze.

It became a Team Sky staple back in 2011, when Brad Wiggins was getting serious about cracking the Tour. Our sports science guru Tim Kerrison, along with Shane Sutton, worked out that Brad was struggling to perform at high altitude, and needed a camp where you could ride without distractions, on empty roads, in perfect weather. The Alps are too wet in May. The US is too far away. Britain doesn't have the climbs. Tenerife has it all.

And it makes you suffer. A minimum of 3,000 metres climbing per day, often as much as 4,500 metres. Everyone pushed to the limit: a heavy sense of 'Oh no . . .' when the alarm goes off in the morning, a heavy dread in the stomach when you go down to see what sessions you have been given. Quicker efforts. Nastier efforts. Less food on the dinner table, no treats in the kitchen. The higher you climb, the more effort you put in, the more the watts on your power meter drop and drop.

Teide looks like the classic volcanic cone. Low on its flanks are pine forests and shallow slopes. On its steep shoulders it is all dark rock and exposed edges. It is the sort of place that doesn't need roads. That means that the few that do exist, you ride again and again and again.

From the south, very few roads wind up to the village of Vilaflor. From there, it is a climb of thirteen kilometres on the only road out of town. From the north-west, through Santiago del Teide and then a tiny place called Chio, it's twenty-eight kilometres of uphill, through the naked lava fields, the road bumpy as hell and horrible to ride. Then there's La Orotava down to the north-east, working your way up a valley and then away from the last vegetation, up to the observatory at 2,300 metres.

Those main routes never get too steep, ramping up to 8 per cent at their punchiest. But there are alternative roads that appear to lead nowhere, tiny cul-de-sacs in the clouds that only the foolish, or Tour de France dreamers, would dare attempt. One takes you to a hamlet called Chirche, up a track that, even in your lowest gear, you have to haul yourself up, long sections at 20 per cent and no-one in any hurry to do it again. We will hit a full-gas effort up there, fifteen seconds apart, all chasing each other through the agony, the competition helping you suck those final drops of fuel from the tank. Everything in the strange landscape feels surreal. Normally, the only sign of life might be the occasional old boy sitting on his porch in a chair. Then, from nowhere, you will round a corner to find a party of schoolkids in the road, who then miraculously part – like a crowd on an Alpine climb – to cheer you on. Did that really just happen?

Later in the day, flat on our backs, we will chew it over just as it spat us out. Anyone reckon they could get up that in their big ring? Someone whose bravado has overwhelmed his recent memory will shrug. Why not? The next day you'll be passing the turning. 'Here we go. Ready to do this?' And then the backtracking will begin. 'Yeah, when I said "Why not?" I didn't mean this year. Anyway, I don't want to injure my knee or something . . .'

There is another route, a road so terrifying that myths and ghost stories swirl around its reputation and exact location. Some call it the steepest road in the world. Tim Kerrison snorted and said it wasn't even as steep as Chirche, just a couple of little ramps. And then one of the team tried to drive up it, and it was so ridiculous that the car couldn't hold its own weight and started sliding down again. So the stats were assessed: up the same vertical height as the famous Sa Calobra in Majorca, around 650 metres, but in 2.5 kilometres rather than almost ten kilometres. That's not a road, it's a wall.

Froomey can climb like no other. So he tried it, got 300 metres in and had to give up. His verdict: 'It's just not possible. It starts silly, kicks up, goes round a corner and, oh my God, what's it doing now?'

It makes you wonder. Why did they build it? How did they build it? It's tarmac. How did they get a steamroller up that? Maybe they didn't. Maybe they had to carry the various parts up and construct one at the top, and then just let it go with the handbrake off, flattening everything in its path until it ran out of petrol and gravity.

Because of Teide's reputation, because it so clearly helped Brad on his way to becoming the first Briton to win the Tour, we are no longer alone on the mountain. In 2014, it was Saxo, with Alberto Contador lounging in the lobby. In 2015, it was Astana, Vincenzo Nibali suddenly rocking up for breakfast with a brisk 'Ciao!'

You'd think our long-term residency there would secure us the best rooms. It doesn't. We don't even get much privacy in the restaurant, where only a folding screen keeps the two rival teams apart. It makes for a slightly awkward atmosphere over the porridge and smoothies, a bit like the vibe in a British B&B when six unfamiliar couples attempt to make whispered conversation over Alpen and black pudding.

To start with, you're very self-conscious. What are they eating? Why hasn't so-and-so come down for dinner? What's that new grain they're all piling their plates? A week in, and it's gone the other way. You're loudly discussing Richie Porte's strategy for the following day's stage at the Giro and you suddenly realise a bloke in a yellow-and-blue tracksuit is looking in your direction, with a rapt expression on his face.

The hotel cares so little for segregation that neither team has its own corridor or wing. You could easily have an Astana rider in the room next door to a Sky rider, which can make for uncomfortable moments in the lift when you both attempt to press the same button at the same time and then have to say a similarly embarrassed goodnight when you're struggling to get your room keys in the slot of adjacent doors.

We don't pick our own roommate – Sky's strategy is to keep it random in order to prevent cliques forming. It can be something of a lucky dip. It could be a real long fortnight if you get a man who prefers his own thoughts to conversation, but I've generally done well: compatriot Luke Rowe in 2015, Mikel Nieve – fellow football lover, as keen as me to watch the FA Cup final – in 2014.

Beyond that it's a tight team, the stripped-down staffing reflecting the austere atmosphere of the training camp.

There will be Tim, a couple of swannies, a physio and a mechanic. The swannies have an area where they can make us omelettes and smoothies and offer a few consoling words as they massage our mangled muscles, but the comforts extend no further. We're all in it together, and there is no wriggle room. This is hard work, heavy rest and more hard work.

Training comes in five-day sections: four days on, one day off, repeat. Each rider has their own specific programme, based around what they will have to do at the Tour and what they need in the tank to get there. As you come down each morning, Tim hands you a sheet of paper. On there you will have two options, both equally horrible: four solo efforts, one race scenario as a team. Sometimes you'll see five efforts, at which point you tend to gulp and think: bloody hell, how am I going to do this?

The race-style runs keep you going. Nothing drags you through your exhaustion like having teammates in front and behind. It will start with Luke or Ian Stannard leading out the first four kilometres, then Wouter Poels, Peter Kennaugh, Nicolas Roche and me pushing on for the next two kilometres before Froomey, the giant-engined Froomey, rides away from us all.

It's never easy. Everyone has a couple of good days, when they enjoy putting the wheel on the others a little, and everyone has a couple of bad days, when it's them watching the wheel in front accelerate away. Climbing towards the summit, there will always be one rider who sits up and rides at his own pace because he has cracked, mentally and physically.

But, because you are never racing against each other for Tour selection, it can still feel like fun, and that drives the collective mindset: get stuck in, do more, don't moan.

It even permeates meal times. So focused is the team that you can feel guilty if you have a piece of fruit between lunch and dinner. Only in professional cycling could a mid-afternoon apple and handful of nuts be seen as a bad thing.

The finest moment you have on Tenerife is the end of your fourth day in the cycle, the start of your precious twenty-four hours of recovery. That night feels like a Friday night when you're at school. And the next night feels like a Sunday night when you're at school, with only half the time for fun in-between.

Cycling being what it is, it's also strictly controlled fun. You delay your breakfast half an hour or so, ride along the plateau at the top to the nearest cafe, linger over a few coffees and ride back to lie on your bed and watch DVDs. That's as rock and roll as it gets. There is a cable car on the mountain that takes you to the very top – over 3,000 metres. The views are supposed to be spectacular. Every year I tell myself I'll do it, and every year I simply can't be arsed. And I've been there on five different occasions.

There is a danger in those few hours of not riding: food. You can hear the swannies' store room calling you, singing its siren song of biscuits, peanuts and chocolate. Except there are none of those things there any more, not for the riders. You can make yourself a smoothie with the blender, but what sort of illicit thrill is that? There used to be a magic drawer, packed with treats that the non-weight-watching swannies were allowed. On our last trip, I managed to not even open it to check, on the rationale that ignorance is bliss; why torment yourself by touching the forbidden Fruit & Nut?

Not all were so strong. You'd occasionally catch one of the lads sneaking out of the room while glancing over his shoulder, a strange lump or two in his pockets. Others would try to use the raw cacao powder that goes into making our mid-ride rice cakes to make a hot chocolate, although that's like trying to make a pint of cold lager with raw hops and water.

All of us go a little stir crazy towards the end of the second week. On the first year's camp there was a carefully organised group breakout, where we all hammered it down to the coast to eat pizza, but you'd never get away with that now. The night of all nights comes on 25 May, when Stannard and I share a birthday. We're allowed to travel down to Vilaflor and not only order a steak but get a glass of wine on the side and a very small cake to follow. It's wonderful for morale but also makes you suffer even more, because once your mouth remembers what sweet tastes like, it immediately craves more.

On Sundays we will ride down to the coast on a long training spin. There you will see club cyclists sitting in the sun, bikes propped up against tables, holding beers and pizza. We ride on, consoling ourselves with wistful talk of the future: when we're done with this game, when we've got kids, we'll come back here, hire a villa and drink all the beers we want.

If that makes it sound like prison, these are walls of our own construction. We understand what Tenerife does to us, and we like the result, if not always the process. But we look forward to flying home, standing in the airport queue for check-in next to blokes in sombreros, 'Thug Life' tattoos on their bellies and raffia donkeys under their arms, two worlds colliding.

Then, when you get to the Tour, Tenerife becomes your great consolation. When you've got Teide in your legs, anything seems possible. This climb's steep? It's no Chirche. This ascent is ten kilometres long? Big deal. I've been grinding up thirty-kilometre horror shows. Bring me your steepest nightmares. I've already conquered worse.

Winning

A win's a win, goes the old sporting cliché. Except it's not. Every win feels completely different.

Winning gold at the 2012 Olympics felt like relief. Winning the one-day classic E3 Harelbeke in 2015 felt like complete joy. Relief didn't get a look-in.

Some of it comes down to expectation. The Great Britain team pursuit quartet were reigning Olympic champions, going into their home Games as world record holders. Lining up for E3, there was no pressure at all. No Welshman had ever won a spring Classic.

Some of it comes down to the aftermath. In London, once our title had been regained, we were free to kick back and kick on, enjoying our medal and everything that came with it. After the Tour of 2015, we celebrated Chris Froome's yellow in a Parisian nightclub until 3.30 a.m. and then, because we were due at Sky HQ in London the next morning, found that a private jet had been laid on to take the riders across the Channel. It kept the collective joy and party mood going even as the hangovers kicked in.

I woke up the morning after E3, huge smile on my face, and remembered within seconds that I was racing Gent–Wevelgem in twenty-four hours' time. Straight out on my bike for a recovery ride, and then into race mode once again: the team are up for it, the boys have ridden for me, let's do this right. As it turned out, I nearly won that one as well, coming in third after the sort of insane day's racing that makes you forget your own name, let alone what happened two days before.

That is how it works in road cycling: it never stops. On the track, it's all about the Olympics. On the road, Classic follows sharp on the muddy tail of Classic. Stage races wipe the slate clean every morning. So you won in a sprint yesterday afternoon? Congratulations. Today you're a nobody at the back, trying to get over this mountain before the cut-off time sends you home.

It happened to me when I won the Tour of the Algarve in 2015. I had barely stepped off my bike when the next day's preparations began. Warm-down on the turbo, find my protein recovery drink, get wet kit off and compression clothing on. My main emotion, as I stood behind the podium waiting for the presentation, was one of frustration. Come on, stop faffing about, let's get on with this.

You can find yourself wanting to hit the pause button, so that you can enjoy it all in fitting style. It's almost cruel. After all those hours spent training and hurting, all the self-denial, karma should allow you to wallow in it, to savour every sweet second. Instead, you pedal onwards with hardly a backwards glance. Nothing matters but the last result. Win the Tour of Flanders, but finish fifteenth in Paris–Roubaix? It's the fifteenth place that sticks.

And what's enjoyment? You can't have a few beers, or even a burger. It's not until the end of the season that you can look back through all those frantic months and think: hey, that was good, back on that wet Sunday in March, wasn't it?

In cycling, you can win without being a winner. Only one guy stands on the top step of the podium, gets the flowers, the champagne, the kisses and plaudits. But he is there because of the seven or eight teammates who delivered him – the teammates who went back to the team car mid-race to get him kit, food and drinks, who brought back the break-aways, who kept him out of the wind, who manoeuvred him into a good position. The man waving from atop the podium is the equivalent of a football striker who scores the winning goal: he finishes it off, but without the goalkeeper and defenders who kept it at 0–0, or the midfielders who won the ball or the winger who delivered the cross, the chance would never have come. Those of us who are the equivalent of wingers, or combative midfielders – and that's the vast majority of the peloton – feel an intrinsic part of that success, and all the satisfaction that goes with it. When Chris Froome won the Tour in 2013 and 2015, we all felt like a part of that win was ours. So too, crucially, did Chris. In 2015, because I had been at the front with Chris for so much of the race, it felt even bigger for me. In 2013 I had been hanging on for long periods, mainly due to a fractured pelvis. Two years later I was a better rider and able to contribute that much more, and that made the satisfaction even deeper.

Winning is a habit. So is losing. Most riders aren't winning, in the same way as most actors are not working. We talk a lot about winning in sport, but only one rider out of 120-odd can win each day. That's an awful lot of losers.

Even the greats lose more than you instinctively recall. Muhammad Ali was beaten five times in his pro career, but it's the epic wins that we remember him for. In the one-day Classics, Tom Boonen and Fabian Cancellara have lost far more than they have won. But their most famous victories create a virtuous circle. The perception in the peloton of them as winners wins them races, even when they're not really in the shape to do so. It's something Steve Peters likes to remind us. Don't think of your rivals as gorillas. They are just riders, same as all of you. Just because you have won a race five times in row, doesn't mean you will win a sixth.

That momentum can carry a whole team. At the Beijing Olympics it was the most glorious, contagious disease, running unchecked throughout the British cycling squad. Everyone who got onto the track thought they would win.

It can just as easily go the other way. The top riders don't win quite enough, the guys working for them lose confidence in what they're doing, the sponsors cut back because they're not happy with the profile they're getting, people lose their jobs.

Confidence can be either a tailwind at your back or a mental slow-puncture. It fundamentally changes the way you race. Do you really believe, or do you just hope? It can be almost frightening to risk it all going for the win, knowing that if you fail you could end up tenth. It's easier to be cagey and subconsciously be satisfied with a top five rather than going death or glory.

When you let yourself believe, it is an exhilarating ride. At E3, I knew when I would attack and how I would try to do it. When I went, there was the liberation of knowing that this was it: beauty or the bust. And then on the team radio it started coming through: G, you've got six seconds. Ten seconds. Twelve. Twenty ... One kilometre to go, the first thought cast into the future: should be okay now. Head down. One more corner. Not until 300 metres remained did I look back behind and let the pleasure wash over me.

At other times, you can be blissfully unaware. During the Tour of 2011 I was part of a break that got away early in the day. During the stage we were to climb the Col du Tourmalet and as we got closer to the summit, riding comfortably at my own pace, I pulled away from the others. This feels good, I thought, although with three kilometres left, I realised we still had another big descent and climb to go that day, and thus maybe I should wait for the next man. Sure enough, an FDJ rider appeared behind me in the distance. I let him come back to me, ready to work together, only to be shocked when he suddenly sprinted away 500 metres from the top. Turned out there was a €5,000 bonus for the first man to clear the Tourmalet. No-one had told me. To be fair, I hadn't bothered to ask. Farewell, new flat-screen TV. Farewell, dream holiday.

Not once in our gold-medal-winning team pursuit runs in Beijing or London did I think about actually winning. You are too focused on each turn, how long you can pull at the front, how close you are to the wheel in front. There are clues if you want them – our coach standing by the finish line indicating what pace we're on, the noise from the crowd every time the differential between the two teams flashes up on the electronic screens. But you don't let any of that in. As soon as you do, your concentration goes, and, when you're riding at 63 kph, millimetres away from the guy in front, that's the last thing you want. You don't look at your coach much – maybe three times, when you're second wheel, to help judge the pace when you go to the front. Sometimes as you come into the home straight you catch a slight glimpse of your rivals on the banking at the far end. But it is only when you do your last turn, when you're on the back, fighting to stay in contact, when you hear the bell, that, for the first time, you know the job has been done.

And that is how you process it: a job that must be done. It's not unknown to finish a team pursuit and be unable to remember anything that happened, so dialled-in were you to the process. That is why, as you cross the line, you feel satisfied. You care about the gold – it's what you've been working towards for three years – but it's not a shock. You can actually feel more of a buzz about seeing you've broken the world record, because it is more unexpected.

That satisfaction really kicks in when you see what winning means to the people you care about. It is these ripples from a victory that finally place it in a context you can appreciate: popping in to Cyclopaedia in Cardiff, seeing the guys you used to ride with out to the Storey Arms when the Brecon Beacons were under snow so happy to see you do well; an older guy who used to give me a kicking on the roads of Cardiff, a chap I still think of as a stronger bike rider, coming up to say hello and well done; Debbie Wharton, the woman who started Maindy Flyers, the woman who got me into cycling, kept me in it and made me enjoy it, sending me messages on Facebook or Twitter: all of them properly chuffed because they're part of it. I hope there are kids down the road from me thinking: Geraint Thomas's mum and dad live over there – if he can do it, I can do it too. Then there are all those you have never met but get in contact via social media. The ripples from that one moment astound me.

With all that at stake, you can understand the despair when it seems a big win might escape your grip. At the Commonwealth Games road race in 2014, when I made my decisive break, the reaction from the other two riders told me I was in better shape than them, that they were racing for second. Then, with less than six kilometres to go, I came round a corner, thought, whoah, that felt a bit spongey, pumped the front wheel hard and, oh no . . .

A puncture? Now? Why? Why? If you've ever lost your phone or passport, you'll know the sick dread that comes with the moment of realisation. Imagine that, but multiplied by ten. Losing your passport as you get ready to board a plane that is taking you on the holiday you have always dreamed of. Losing a phone that has all the photos and music on that you've ever cared about and that are not backed up anywhere else.

I looked back. No support car. I was in slow motion and everything around me in fast forward. How can this be happening? Why me? Why now?

And then the bloke arrived with a spare wheel, a man who has changed a wheel at speed a billion times, and suddenly his fingers were like sausages. Seconds seemed to become minutes. At any moment I knew a swishing sound coming down the street would signal the sprinting pass of my two pursuers. Still he fumbled. I'd had no hope of the gold. I had been in bits coming off the Tour. And then the break, and a genuine sense that this miracle could really happen, only for it now to all fall away.

I probably should have said to the bloke: 'You're doing fine. Calm down. No pressure.' Instead I caved in: 'COME ON!'

He made it, of course, finally tightening that skewer with my lead still alive, and in doing so inadvertently made the home straight an even more emotional experience. It was gone, it was on, it was gone, it might be back . . . I've actually done it.

Here's another strange thing about winning: when a friend or teammate bags a big one, 99 per cent of you will be delighted for them. One per cent of you will be a little bit jealous.

When I won on the Algarve, Ian Stannard texted to congratulate me. A week later, he won the big Omloop Het Nieuwsblad one-day race in Belgium. It was brilliant, especially the way he'd won it, and I was made up for him. But part of you hurts. I want that feeling again. It's only a week ago but it's already gone. Somebody else has got that feeling now, and I want it back. Those two contrasting emotions can coexist in your brain.

It's the competitor in you. You cannot damage yourself every day as you must to become a road racer unless you are abnormally competitive. I don't like to admit it, but I am.

I will lose a board game at Christmas with the family and be genuinely angry. I will lose a game of squash on holiday, having never played it before, and be furious.

I can at least rationalise it. It's only a board game. Squash? Not my sport. Mark Cavendish cannot. If he loses a board game, the board itself might not survive. If he's still in the room after losing, rather than somewhere else kicking something, you've got away lightly.

But he's used to winning. It is his addiction. And every win matters.

Race Day

Stages can vary. The weather can be all over the shop. What doesn't change is the desire to be asleep for as long as possible. And then . . .

7.55 a.m.: Wake up, slightly begrudgingly. Roll over, swing your legs onto the floor and make the first subconscious check of how they feel. No time for fashion choices or a pre-breakfast beauty regime – that's been trumped by sleep. Clothes on and out of the door. My regular room-mate Ben Swift is slightly different; he likes to spend a good ten minutes in the toilet, sprucing himself up. Most of the time I won't need an alarm. Instead, I'll be woken up by different beauty products clattering around the bathroom tiles.

Before heading down to breakfast, we stop off at the doctor's room. Jump on the scales. Whether you look at the result on the screen depends on the time of year. Early season, when you haven't been weighing yourself regularly, you tend to avoid the result. It's better to think that you're seventy-one kilogrammes than to know you're in fact 72.5 kilogrammes. During the Tour, you'll confront it, not least because you have been on the scales every day since the start of May. There are no hidden surprises. The doc will then test your hydration levels by taking a urine sample, which becomes more important in the warmer conditions of the Tour Down Under, Tour de France or Vuelta. Throughout this sometimes invasive process he will also be gently questioning you about your sleep and assessing your mood. I'll be better in ten minutes, Doc.

8.00: Breakfast, always three hours before racing begins, and one of the most pleasant points in the day. There is no formal seating arrangement but, as always, riders take comfort in routine and sit without thinking in the same seat where they ate dinner. The chef asks if you would like an omelette. Ham, please, and stick in three eggs. On the table are flasks of smoothie, bowls of fresh berries and four different types of milk: almond, soya, rice, cow. Then there's usually fresh bread the chef has made, pots of honey, jams and spreads, the chef's very popular almond butter, a big vat of porridge, Special K and muesli. A permanent fixture is a packet of rye bread. It's never opened or touched but continues to come with us around the world. Pride of place goes to the hardest-working piece of equipment in the team, the espresso maker. Once the caffeine kicks in, the various silent zombies who have staggered in slowly turn human and remember that they can speak. The first sprint of the day comes, not forty kilometres into the stage, but if Heinrich the chef decides to bring out some fresh fruit scones or pancakes. As you leave breakfast, there will be a laundry basket in the corner containing the freshly washed and dried kit. Most of the time I will forget and get back to the room before bellowing, 'Ah, balls, my kit . . .' Being a cyclist, you don't walk back down. It's too far, I've got to race. You gamble that one of your teammates notices you've forgotten it and brings your kit up with them.

8.45: There's always a little sadness that the best meal of the day has come to an end. But packing calls, even though you haven't unpacked, merely unzipped the bag and taken out your washbag and fresh boxers. Now to pack your kit for the day's racing – generally no harder, since you usually just use the same kit as the day before, which is in the laundry bag you just forgot to pick up. At a Grand Tour, your suitcase is so full of different items of kit that it can weigh more than you do. Just like anyone else who goes away, we're guilty of overpacking; only bad weather or crashes actually require a spare to be brought out, but you never learn. Once bags are done, another question: does the hotel TV have any channels in English? Stare blank-faced at BBC World for ten minutes, taking nothing in.

9.00: Back in the dark ages, a printed list of names and room numbers was stuck on the lift door, so that everyone knew where everyone else was. Next to it would be the list of timings: bags collected at this time, onto the bus by that time. Except, once Brad became Wiggo, we realised that giving out such detailed personal information was probably less than sensible. Instead, there is now a closed group on WhatsApp that we all subscribe to. That tells us everything. Sure enough, bang on time, there's a knock on the door – the swannies are here to drop off our cleaned kit and pick up our suitcases.

9.10: The bus departs promptly. Christian Knees will always be on there first, waiting for everyone else. Maybe it's a German thing. Some riders like to slip into their kit before leaving the hotel to get in some quality chamois time, and Christian is certainly one of these. He'll be sitting there in the front of the bus with his cycling shorts on, along with compression tights, cycling socks over the top, a sleeveless undervest and a hat on. It's a sight to behold. I prefer to stay in my joggers. It is not yet time to strip for battle. Each man has his own dedicated seat on the bus, and with that comes comfort. To be suddenly switched to the other side would freak you out as much as instant coffee.

9.30: Time to top up the tanks. A big bottle of pineapple or grape juice is waiting for us at our seats. This is the time I use to put my numbers on. Most guys take a lot of care trimming these down and pinning them to the pockets of their jersey in aerodynamic fashion. It's like our own surgical operation, and intensifies in importance if you are wearing a skinsuit. It is one of the great secret arts of the peloton, and almost completely useless outside it.

9.50: As the bus parks up at the start, it is time to remind yourself of the tests that lie ahead. You might have examined the stage profile in the official race book the night before, but most of the time, I tend to leave it until the next day. If you've just had a solid day on the bike, the last thing you want to do is examine closely the pain you're going to endure the next day. Plus you need your sleep, and studying the race book before bed can give you nightmares. So, probably over another coffee, you will have another scan. Whoah. That looks big.

10.00: Time for a team meeting. If the stage is short and simple, so too will be the meeting. If it is long and painful, likewise. All but the riders and bosses leave the bus – swannies, physio, doctor, mechanics. The lead directeur sportif (on the Tour, this means Nico Portal) will stand up first, pulling the blinds down on the coach windows and the big screen at the front to create both privacy and focus. He will take us through the map of the route, stage profile, spell out the objective for the day, ensure everyone knows their specific task and give us the weather forecast. Using Google Street View, he will then show us exactly what the last climb or run-in to the finish looks like. Dave Brailsford and Tim Kerrison stand at the back and watch. When Nico is done, Dave takes his turn.

10.20: Let's get ready. On goes the music via someone's Spotify playlist. Expect some complaints and some desperate defence ('This can't be mine'; 'You've pressed the wrong one).' There's everything from house music to Taylor Swift and German hip-hop: blame Knees. Embrocation is rubbed into your legs. You pull your shorts on. Adrenaline climbs, because the battle is near.

10.30: To the practicals. Always leave going to toilet as late as you possibly can. You will be capable of peeing on the go during the next five hours, but anything more than that can be awkward.

10.35: Jersey on, radio into its pocket at the back of your shorts, race food laid out on the little space by your seat. Message your partner: 'We're just about to go off, speak to you later.' Shoes pulled on and wound up tight. One last coffee. There's always time for one last coffee.

10.40: Okay. Helmet and glasses on and totter off the bus. A cheery hello from a few punters, over to the mechanic to get your bike and onto the turbo trainer to warm up. As soon as you're pedalling, there is an instant sense of comfort. You are doing what you are used to doing. It feels natural, and you feel ready. Once sweat is on the brow, fill your rear pockets with race food and take some calming breaths.

10.50: A swannie will open up the airport-queue-style barrier around the bus and clear a narrow path through the onlookers for you to get through. You go through all the crowds to sign on. It's a small official job to tick off, but on the Tour they are strict as old headmasters about it. In 2011, I missed the cut-off time three days in a row and was on the wrong end of a monstering from then-DS Sean Yates as a result. 'Right. We've been fined because of you. And if you miss it tomorrow, we get thrown off the race!' The UCI have since brought in a rule that if you do miss signing on (which closes promptly, ten minutes before the race goes), you will not be allowed to start. I'm now always on time.

10.55: Still calm, still pretty chilled. With five minutes to go until the start of a team pursuit on the track it is awfully intense. On an ordinary road race stage you have more time to get into it, and your nerves simmer accordingly. You might chat to a few lads from other teams to get a different perspective on the day. If you're feeling good, there is more chat in you. If you're weary, if you're dreading the stage, you just want to get to the start. Head down, shades on, zero eye contact.

10.58: The jersey wearers – yellow, green, polka dot, white – line up, shoulder to shoulder on the start. The rest of you can start where you want. Because the first few kilometres is a neutral zone, there will be no racing, and therefore there is no rush. Local dignitaries may grasp a few famous paws. At the start of the first stage of the Tour in Yorkshire, the Duke and Duchess of Cambridge shook the hands of all the Brits and all the past winners: Chris Froome, Mark Cavendish, Adam Yates, Andy Schleck, Alberto Contador, reigning world champion Rui Costa. Fast forward two weeks and every single one had retired from the race, injured, crashed or both. I was the only man left pedalling, the only rider immune from the Curse of the Cambridges.

11.00: And away we go. Through the neutral zone, the action dependent on the day ahead. If it's a tough start or a breakaway day then it'll be frantic, everyone jostling for position before 0 kilometres in the style of yachtsmen at the Olympics.

11.05: The flag drops and the race is on. Suddenly every-thing becomes simple and clear: I'm a bike rider, riding my bike. That is all that matters.

16.00: Phew. Day's racing done. How was that for you? As we come to a halt after crossing the finish line, our swannies are the first people we see. They put a recovery drink into your sweaty palm and point you in the direction of the team bus. There, another swannie will pop your bike on a turbo trainer in a cordoned-off area and you will warm down for ten minutes, signing a few autographs as you unwind mentally too from the travails of the afternoon. The bus is never more appreciated than in these moments when your heart is still going and your legs have little left – up the steps into its cool privacy, blinds down over the windows, a cocoon where the weary can recover. We will take it in turn to use one of the two showers, then pull on warm, clean clothes and dive into the fridge for the food that Heinrich has prepared – quinoa salads, fresh tuna, cold chicken. In that time, Dave Brailsford and any riders will have conducted all the post-race interviews they need to do; if we have a rider in the leader's jersey, their extra media duties mean they will be the last man on the bus. Should someone be called away to doping control, a car will wait for them. Like all buses, the Team Sky version must stick to its timetable.

17.00: You might imagine that we always stay very close to the finish. Why book a hotel that's nowhere near the day's end? Partly it's because you are one of 180-odd riders. Multiply that by the number of support staff, mechanics, chefs, media and punters that attend each stage and you can see that most towns simply do not have enough beds. Sometimes we have finished a stage, driven an hour to the hotel, got back on the bus the next morning and done the exact drive in reverse to start the next stage in the same place. The rule of rest applies as always: better to travel that evening rather than lose precious sleep in the morning by having to get up two hours earlier. Sometimes, as when you finish atop a mountain, there will be a Tour traffic jam down the tight turns and twists of the climb you have just ridden up. It all takes time, which is when the humble DVD comes very much into its own. It also helps when your mates are on the same race as you. You spin away the hours with reflections on the day endured and anticipations of happier ones ahead – rest days, stag dos, days at home on the sofa, worrying only about which sports channel you will flick to next.

17.30: Let's assume it's been a simple half-hour transfer. When you pull up outside your hotel, a member of Team Sky will greet you in the lobby with your room key and instructions where to go. When you open the door, your suitcase will be waiting for you, with your own mattress topper, pillow and sheets laid out perfectly. That's where the five-star treatment ends. Most of the time you're staying in budget hotels with rooms so small there isn't enough space to open your suitcases and leave them open. Imagine Ronaldo and Messi rocking up to one of those hotels the day before a Champions League final.

18.00: There are five swannies for nine riders. So you will either go straight in for your massage – ideal scenario – or have an hour's wait. If it's your turn to go second, you will hardly fill the time with any great spurts of activity. If you have a niggle, you might slouch off to see the physio. If you don't, you'll lie down on your bed. Ah, sweet relief. Clambering onto the massage table is one of the best parts of the day, at least until the swanny finds a gigantic knot in your calf and decides to take it on. The pain can be so excruciating that it makes you feel thirsty. Sweat pouring out of you while you call the swanny everything under the sun. They may not know Welsh swear words, but they get the drift.

19.15: With forty-five minutes to go until dinner, this is the perfect opportunity to get ahead on that DVD box set you've been working your way through. You might look at the next day's stage in the race book, but, more often, *Game of Thrones* will win that particular battle. At some point, either halfway through your massage or somewhere in the Seven Kingdoms of Westeros, the DS will come round to ask how you are. Was anyone struggling? Are there any issues he should know about? It is a gentle sort of debrief, but it is essential all the same.

20.00: Ah, the sweet smell of dinner. I've been thinking about you since breakfast. A sushi starter, more tuna and chicken, some rice and quinoa. A little fruit-based dessert to finish, perhaps a decaf coffee. On an easier day, a few of us might hang around the dining room for a little light conversation. If it's been a brute, the stage brings silence.

21.30: As a cyclist, you can never do enough lying on your bed. Now is the time to catch up with your partner on the phone, or knock off your third *Game of Thrones* episode of the day. Your energy levels will dictate your preference.

23.00: Lights out. With 120 miles in your legs, you tend to fall asleep sharpish. If it has been a long day, or a thriller, or you've overdone the caffeine gels, you can lie there a little too buzzy. You don't mind too much. You are lying down. Job done.

Me and Sa after the 2015 Tour, Welsh cakes in tow. She is dressed for the occasion – I was just happy to be out of team kit!

Acknowledgements

I'd like to thank Sara for all her help with this book, but maybe more for everything with life in general. She's always there with a sensible head on; we make a great little team. Howell and Hilary Thomas, my mum and dad, for giving me the best start in life. My brother, Alun. My aunties and uncles Chris and Ade, Glyn and Menna for travelling all over Europe to support me. And the rest of my extended family. My in-laws Beth and Eif for all their help off the bike. Rhys, Carys and Blanche, mainly for entertaining Sa when I'm away. The rest of their family around Cardiff and up in the Gogs. Ian Middleton and Ed Clancy, my best men. All the boys back in Cardiff, for all the great nights.

Debbie Wharton and everyone down at Maindy Flyers for helping me love the sport. Whitchurch High, for allowing me all that time away. Mr Williams for letting me leave the school rugby team -   George North should count himself lucky. Ian and Meeky down at Cyclopaedia. Darren Tudor, my first coach, who got me training properly and for a purpose. Dave Brailsford, for his vision and dedication in building one of the strongest cycling nations around. Shane Sutton, for spotting me, taking me under his wing and always being there. Matt Parker, a sport scientist who along-side Shane got us to Beijing in top shape. Rod Ellingworth, for all those hard yards in the academy. Tim Kerrison, my coach, for helping me continue my progression. Everyone at British Cycling and at the Manchester Velodrome. Team GB. Team Barloworld, my first professional team. Claudio Corti, team manager at Barloworld, for giving me some great opportunities and always believing in me.

To my best mates Ian Stannard, Luke Rowe, Rob Partridge, Dale Appleby, Steve Cummings, Mark Cavendish, Ben Swift, Bradley Wiggins, Steven Burke, Pete Kennaugh, Chris Froome and Paul Manning; we've been through some amazing stuff together, from Olympic Gold to Junior Tour of Ireland. And to everybody else who has helped me along the way, from riders and soigneurs to physios, mechanics and nutritionists.

Luke Lloyd-Davies and the great team at Rocket Sports. Richard Milner and all the brilliant hard-working team at Quercus. David Luxton. Gayle Thrush, the first PR/agent to genuinely care about me. And obviously a huge thanks to Tom Fordyce for listening to my stories, putting them all together and dealing with all my questions.

And lastly all you guys! Thanks for all your support from the velodromes of Maindy to London, the roads from South Wales lanes to the Alps, in the rain and sun. Everyone on social media - I appreciate every single word from every single one of you. Thanks!

Credits